Algeria

Algeria

A Study in Competing Ideologies

Kay Adamson

CASSELL

London and New York

Cassell
Wellington House
125 Strand
London WC2R 0BB

370 Lexington Avenue
New York
NY 10017–6550

First published 1998

British Library Cataloguing in Publication Data

A catalogue record for this book is available from the British Library.

Library of Congress Cataloging-in-Publication Data

Kay Adamson
    Algeria : a study in competing ideologies / by Kay Adamson.
      p.   cm.
    Includes bibliographical references and index.
    ISBN 0–304–70012–6 (hbk.) — ISBN 0–304–70013–4 (pbk.)
    1. Algeria—Economic policy.   2. Algeria—Economic conditions—
    1962–   I. Title.
  HC815.A6   1997
  338.965—dc21
                                     97–8712
                                        CIP

ISBN 0–304–70012–6 (hardback)

     0–304–70013–4 (paperback)

Designed and typeset by Ben Cracknell Studios
Printed and bound in Great Britain by Bookcraft (Bath) Ltd
Midsomer Norton

Contents

Tables and Figures

Abbreviations and Acronyms

AGTA	Amicale Générale des Travailleurs Algériens (General Association of Algerian Workers)
AIS	Armée Islamique du Salut (Islamic Salvation Army)
ALF	L'Avenir de la Langue Française (The Future of the French Language)
ALN	Armée de Libération Nationale (National Liberation Army)
ANP	Armée Nationale Populaire (People's National Army)
ASCOOP	Association Coopérative (Cooperative Association)
BCA	Banque Centrale d'Algérie (Central Bank of Algeria)
BNA	Banque Nationale d'Algérie (National Bank of Algeria)
CAPCS	Coopérative Agricole Polyvalente de Services (Agricultural Cooperative Council for Multi-purpose Services)
CCAA	Conseil Communal d'Animation de l'Autogestion (Communal Council for the Co-ordination of Self-management)
CEFIC	Centre Européen des Fédérations de l'Industrie Chimique (European Centre of Chemical Manufacturers' Federations)
CFDT	Confédération Française Démocratique du Travail (French Democratic Labour Confederation)
CFP	Compagnie Française des Pétroles (French Petroleum Company)
CFPA	Compagnie Française des Pétroles d'Algérie (French Petroleum Company of Algeria)
CFTC	Confédération Française des Travailleurs Chrétiens (French Confederation of Christian Workers)
CGT	Confédération Générale du Travail (General Labour Confederation)
CNGSE	Commission Nationale pour la Gestion Socialiste des Enterprises (National Commission for the Socialist Management of the Firm)
CNO	Commission Nationale Opérationelle (National Operational Commission)
CORIF	Conseil de Réflexion pour l'Avenir de l'Islam en France (Council for Reflection on the Future of Islam in France)
CPA	Compagnie des Pétroles d'Algérie (Algerian Oil Company)

CREPS	Compagnie de Recherche et d'Exploitation du Pétrole du Sahara (Saharan Oil Research and Exploitation Company)
CRUA	Comité Révolutionnaire d'Unité et d'Action (Revolutionary Committee for Unity and Action)
CSLF	Conseil Supérieur de la Langue Française (Higher Council on the French Language)
DA	Algerian Dinar
DAA	Direction des Affaires Arabes (Ministry of Arab Affairs)
DGLF	Délégation Générale à la Langue Française (General Authority for the French Language)
Diccilec	Direction Centrale pour la Lutte contre l'Immigration et l'Emploi Clandestins (Central Authority for the Struggle against Illegal Immigration and Employment)
ELF-ERAP	Essences et Lubrifiants de France – Enterprise de Recherches et d'Activitiés Petrolières (Petrols and Lubricants of France – Petroleum Operations and Research Enterprise)
ENA	Étoile Nord-Africaine (North African Star)
FFS	Front des Forces Socialistes (Socialist Forces Front)
FIS	Front Islamique du Salut (Islamic Salvation Front)
FLN	Front de Libération Nationale (National Liberation Front)
FNRA	Fonds National de la Révolution Agraire (National Fund for Agrarian Reform)
FNTM	Fédération Nationale des Travailleurs de la Métallurgie (National Federation of Metallurgical Workers)
GPRA	Gouvernement Provisoire de la République Algérienne (Provisional Government of the Algerian Republic)
HCMF	Haut Conseil des Musulmans de France (High Council of Muslims of France)
MARA	Ministère de l'Agriculture et de la Révolution Agrarie (Ministry of Agriculture and Agrarian Reform)
MNA	Mouvement National Algérien (Algerian National Movement)
MTLD	Mouvement pour le Triomphe des Libertés Démocratiques (Movement for the Triumph of Democratic Freedoms)
OAPEC	Organization of Arab Petroleum Exporting Countries
OAS	Organisation Armée Secrète (Secret Army Organization)
OCRA	Organisation Clandestine de la Révolution Algérienne (Underground Organization for Algerian Revolution)
ONI	Organisation Nationale de l'Immigration (National Immigration Organization)

ONRA	Office National de la Réforme Agraire (National Bureau of Agrarian Reform)
OPEC	Organization of Petroleum Exporting Countries
OS	Organisation Secrète (Secret Organization)
PCA	Parti Communiste Algérien (Algerian Communist Party)
PPA	Parti du Peuple Algérien (Algerian People's Party)
RADP	République Algérienne Démocratique et Populaire (People's Democratic Republic of Algeria)
RGA	Recensement Général de l'Agriculture (General Agricultural Census)
RGPH	Recensement Général de la Population et de l'Habitat (General Census of the Population and Habitat)
RP	Refah Party (Welfare Party)
RPR	Rassemblement pour la République ('Uniting for the Republic')
SAP	Société Agricole de Prévoyance (Agricultural Provident Society)
SAR	Secteur d'Amélioration Rurale (Rural Improvement Sector)
SIP	Société Indigène de Prévoyance (Native Provident Society)
SN	société nationale (state enterprise)
SN Repal	Société Nationale de Recherche et d'Exploitation des Pétroles en Algérie (State Enterprise for Petroleum Research and Exploitation in Algeria)
SNED	Société Nationale d'Édition et de Diffusion (State Publishing and Distribution House)
SONATRACH	Société Nationale pour la Recherche, la Production, la Transformation et la Commercialisation des Hydrocarbures (State Enterprise for Research, Production, Transport, Processing and Marketing of Petroleum)
SONIC	Société Nationale des Industries de la Cellulose (National Society of the Cellulose Industry)
SOPEFAL (Erap)	(An umbrella group representing French oil interests in Algeria)
UGSA	Union Générale des Syndicats Algériens (General Union of Algerian Trades Unions)
UGTA	Union Générale des Travailleurs Algériens (General Union of Algerian Workers)
USTA	Union des Syndicats de Travailleurs Algériens (Union of Algerian Workers' Trades Unions)
VSNA	Volontaire du Service National Actif (National Active Service Volunteer)

Acknowledgements

It would be impossible to thank individually everyone I would like to, and there are a great many people who have in one way or another helped this project to completion. To all of those I owe a considerable debt of gratitude as they may have wondered if the project would ever be completed. However, in a final summary I should like to mention Tony Hepburn who first suggested that I think about turning a doctoral thesis in economics into something more readable; the University of Sunderland who provided me with a six-month period of research leave which enabled actually rewriting it; Joan Hartley and Rob Dixon who ironed out the technology; the University of Leeds, and Rodney Crossley who saw the thesis through to its end and supported the original research, but who probably would not recognize much of it now. I want also to mention Dr John Wansbrough of the School of Oriental and African Studies who made me think about North Africa in the first instance; the late Ernest Gellner who tried to make a historian think sociologically; Ian Clegg who very kindly gave me much of his material on autogestion; and Dr Michael Brett of SOAS who always encouraged me when I most needed it. Jane Greenwood at Cassell is owed a special thanks for being prepared to risk the idea in the first place, as is Helena Power, who saw it through to its conclusion, and Mark Fox, who helped eliminate many of the errors which otherwise would have gone unnoticed. Personal thanks to Marie Stinson and Diane Kelly who have always been there, and also to Viv Waugh; and finally a very special thanks to Allan Arnaud for rekindling the desire to write and for providing the perfect environment in which to complete the project.

This book is dedicated to the memory of my father, George Adamson, journalist and writer, who died on 19 February 1998.

Introduction

In focusing on Algeria, this study aims to show that the political crisis of legitimacy in Algeria today which has resulted in the deaths of some 50,000 people[1] during the last five years is not just an issue for Algeria but is also a lesson for the limitations of western economic and political analysis. Interest in Algeria today is either because it is seen as the next site of an Islamist government or because of fears that the internal struggle for hegemony between the government and the Islamist groups will be transferred to Europe, and more particularly to France which hosts the largest Algerian immigrant population in the European Union. These concerns are very different from those which aroused widespread interest in Algeria in the 1960s and 1970s. Interest at that time came primarily from among western radicals who believed that Algeria had found a solution not only to the problems of colonization and decolonization but also to the organization of a socialist economy. Then Algeria was perceived as offering a positive example of what could be achieved by a newly independent Third World nation. However, in spite of the optimism with which the post-independent Algerian state was initially viewed, perspectives on it would change quite quickly – not because anyone thought there might be a civil war or a struggle for hegemony between competing discourses on the form and content of the late twentieth-century Muslim state, but because it was felt that Algeria's radical socialist experiment based on *autogestion* (or self-management) was being consumed by an increasingly bureaucratic state. As a reflection of reality, this was indeed what happened; but the reasons why it happened are at the same time more complex than was thought and more interesting, as they serve to illustrate the fragility of the experiment itself, the weaknesses of the theorization of the character of a socialist economy, and the Algerian state's own dualism. Both the fragility of the experiment and the issue of the weaknesses in the theorization of the socialist economy are bound up with the issue of dualism. The dualism which characterized the Algerian regime was manifested in a political discourse which employed the language of socialism but which employed the political and economic practices with which the Algerians were most familiar, namely the French *étatiste* model. It reflected the fact that the Algerians like the western radicals – even if they did not share their widespread disillusionment with both capitalism and soviet-style economies – knew relatively little about what shape a socialist state or a socialist economy should have.[2]

Post-independent Algeria provides an opportunity to study the impact which a particular choice of economic development policies had on a country situated at the intersection of five worlds – Europe, the Middle East, Africa, the Third World and the Muslim world – each of which had an influence on the character of the post-independent state and the policy choices which were made. Europe was represented by the colonial power, France, and was present in language and in political and economic institutions. The Middle East represented the Arab world, the language of which the nationalists of the 1930s had envisaged as the means by which the people's soul would be reawakened and which the post-independence governments also invoked to represent their new world. Africa is involved because in continental terms Algeria had been an entrepôt for the cross-Saharan trade and the ambivalence of that location on the edge of the Arab world and north of the Sahara also has an impact on the tension between the geographical and the ideological positions. The Third World has its place because colonization had left an economy and state poorly adapted to the demands of post-independence economic development. Finally comes the Muslim world, reclaimed through the idea of an Arab identity but a world in the process of transformation, in which increasingly events outside of the Middle East were changing its character. Consequently, post-independence Algeria offers an occasion to examine critically the options available at that juncture for economic development; and how, when the choices were made, they were affected by the impact of and the interaction between the internal and the external environments.

Algeria illustrates some of the problems which were posed by the need to operate its economy globally while its internal economic and political infrastructures were poorly developed. In the early 1960s, Algeria appeared to possess all the required resources to make a successful entry into the global economy. However, by the mid-1970s, it was clear that it might have entered the global market but that it had not done so in such a way that benefits accrued internally. It became increasingly evident that the economy had failed to develop in a sufficiently holistic manner to provide for both capital investment and for political and social needs, so that when economic problems began to arise so did political and social problems, with the result that, at the beginning of the 1990s, the attempts to provide for political and social expression caused the implosion of the whole edifice. The immediate cause of this implosion was the decision to annul the second round of elections due to take place in January 1992 because of the certainty of a victory by the Islamist party, the *Front Islamique du Salut* (FIS – Islamic Salvation Front). Since then, the political situation has continued to deteriorate as armed resistance groups proliferate and state repression intensifies, and there has been no economic recovery.[3] However, the extent to which economic recovery has been affected by political repression and the actions of the armed resistance groups is more difficult to assess; the impact of the military struggle for power on the daily lives of individuals and families, on human rights and on freedom of expression has resulted in their further deterioration.[4] The question which is then posed is how to make sense of this failure. It can probably only be understood if it is placed in the context of not only a particular history but also a particular colonial relationship. The importance of both of these and the interaction between them is that this particular historical experience is responsible for the subsequent configurations and weaknesses of social and economic structures. Furthermore, a second major historical factor is the interaction between Algeria's former status as one of the outlying regions of the western Muslim world and its subsequent special status within the French colonial empire, which helped create the particular conditions of Algerian decolonization and post-colonial choices.

Algeria's potential economic wealth derived from its Saharan oil and gas reserves. The country's programme of economic development was based on a commitment to full industrialization of the economy, and the adoption of a discourse of socialism. As a result, post-colonial Algeria is an example of a particular optimistic view of the possibilities for economic growth which, in the 1960s, was thought achievable. Algeria's experience illustrates the impact that adoption of this type of economic programme and political discourse had, and provides an example of the limitations of this particular model of economic development. Problems arising from the adoption of this model were apparent by the early 1970s, and the death of Boumediene in 1978 can perhaps be seen retrospectively as a marker in the increasingly problematic nature of his strategy. However, it is also useful to recall that at his death, Algeria's economic problems appeared to be less serious than those of her immediate neighbours, Morocco and Tunisia. In fact, Morocco's economic problems were to lead to the intervention of the International Monetary Fund in 1980 and the rescheduling of its debts. Algeria's own debt rescheduling would become an issue of the 1990s.

Although the precise nature of the interaction between the economic and the political now receive greater attention than they did during the

1970s when the emphasis was on the economic, it would still seem to be the case, as the debates on economic restructuring in Central and Eastern Europe illustrate, that many economic policy analysts continue to operate as if the political were a marginal consideration.[5] The debates which led to progressive economists recommending the economic development model which Algeria adopted took place against a series of discourses on 'development' which operated within narrowly defined parameters and which tended to concentrate on current, immediately visible social phenomena. Both those at the centre and those associated with the radical left tended to produce models based on universalistic models. On one side there were those models which argued that there was only one process of industrialization and that was the route by which Western Europe had industrialized. These have been characterized under the heading of 'modernization theory'. The most sophisticated exponents of this school were D. C. McClelland (1961) and Daniel Lerner (1964). This used a balance-sheet type approach in which Third World countries were measured against a Western European norm.

However, on the other side, radical researchers despite their critique of this model also tended to work from a universalistic norm. The major characteristic of these 'left' critiques of Third World states was their tendency to project on to them an idealized and abstracted notion of socialism. The origin of their discourse was a combination of the absence of actual Marxist socialist experience in Europe and the belief that, were classical Marxist texts followed, it would be possible to create a true 'socialist' state. At the same time, their ability to project successfully this discourse on to the Third World state was dependent upon, as well as reinforced by, the Third World state's own discourse and wish to claim for itself a socialist character. Algeria provides the example of this kind of interactive discourse. The question of 'Algerian' as an example of some ideal type was particularly marked in those studies which focused upon *autogestion* (self-management), examples of which are Ian Clegg (1971), *Workers' Self-Management in Algeria*, and Gérard Chaliand and Juliette Minces (1972), *L'Algérie indépendante*. Certainly, the reality of autogestion in Algeria was not to reflect the ideological premises of self-management as an alternative form of socialism. However, the nature of the critical analysis which was made of autogestion, and especially its eclipse because it was focused on autogestion as an authentic socialist paradigm, made the subsequent critique of agricultural policy subject to the issue of authenticity. The debate over agricultural policy is the subject of Chapter 5.

These 'left' critiques in many ways illustrate the types of hegemonic discourse about the Third World which were to become the subject of

Edward Said (1978), *Orientalism*. However, they also illustrate the problems of a social science discourse whose origins and methods are firmly in the metropolis. However, in the sense that it is the researchers of the metropolises who will continue to dominate social research in these areas, it is also necessary that this privileged position is used to reflect on the discourses which they have used. To make sense of a world whose share in the history of the metropolis is through the agency of empire requires that the role which each has played in the history of the other is accounted for. The study of the Algerian experience provides a particularly clear illustrative example of just how dependent the histories of each are upon the other. This is the subject of the discussion in Chapter 7, which examines how each has played and continues to play a formative role in the social, political and economic life of the other and how, more particularly, the Algerian–French relationship is an example of Bhabha's (1990: 218) 'repressed history'.

However, in order to explore the processes by which this 'repressed history' is created, the method employed is one in which there is a constant juxtaposition of the ideological with the practices of economic policy. Each of a number of agents which are considered to have influenced the Algerian polity and affected economic policy decision-making, and therefore the political configuration of the state in the post-independence period, are explored. This means that – although this is principally a study of political and economic discourses of the Boumediene period – in order to situate these historically, it was felt necessary to provide a brief introduction to the social, political and economic structures of the pre-colonial period. As a result, Chapter 2 discusses both the characteristics of Ottoman Turkish rule in the provinces and the social and economic structures which prevailed at the time of the Ottoman Turkish conquest in the sixteenth century. This is followed by a discussion of the impact of colonization and the colonial project on these base social and political structures. In the following chapter, the focus is on Islam and the character of Muslim practice in Algeria, in which there is some discussion of the relationship of Islam to the state and of the state to Islam. The emphasis is on the integral role of Islam, both in ascendance and in eclipse, to the foundational social and political structures. It is argued that to some extent the success of the colonial project depended upon the marginalization of Islam and that one of the principal means by which this was achieved was the denial of colonial citizenship to Muslims and the appropriation of the word 'Algerian' by the European settler population. The result was that the understanding of the public or political role of Islam was distorted and misunderstood. The impact of the rise of Islamist movements in Algeria has had the result of refocusing attention on Algeria's Muslim heritage. However, this has often been in a way which suggests that it is not an integral part of the history and social structure of the society. In an important study of Muslim practice in Algeria, *Les Versets de l'invincibilité, permanence et changements religieux dans l'Algérie contemporaine* (1995), the effects of this neglect of the political role of religious practice are examined by Fanny Colonna.

For some time now, Muslim writers such as Akbar S. Ahmed (1991, 1992) have pointed out that the secularization of western societies has tended to result in, at best, simple omission and, at worst, active hostility towards the role which religion may play in the conduct of both personal and state affairs within society. The secularization of western societies has been attributed to the philosophical developments which were set in motion by the Enlightenment (Said, 1993). However, it is probably also true to say that – although the western philosophical tradition since the Enlightenment has distanced itself from the view of the integral relationship between religion and society, and although in general western societies (if religion is measured in terms of attendance at Christian churches) appear to have moved away from religion as a central part of their identity – nevertheless such societies when challenged (and quite often the challenge is by Muslims) actively reassert their Christian identity. This reassertion of a Christian identity of the Western European state is also considered in Chapter 7: Algeria and France. Moreover, within the boundaries of the colonial project, religion and Christianity were an integral part of that project. Furthermore, Christianity historically has had a powerful influence on the shape of the Western European state as well as underpinning much of the political philosophies adhered to. The underestimation of the influence of religion means that both the role which Christianity played in the French colonial project and the influence which Islam has had on state and society have been both underplayed and exaggerated.

In Chapters 4, 5 and 6 which are concerned primarily with economic policy, and with the conflict between economic policy aims and objectives and the political discourse within which it was situated, a number of themes are used to centre the argument that the study of Algeria is, in effect, a study of competing ideologies. The question of the denial of religion and its place in the structuring of the state has already been mentioned. Other themes are the role and effects of western capitalism in its *étatiste* French form; the specificities of the Algerian economic strategy; the Algero-Franco relationship itself; the impact of a Third Worldist socialist rhetoric as the means by which the post-independence Algerian state attempted to negotiate internationally a viable post-independence economy and polity; and, finally, the role of international bodies such as the European Union. As a result, Chapter 2 focuses on the underlying social structures which were the base on which the colonial project was built and which help to provide an explanation for the failure of both the colonial project and the Boumediene project. Chapter 3 concentrates on Islam, how the discourses have been constructed and the critical 1930s period. It also discusses the use of women in defining the parameters of both the colonial and the national project. There is also some discussion of the international context within which the Algerian project was formulated, including the dominant ideologies of the state and economy in Muslim societies in which the influences of both Nasser and Mustafa Kemal played a role.[6] The study will also argue that the principal pillars of this strategy were put in place during the period 1965–78, the period of the Boumediene presidency, and that its failure reflects a combination of the internal weakness of civil and political institutions and the character of the economic models used. These are the subject of Chapters 4, 5 and 6 which aim to show why the political and economic strategies of the post-independent state were unable either to deliver a better life to Algeria's rapidly growing urban population or to satisfy the aspirations of those who had benefited from the development of mass education.

While I do not intend to diminish the role that internal factors have played in the collapse of the Algerian ideal, nevertheless all criticisms which are made, and particularly those which relate to economic policy-making, have to be viewed within the overall structural constraints within which such countries have to operate. The notion of even the possibility of radical economic change seems today even less probable than in 1962 when Algeria gained independence. The collapse of the former Soviet Union, and the adoption by all the countries of the former eastern bloc of policies which aim to restructure their economies on capitalist lines, have suggested that in reality states have only one option and that is entry into the capitalist market. Chapters 7 and 8 are therefore essentially concerned with the relationships between Algeria and the external world in which the Franco-Algerian relationship is important, as is Algeria's relationship with the European Union and the Muslim world community. How these impact on both external and internal Algerian relations is the subject of Chapter 8. The post-independence Algerian state has been shaped both by its own past and by the world around it; if even to a small extent the arguments which are presented help to better understand why the Algerian experiment went wrong, then perhaps this study will have diminished a little the distance which separates Europe from the worlds it colonized.

Notes

1. Figure reported in *Le Monde*, 20.11.96 and based on a report carried out by Amnesty International published 19 November 1996.
2. The understanding of how little was known about how a socialist economy might function has been highlighted by the political collapse of the Communist party governments in central and eastern Europe. In the 1960s, the western left sought alternative models to the dominant socialist paradigm of the soviet-style economies. However, as Algeria illustrates, this was an area of experiment, the outcomes of which no one could really anticipate.
3. *Le Monde*, 12.1.96 reported that, in the September 1995 review by the International Monetary Fund of the adjustment programme by the Algerian government, it was shown that two of the eight stated criteria had not been met. The first concerned the amount of credits distributed within the economy, caused in particular by the failure to reform the public sector; and the second, arguably more serious, that foreign exchange reserves had not obtained the desired levels while at the same time continuing to fall.
4. For example the targeted assassination of journalists, writers and academics as well as mass bombings by the Islamist resistance groups, and suspected similar counter-attacks by the security forces. The government's suppression of any form of opposition can be illustrated by the arrest, trial and imprisonment of the cartoonist Chawki Amari who worked on the private daily *La Tribune*. Chawki Amari was accused of a 'drawing offence' (*délit de dessin*) and was imprisoned on 4 July 1996, and his trial and conviction were completed by 31 July 1996. Despite calls by the prosecution for an eighteen-month custodial sentence, he was given a three-year suspended sentence. At the same time, the paper's editor was given a one-year suspended sentence with publication of the journal suspended for a further month. See *Le Monde*, 2.8.96 and 5.9.96 and *Libération*, 31.7.96.
5. The best known example of this kind of economic policy analyst is Jeffrey Sachs of Harvard.
6. The Algerian project may be called a Kemalist state project because of the choice of governmental form made by Algerian politicians at independence. Their choice can be interpreted as an attempt to build a modernistic state after the Turkish pattern. The word Kemalist is derived from the name of the founder of the post-Ottoman successor Turkish state, Mustafa Kemal (Ataturk), who attempted the construction of a secular state on the western model which would be able to compete economically with the established capitalist states. It was also itself an *étatiste* political model.

2

Historical Origins of the State in Algeria

This chapter seeks to explore how the particular configuration of institutions and historical experience of the geographical area which became the post-independent nation-state of Algeria predisposed that state towards the bureaucratic modes of organization which the Boumediene Presidency helped to establish and which form the backdrop to the 1991–2 crisis. This will allow a consideration of how even a relatively economically advanced pre-colonial state became subordinated to a colonial power which was neither significantly more prosperous nor politically more stable, but which through its colonial relations was able to develop its own economy while that of its colony atrophied. The focus here is on social and economic structures and the impact on them of colonization, whereas the next chapter will look in more detail at questions of ideology and the role occupied by Islam in such processes. The aim is to provide some basis by which it may be possible to answer the question of why, in 1962, Algeria appeared to promise so much not only to its own population but also to many outside and yet through its subsequent history has appeared to fail to fulfil this promise.

In his Preface to the English translation of Ageron's *Modern Algeria*, Michael Brett suggests that French policy towards Algeria was characterized by a dualism which on the one hand incorporated Algeria into France but on the other kept it as far as possible separate from the metropolitan country. The result was Algeria's isolation from the rest of the world, with the consequent effect of rendering its problems parochial (Ageron, 1991: vi). This issue of dualism and the character of French policy towards Algeria is a question which forms a recurring theme within this book and is the subject particularly of Chapter 7.

However, before making a more detailed examination of the form and practice of French colonial rule in Algeria and the impact which it had on the pre-colonial society, some understanding of the ideas which underpinned the French colonial project is necessary. A starting point for understanding both the wider framework and the specificities of this project is provided by Anthony Pagden's study (1995) of the ideologies of colonization of the three major imperial powers, Spain, France and

Britain, *Lords of All the World*. Pagden's primary concern is with the colonial projects of these three powers in the Americas, as he argues that it is in the struggle in the Americas that the ideologies of empire (which these three primary imperial powers came to adopt) are developed (Pagden, 1995: 4). However, the exploration of the ideologies of empire in the Americas is also a means to explain the conditions which predisposed these three countries to develop overseas empires. At the centre of his argument is the idea that all three sought to some extent in these projects to emulate and recreate the Roman Empire. However, in practice, only Spain could ever genuinely claim to be in some way Imperial Rome's successor and only because it was able to draw upon an external legitimation provided by the Pope. This was an endorsement of the imperial project which Britain and particularly France sought but never obtained: Britain because it was outside the Catholic world after the sixteenth century, and France despite the efforts of Francis I; and the later attribution to the French king of the title 'the eldest son of the Church' (*le fils aîné de l'église*)[1] was never achieved. French interest in North Africa can be seen in this light, in the sense that North Africa had been subject to Roman imperial rule, thus the creation of a French empire in North Africa could be said to be a recreation of that empire. Certainly some of the concepts which it employed are reminiscent of those which underpinned the Roman empire, such as being possessed of a civilization for export and a mission to convert the pagan/barbarian. French attitudes to empire exhibited a certain tension between the idea of it as 'a source of honour' (Pagden, 1995: 126–8) and the view first expressed by Talleyrand in 1797 (quoted in Pagden, 1995: 126) of empire as being a source of commercial and agricultural profit. However, Talleyrand was also to argue that it would be better for the French empire to be based on the Greek model rather than the Roman model. In spite of views such as these, which were themselves a reflection of France's dual heritage of, on the one hand, the new republic of which Talleyrand was a member and, on the other, the monarchial tradition, in practice, the French empire tended to emulate the characteristics of the Spanish empire, including the incorporation of the colonies into the *metropole* (motherland).

An earlier commentator on the French ideology of empire, the French colonial historian Henri Brunschwig (1964: 13), drew a distinction between the motivation which lay behind the British quest for empire and that of the French empire. He also argued that the French imperial project exhibited a certain tension between empire as 'prestige' and empire as 'profits'. However, even if the primary motive of the imperial project had been prestige, the profits of the sugar trade in the early half of the seventeenth century and their impact on metropolitan France went some way towards a shift of perspective which would cause the philosophers of the Enlightenment such as Montesquieu to view the primary purpose of the colony as a source of commercial profit (Brunschwig, 1964: 14). Such a view of empire would change when this empire collapsed in the wake of the defeat of Napoleon. Although Brunschwig's principal argument is that France did not need colonies and that the colonies acquired by the middle of the nineteenth century, namely Algeria, Senegal and Cochin-China, were of little direct benefit to the French economy (1964: 18); this did not prevent individuals, whether individual businesses or colonial officialdom (including army and navy officers) from deriving considerable benefit from the empire (1964: 163–6). The importance of the role of members of the two armed forces of the army and navy in the colonial project, which Brunschwig suggests, is the focus of Patricia Lorcin's (1995) study *Imperial Identities*, while Philippe Lucas and Jean-Claude Vatin (1975) in *L'Algérie des anthropologues* also draw attention to the other role played by the military in France's colonial project, that of scientific commentators on the life and mores of the peoples whom they were engaged in conquering. Algeria illustrates just how important the role of the military in the colonial project was, where they simultaneously played the roles of conquerors, administrators, ethnologists and anthropologists. It can be argued that the military were able to play such an important role because doing so allowed three aims to be achieved. In the first place, conquest itself extolled the glory of France. Secondly, conquest offered key opportunities for Frenchmen to gain promotion and both economic and social success. Thirdly, through their primacy, the military were able to maintain the colonial project even when, politically, such projects were unpopular at home. Their capacity to do so stemmed from their control of information and knowledge about the colony. That the military were so important is a reflection of the institutions which were established after the 1789 Revolution. Thus, the leading education institutions of the post-Revolutionary period, such as the prestigious *Grandes Écoles* and specifically the *École Polytechnique*, were military in origin and retained certain of their traditions until relatively recently. As an illustration of both the penetration and the interconnection between French military and civil life, the *École Polytechnique* is a supreme example: founded in 1794, under the tutelage of the Army Ministry, its purpose was to train for the state both the highest grade civil and military engineers.[2]

The importance which can be ascribed to the military in the pursuit of the colonial project in Algeria (Lorcin, 1995) needs to be set against the civilizing mission described by Pagden (1995) and the duty, leading from the French Revolution, to unite in common purpose with the peoples of the world (Brubaker, 1992: 44). This in turn gave rise to notions of assimilation. The first, an idea of personal assimilation which would give to the individual both actual and potential equality; and secondly, assimilation which was administrative, political and economic. Crowder (1968: 167) suggests that the first of these notions was soon abandoned, except in its effects on a small colonial elite, leaving the second to be pursued. However, although the idea of personal assimilation may have slipped out of focus as the Empire expanded, it never entirely disappeared; it had inspired Toussaint L'Ouverture's revolution in San Domingo in 1791 (James, 1991) and would inspire the cultural renaissance movement of Césaire and Senghor (Hall, 1995: 10); and its continuing presence can be captured in the word and the idea of *la Francophonie* (a French-speaking cultural world).[3] These competing discourses form a central part of the colonial project in Algeria in which Algeria as a geographical area was considered an integral part of France, but the majority of its inhabitants because they continued to wish to be Muslims were excluded from citizenship for the totality of the period of colonial rule (Lebovics, 1992: 122–3). It is only possible to make some sense of the dualistic nature of the French colonial project in Algeria if the colonial project itself is explored in the light of the nature of the state and civil society which it encountered.

Pre-Ottoman Turkish traditions of state and society in the Maghreb

The starting point for a nearly contemporary study of pre-Ottoman Turkish traditions of state and society in the Maghreb is undoubtedly the work of the fourteenth-century North African philosopher and historian, Ibn Khaldūn.[4] The importance of Ibn Khaldūn's *The Muqaddimah* stems not only from the fact that it provides an account of the nature of state and society in the Maghreb just before the Ottoman seizure of power in Algiers in 1534, but also because it has become a reference point for interpretations of the condition of North African society at the time of the French conquest. The Anglo-Saxon anthropologist and writer on Islam Ernest Gellner[5] utilized Ibn Khaldūn's theory of history in conjunction with Durkheimian sociological theory, and more especially Durkheim's distinction between mechanical and organic solidarity (Durkheim, 1964), to construct a view of the nature of society and societal formations in North Africa in particular but also within the Muslim world generally. The French geographer Yves Lacoste is another of these interpreters, and in his book (1984) *Ibn Khaldoun: The Birth of History and the Past of the Third World* he argues that Ibn Khaldūn can be seen 'as one of the founders of History' (1984: 1) and his work as 'a major contribution to the study of the underlying causes of underdevelopment' (1984: 2). In Lacoste's view, what Ibn Khaldūn provides is an explanation for the absence of the conditions which would have led to the creation of a bourgeoisie capable of creating the social and political conditions for economic development (1984: 4).

In essence, both Lacoste and Gellner are concerned with the conditions under which modern capitalist – and therefore industrial – society has emerged, and Ibn Khaldūn provides them both with an image of otherness which can be used in support of their very different views about its future. While Lacoste interprets Ibn Khaldūn's study as history and essentially the study of a historical 'period of ossification punctuated by intermittent crises' (1984: 5) which effectively creates the conditions for later colonization, Gellner interprets Ibn Khaldūn sociologically as a 'theorist of *social cohesion*' (1981: 86). Gellner is also using Ibn Khaldūn as a means to explore the reasons why society and economy in North Africa seem not to have had the conditions necessary for the emergence of industrial society. In Gellner's view such an explanation is provided by Ibn Khaldūn's description of the way in which societies are bound together, which Gellner summarizes thus: 'On the one hand there is the cohesion, the capacity to identify with the group and internalise it, which is exemplified by tribal society; and on the other, the lack of cohesion in urban society, despite or indeed because of its "organic character", i.e. its highly developed division of labour.' (1981: 86–7), which is the characteristic of modern industrial societies. This is accompanied, Gellner argues, by the following premiss that 'the cities, though offering very little by way of *political* contribution to society, are *economically* indispensable.' (1981: 87), which he further argues represents 'the principal partners in traditional Maghrebin society – tribesmen and townsmen' who, significantly, are also contemptuous of each other.

However, although the distinguishing of 'tribesmen and townsmen' may not itself be problematic, its use has become embodied in a view of North African society as divided between two ethnicities: Berber and Arab. This view of Algerian society as comprised of two ethnicities which in turn could be equated with a positive and negative character has also passed into the popular imagination, as Lorcin (1995: 2–13) persuasively argues, through the manner in which Maghrebi society was observed and recorded by the scientific studies carried out by the first military administrations in Algeria. These studies also embodied a juxtaposition between uncorrupted and democratically organized Kabyles and corrupt and despotic Arabs. It was a view which was based in large measure on the military and political realities of the time but it carried with it the idea that it was possible for the colonial administration to deal with the former but not with the latter. Jacques Berque described this view of Maghrebi society by the colonial regime as the image of a Berber reservation (1967: 217–19). Lorcin argues that Ibn Khaldūn had relatively little impact on the construction of French ideas about Algeria during this formative period.[6] However, Lorcin also suggests that it is more difficult to evaluate the impact of Ibn Khaldūn on studies produced in the second half of the nineteenth century and, to illustrate this, she includes a quotation from the colonial historian Émile Gautier writing in 1931 whose view was that 'For all his genius, he has an oriental brain which does not function like ours. He cannot be read like Titus-Livius or Polybius or even Procopius. He has to be interpreted, transposed.' (Lorcin, 1995: 108) In spite of this apparent disdain, Lacoste argues that in fact Gautier actively misinterprets the opposition which Ibn Khaldūn makes between 'the rural population, the people of the *bled* – a category which includes both nomads and sedentary farmers – and the townspeople and farmers who live near the towns' (Lacoste, 1984: 67) to reinforce the colonial proposition which is at the centre of Lorcin's argument 'Nomadic–Sedentary, Arab–Berber antagonism' (Lacoste, 1984: 68; Lorcin, 1995: 74–5). The use of the terms 'Berber' and 'Arab' beginning with that by Ibn Khaldūn himself has therefore caused much difficulty because they are used both paradoxically and interchangeably not only to describe the peoples of North Africa but also to distinguish unfavourably between them. Thus the words are not neutral constructs but are intended to convey a range of meanings not only about the peoples themselves but also about how they are and have been seen by others. The symbolic content of these words is illustrated by the use in contemporary France of the word 'Arab' simultaneously as a collective term for immigrants and as a term of abuse.

In constructing a picture of pre-Ottoman Turkish state and society in the Maghreb from *The Muqaddimah*, one finds three concepts used to underpin Ibn Khaldūn's study (and which have been employed by contemporary writers such as Gellner). They are *'umran* (civilization), *'asabiyah* (group spirit) and *badawah* (desert life or attitude). In contrasting the different lives of the Bedouin and the sedentary people, Ibn Khaldūn is also concerned with the processes of urbanization (1967: I, 252–3) and the impact which this has on individuals and groups. His discussion of the role of *'asabiyah* is of particular interest because of the description of the processes which lead to the transformation of a society based on closely knit groups of common descent to one in which groups continue to emphasize purity of lineage or descent but in practice assimilate new members who then assume the accepted group line of descent (1967: I, 267–8). To illustrate this process, he gives an example of a group, the Zanātah, which claimed to be of Arab origin through descent from the 'Abbasids even though there was no record of any 'Abbasid having set foot in the Maghreb.[7] However, Ibn Khaldūn also argues that power resides with those who can convince themselves and others of their superiority of descent (1967: I, 277). In spite of the importance of descent manifested through the idea of 'house' (1967: I, 273), Ibn Khaldūn sees power as both personal and transient with the result that it is usually only possible for a single group to retain power for a maximum period of four generations (1967: I, 279). At the same time, power can be legitimated and strengthened through religious feeling – a view which is essentially reflective of Ibn Khaldūn's own experience of the contemporary history of the Maghreb and Spain in which religious belief had sustained the seizure of power by two extraordinary dynasties, the Almoravids and the Almohads (1967: I, 321). In other words, the maintenance of secular power requires religious sanction; thus Ibn Khaldūn's analysis of the actuality of power restates the foundational link within the Muslim world between the secular and the sacred. In this sense, without identification with and adherence to Islam, state power cannot be obtained.

In understanding economy and society in this period, the most important chapter is Chapter IV (1967: II, 235–307) for it is in this chapter that Ibn Khaldūn suggests reasons why the economy of the Maghreb had not experienced the same levels of growth as other parts of the contemporary Muslim world, including Spain. Central to his argument is that the most powerful elements characterizing Maghrebi society, namely group feeling and common descent, are representative of a rural-based society and economy. Not only are they features of society which are more attuned to the patterns of rural life, they also actively inhibit the emergence and growth of towns and cities (1967: II, 266). Ibn Khaldūn argues that 'profit is the value realized from labor. When there is more labor, the value realized from it increases among the [people]. Thus, their profit of necessity increases.' (1967: II, 272). Consequently, the absence of great cities in North Africa meant that there was no base upon which a dynamic economy could be built. Similarly he argues that labour specialization can only occur when there is both a sufficiently large concentration of population and a stable government. In the Maghreb, he argues, no single group had ever held power for a long enough period for this to occur. He argues that neither the Romans who only controlled the coast nor the Arab conquerors of the seventh century were able to create the political conditions for economic growth (1967: II, 287–90).

To conclude this brief snapshot of North African society in the fourteenth century, it can be seen that Ibn Khaldūn's dialectical relationship between the countryside and the city is also the portrayal of a system of revolving power. In this system, a dynasty builds up its power base and strength from the position it holds in the countryside. It then uses that strength to acquire authority over the towns and cities but the fact of having acquired such authority begins the process of the decline of its power. It is this view of the cyclical nature of power which Gellner combines with Durkheim's concept of 'mechanical solidarity' to construct the notion of segmentary society in the North African context. This concept of revolving power between town and countryside also employs the concepts of Bled el-Makhzen (land of government) and Bled es-Siba (land of dissent) which have been used subsequently to explain, for example, the structure of politics in Morocco (Waterbury, 1970).

The question of the nature of Algerian society, its social structures and its peoples was not only a discussion which preoccupied the colonial administrators, it also became a point of struggle over the nature of knowledge as the period of direct colonial occupation began to draw to a close. Our discussion here illustrates how a single text, namely Ibn Khaldūn's *The Muqaddimah*, has been used by different authors in different ways to interpret state and society in North Africa. More recently it has been accorded a universal importance in the development of historical ideas. Here Ibn Khaldūn is seen by the historian Alex Callinicos as a transitional figure between ancient and modern conceptions of history (Callinicos, 1995: 62–3). Callinicos suggests that Ibn Khaldūn integrates 'a proto-materialist conception of history with a classical theory of constitutions' which is summed up in the phrase 'Dynasties have a natural lifespan like individuals' (1995: 62–3; Ibn Khaldūn, 1967: I, 343).

The organization of the Ottoman Turkish state and the Beylik of Algiers

Ibn Khaldūn provides a context for the basic pattern of organization of rural and urban society in the pre-Ottoman Turkish period, and his discussion poses questions about the capacity of successor regimes to create the necessary stability for bringing about the social and political changes needed to create the conditions required for economic development. The importance of the Ottoman Turkish state in

Maghrebine history is that for almost three hundred years it was the principal geopolitical power in North Africa, which means that its influence forms an essential part of the picture of state and society in the region. The creation of the Ottoman Turkish empire began in the fourteenth century; at its greatest extent at the end of the seventeenth century, it stretched from Hungary and the Balkans to the borders of Georgia and south to Mosul in northern Iraq, the Yemen, Egypt and west along the southern shore of the Mediterranean as far as modern Morocco (Lewis, 1995). Ottoman expansion into North Africa began in 1517 with the conquest of Egypt and was followed in 1534 by the incorporation of the Algiers corsairs through the appointment of Khayr ad-Din as Capudan Pasha (Admiral of the Sultan's fleet), the taking of Tripoli in 1551 and the recapture of Tunis from Spain in 1574. Although the Ottoman Turkish Empire was the major political power in North Africa, it never controlled Morocco nor was its control entirely unchallenged as for most of the sixteenth century, there was an open struggle with Spain for control of the Mediterranean seaways. At the time of the establishment of the Algiers corsair state in 1516 by Aruj ad-Din, Spain had a network of defensive forts along the North African coast which had been established between 1509 and 1511 by Ferdinand II (Braudel, 1973: 855); while Oran had been occupied in 1505 and Spain (apart from a short period between 1708 and 1732 when it was controlled by the Beylik of Algiers) would retain control of the city until 1791 (Lespès, 1934; Braudel, 1973: 856–7).[8]

Ottoman Turkish rule fulfilled one of the criteria that Ibn Khaldūn argued was necessary for economic development to take place, namely the longevity of geopolitical control. However, like the earlier Roman and Christian empires Ottoman Turkish control was largely confined to the coastal region and the cities, thus the extent of its influence over the population at large has to be seen as limited. Furthermore, the establishment of the corsair state of Algiers in 1516 was the prelude to a period of almost a century of struggle with Spain for hegemony in this part of the Mediterranean (Braudel, 1973). Ottoman Turkish suzerainty has consequently to be seen through two prisms. The first is the prism of the corsair state; and the second that of its status as a province of the Ottoman empire. In the case of the corsair state of Aruj and Kayr ad-Din, the primary purpose for its establishment had been as a base to control the seaways and therefore to be better placed to carry out the piratical raids on which the economic wealth of the state was dependent. When Khayr ad-Din became Admiral of the Sultan's fleet, such activities were incorporated within the naval strategy of the Empire. However, as a state whose orientation and wealth were towards the sea, there was no pressing need for the state to have control of the interior. The state needed control of the hinterland around the urban centres in order to ensure that these centres were adequately provisioned, but its primary focus outside of its corsair activities was the cities as centres of administration and commercial activity. The result was that agriculture was perceived as a secondary activity.

As a province of the Ottoman Turkish Empire, its administration was located around two authorities, the *Bey* who was chosen from the military class to represent the Sultan's executive authority; and the *qadi* who would be a member of the *'ulama* (teachers of the law), and whose job it was to represent the Sultan's legal authority. The administration of land itself within an Ottoman Turkish-controlled province occurred under the auspices of what is called the *timar* system. The starting point of the timar system was that all land was the property of the state with, however, two principal exceptions: *mulk* or freehold land, and *wakf* lands or endowed property. Mulk land gave to the peasant who worked it the status of hereditary tenant and, although he could pass his land rights on to his son, he could not sell the land or provide for its grant or transfer outside of these limits. However, whenever the state was weak, private property in land was created. Wakf lands were usually endowed to provide revenue to the Muslim authorities but it was also a means by which those not entitled to hold land themselves, for example the women of the harem, could endow the use of the land and thus provide for their descendants. Immediate local control of land lay in the hands of the *sipahis* who formed the cavalry levies of the Empire. The sipahis did no agricultural work themselves but were entitled to receive from the mulk labourers certain services. The restrictions on the ownership of land, coupled with the emphasis on political influence as allied to proximity to the centre of power (whether the Sultan or the local regional centre), helped to give impetus to the growth of cities. A further feature of Ottoman administration was that importance was measured in terms of the degree of proximity, whether lands or people, which was held to the sovereign; thus the Beylik of Algiers was in this context of much less importance to the Sultan than a province closer to the centre would have been.

Although Ottoman Turkish sovereignty was to prove remarkably durable, during which time notions of frontiers and sovereignty within the Beylik began to evolve, these processes had not begun to create a homogeneous society. This was due partly to the heterogeneous nature of the province geographically, and consequently in terms of its economic activity; partly because of the dual character of its foundation; and partly also as a consequence of the internal changes which had begun to take place within the beylik as its links with the Ottoman centre became increasingly tenuous. This last process was a natural consequence of the sheer distance which separated the Beylik from the Ottoman heartlands and which the passage of time accentuated. It was also, however, the consequence of the limited character of Ottoman Turkish rule in the Beylik of Algiers. While the coastal plain, the Mitidja, had certainly owed allegiance to the Dey,[9] a position reinforced by the partition of land there among nominees of the Ottoman administration, other parts of the Beylik, and more particularly Kabylia, had been scarcely touched by the presence of an Ottoman Turkish administration in Algiers.

How the impact of colonial rule is understood depends to a considerable extent on the characterization of society and economy within the Beylik on the eve of colonization. However, any such description is inevitably read within the context of subsequent European colonization. Various attempts have been made to place the society and economy of the Beylik within a global theoretical framework. Among these have been Lacoste's 'military democracy' based on the idea that what you had were 'tribally-based societies in which an aristocracy that is still very much integrated into the tribe uses the complex influences it can exert (blood ties, client or vassal relationships) in order to lead a group of armed men to military victory' (1984: 30–1); subsequent victories lead to this tribal aristocracy becoming more differentiated and consequently evolving into a ruling class. Lacoste also argues that 'The military power of a group of tribes is not enough, and profits from trade are essential' (1984: 31). Gallissot[10] suggests that the first step towards understanding the Algeria of 1830 is the recognition of the fact that it was 'overwhelmingly rural (95% of the population and very dispersed)' (1971: 148) but also a society in which was found an 'aristocracy of government civil servants who were both political and economic, and military and urban but superimposed on a rural aristocracy which was more warrior than military and sometimes also religious' (1971: 160). Gallissot also argues that it is the presence of this military ruling class of civil servants which differentiated the social structure of the Beylik from European feudalism (1971: 164) and gives it the appearance of an Asiatic mode of production (1971: 169). In response Valensi suggested that what was in fact being discussed was 'the archaic mode of production' (1971: 223); whereas Nouschi (1971: 181) rejects all of these attempts at modelling, arguing that they are unhelpful.

More recently, Samir Amin has attempted to place such societies within the framework of what he calls 'tributary culture' (Amin, 1989).

All of these attempts to provide a theoretical framework reflect the problems which are faced when describing societies which are not within the main European paradigm that gave rise to the development of modern capitalism. What follows is therefore intended to provide an image of such a society, as far as possible within its own terms: a society which, although both relatively prosperous and governed by a military oligarchy, was ultimately not strong enough militarily to resist the sustained military campaigns which France would undertake after the initial seizure of Algiers in 1830. The fact that the Beylik and the local powers subject to it failed to resist the French army should not lead to the assumption that viable social, political and economic relations did not exist. In one sense, one could regard the French military expedition as no different from other military campaigns in the region, and which are the subject of Ibn Khaldūn's history. What was different about the French military campaign was that it would be conducted in the Beylik, but behind it lay the changes in the basic structure of economic and social relations which would enable France and its European neighbours to enter the stage of modern capitalism. Consequently the regime which was subsequently introduced was based on principles fundamentally different from those which had accompanied previous changes of political and military power.

The picture which Gallissot paints of the Beylik on the eve of colonization is one where a number of the major towns such as Algiers, Constantine and Médéa had begun to function as independent economic centres with a parallel concentration of private property within them. In some of them, and Constantine is one example, there were the beginnings of what might become important manufacturing centres. In the countryside, local notables were beginning to develop a distinctive presence, drawing their influence and power from religion and in particular from their control of the *habous* land.[11] Accompanying these developments was the emergence of a hierarchical chain of authority in which was embodied a system of patronage based on genealogy. Although Gallissot estimates that some 95 per cent of the population was living in the countryside, it must always be remembered that cities and towns have played a major role in life in the Muslim world and the Beylik was no exception. Algiers itself was a city of some 100,000 to 130,000 inhabitants; and although Oran's population under Spanish control had declined from 25,000 in the fifteenth century to 10,000 in 1738, the return to Ottoman hands in 1791 led to it replacing Mascara as the western capital in 1792. Other towns were the regional capitals of Constantine and Médéa, as well as the former Zayyanide capital of Tlemçen.

In 1830, the ruling class in the Beylik of Algiers spoke neither Arabic nor Berber, the two principal languages of the indigenous inhabitants of the Beylik; furthermore, in principle this ruling class was alien, drawn from other parts of the Empire. This was because the Ottoman Turkish empire drew its administrative personnel primarily from the Balkans (although also from Georgia and the Caucasus) and then educated it in Turkish. However, in the Beylik of Algiers, mirroring developments in other parts of the Empire (Lewis, 1995: 126), the underlying military code of the Janissaries had broken down. It had, for example, become quite common for a Janissary who had some years' experience and therefore contacts within the local community to marry into it – an event witnessed by the growth within the Beylik of the *kouloughli* (the children of Janissaries and local women). The social position of the children of these marriages was determined by the religious status of the mother. Where the mother was Muslim, the children's social position was determined by her social position and they were not eligible for membership of the *Oldjach*.[12] Where the mother was Christian, they usually inherited their father's status. Another example of localization was that, in the regional Beylik, it was not unusual for non-Ottoman cadres to be used in the administration (Vatin, 1974).

At the centre of the administration of the Ottoman Beylik of Algiers was the Dey, who since 1689 had been elected by the Oldjach. The Beylik itself was then divided into three regional Beylik: Constantine in the east, Titeri in the south (capital: Médéa), and Oran in the west; the coastal plain of the Sahal and the Mitidja was under the direct control of Algiers. This area was further sub-divided into four *outhans* or cantons which were administered by *Caids* with the outlying areas of Algiers itself being administered by officials called *Chioukh* (Vatin, 1974). The regional Beylik too were subdivided into *outhan* or *caidat*. The regional Beys were appointed by the Dey and not from Istanbul. They were supposed, however, to reaffirm their appointments every three years by presenting themselves in Algiers to pay the *denouche*.[13] In practice, however, Algiers exercised little authority over them and they were able to enjoy considerable autonomy.

The central administration of the Beylik of Algiers was based around four officials: the *vekilhardji* (or Minister of the Marine), the *khaznadji* (or Grand Treasurer), the customs' administrator and the *agha* (or military governor) of the Algiers garrison; in general terms, this pattern was duplicated in the regional Beylik. This was the inner administrative core of the Regency. However, the administrative remit of the Beylik did not extend over the whole of colonial Algeria; Kabylia and the greater part of the Saharan region were never fully under Ottoman Turkish control. They were able to remain largely outside Ottoman control primarily because of their geographic position and because of the Beylik's commercial orientation to the exterior. Kabylia was also a mountain region of isolated hamlets perched on the hill slopes where, because of its geographic isolation, its peoples had been less influenced by the Arabic language, and the dominant spoken language – Kabyle – had etymologically different roots. Similarly, the nomadic tribes of the Sahara also retained their original languages and were isolated by the difficulties of retaining any kind of central control over such a harsh environment dependent upon nomadic pastoralism.

If there were certain areas within the Beylik where the Ottoman Turkish administration exercised virtually no control, such as Kabylia and the Saharan region, their control over the remainder of the Beylik was to a large extent determined by the limitations of the social structures which pertained in the Beylik. Their categorization as the Berber areas of Algeria is in the light of our earlier discussion, probably misleading in the sense both that language does not necessarily mean different ethnic origin and that for political and religious reasons, groups often sought to acquire a genealogy of Arab descent. However, it is possible to delineate an area in geographic terms where the influence of the Arabic language was weakest. This comprised the Aurès, the Djurdjura and Kabylia plus the nomadic tribes of the Sahara: the Zenaga and the Tuareg. The structure of social organization of those other than the transhumants and pastoralists was that of a society where social organization was located at the village. A village would group together three or four hamlets and the villages themselves would be grouped together in cantons, and then the cantons would together form a federation which made up the tribe. The final level within this social system was the confederation which was an assembly of many tribes loosely claiming a common ancestry. At the level of the confederation, alliances would shift; there were no predetermined groups – in other words, the segmentary system alluded to by Ibn Khaldūn and analytically developed by Anglo-Saxon anthropologists such as Ernest Gellner (1969, 1981).

It is obvious that such a fluid socio-political organization presented many problems for a central government, and it was to have repercussions throughout the colonial period and the independence struggle. The Beylikal government's solution was to utilize the various levels of organization within the groups themselves and juxtapose an official hierarchy whose responsibilities were to the central administration, the aim being to formalize informal structures in order to be better able to collect taxes.

Economy and social organization in the Beylik

At the centre of administration in the Beylik, therefore, was this alien ruling group of Ottoman Turkish servants, and it was this group which controlled the appointment of administrative officers to the rest of the Beylik. In order to consolidate its position, then, it sought alliances with a section of the local population usually referred to in the literature as 'Moors'. This is a very vague term used to depict a wealthy urban stratum of local inhabitants who would have derived their position from their role in trade and commerce and the corporations/guilds. They included within their number Muslims descended from the Muslim diaspora from Spain. Although their wealth was not derived from land, some of them did own small properties in the Sahel which were worked by tenant farmers. It was the Moors who followed Ottoman Turkish social customs such as the harem and whose households contained slaves. The Moors did survive the period of colonization although their social and economic position was considerably eroded during that period.

External to these major stratifications, but playing an important role in the economic life of the Beylik, were two self-identified groups: the Mzab and the Jews. The Mzab were Muslim but they were Muslims who belonged to an exclusive group called the Ibadi.[14] Consequently, to maintain their exclusiveness, they had geographically confined themselves to five cities on the edge of the Sahara, of which Ghardaia was the principal town. Although they farmed the surrounding oases with the aid of slave labour, their primary occupation was that of traders. While the Mzab were members of an unorthodox Muslim group, they were nevertheless Muslim, which by definition the Jews were not. The position of Jews in North African society is complex, however, although at this period the relationship between Jew and Muslim more nearly reflects the relationship between the two communities which had prevailed in Muslim Spain, in part because North Africa, from the fifteenth century onwards, became one of the refuges not only for Muslims expelled from Spain by the Reconquista of Ferdinand and Isabella but also for Sephardic Jews. These new immigrants augmented a native Jewish community in North Africa which predates the coming of Islam into the region in the eighth century AD and which shared much socially and culturally with its neighbours who had adopted Islam. The impact of the Spanish Reconquista with its accompanying dispersal of the Spanish Jewish community to North Africa, Italy and the Ottoman capital, Istanbul, provided the Beylikal governments with access to a community which had links with both the Christian and the Muslim worlds. At the same time Jews often held posts of financial advisors to the governments of the Beylik.[15] Jews were not confined to Algiers: Oran also hosted an important Jewish community engaged in commerce and banking (Vayssettes, 1858-9; Eisenbeth, 1952).

Algiers' prosperity was based on her choice by the elder of the Barbarossa brothers, Aruj, as the capital of the Beylik and the centre of the corsair trade. A natural sea port, the city of Algiers was a tightly clustered collection of whitewashed buildings climbing up the hill behind which extensive suburbs provided the city with her agricultural requirements. Constantine, the capital of the eastern Beylik, was an Islamic centre dominated more than Algiers by large local families.[16] It also occupied a strategic position in commerce with Tunisia. Tlemçen, the historic capital of the Zayyanides, was a city with a rich cultural heritage. Oran was the port of entry for Tlemçen; not only did it import fine goods from Europe but it had also acted as the entrepôt for the trade traffic across the Sahara (from places such as Sidjilmasa and Tafilalet in the eastern Sudan, which were sources of such diverse products as gold and salt). From the Beylik, Europe bought fine cloths (damask, satins and taffetas), glassware, spices, perfumes, cork, skins, dried fruits, and oil for use in the European soap works. After 1791 when Oran returned to the Beylik and until 1830, the main commerce from Oran's port was the export of cereals – with one merchant alone in 1829 exporting approximately 95,000 hectolitres (of largely hard wheat) to Gibraltar, as well as livestock and wool (Vayssettes, 1858-9).

While the primary purpose for the establishment of the Beylik had been the control of the western Mediterranean sea routes, trade was also an important element of its economic life. This meant trade not only with the eastern Mediterranean but also with Scandinavia and North America and, in the early years of its life, the trans-Saharan trade in gold (Braudel, 1972: I, 474-5). Merchants from the Beylik also had permanent trading houses in Marseilles and Gibraltar (Eisenbeth, 1952; Julien, 1919; Spencer, 1976). While the Beylik gained important revenues from its commerce and from the corsair trade, there was also tribute from foreign consuls in return for the right to set up consulates in the capital, and from lending money at interest and from taxation. Taxes were paid on land, on goods and as customs duties. Taxes on land were received largely in kind – for example, the *hokour* was paid according to how much land two oxen could work in a season; and *achour* was a tithe on corn and barley. The outlying tribes paid a money tax but this was frequently commuted to a tax in kind. These taxes and a number of other smaller taxes paid largely on an individual basis went under the name of *gherama*.

In the towns, the small shops and the trades were liable for two taxes: a basic rate tax and an occasional additional levy. The gardens and other urban property were also taxed, the former paid at the rate of each pair of oxen used in tillage. The Beylikal state also made use of special levies as a means of obtaining revenue to finance its public works.

According to Vatin (1974), there were three main types of land tenure. These were *habbous* land (or land left in trust) and *melk* (or private property, frequently also with family connotations) which have already been mentioned; and *arch* (or the collectively attributed lands of the tribes). Vayssettes (1858–9) describes three further types of land in the Beylik. These were *azel* or land which was given to individuals in return for service, etc.; *djouabria* or land which was subject to a fixed term based on the amount of territory under cultivation; and finally, land which was worked under the *khamessa* system. The khamessa system is considered to be a uniquely North African feature and was a system of agricultural contract under which the tenant retained a quota part of one-fifth of the produce of the land which he occupied and worked, the remaining four-fifths representing the rental required by the landowner. It was found largely in the Sahel region and survived through to independence. Finally, there were the large state-owned farms of the Mitidja which were worked either by labourers or using the khamessa system. These supplied the grain whose export to France was what precipitated the invasion of the Beylik in 1830. Other property to be noted was that owned by the trade or manufacturing guilds. Further areas of property and land use were the gardens which were to be found in the cities, and the *fahs* which surrounded the cities. Some of these gardens were worked by slaves, but in the main they were worked by gardeners who paid tithes or kept half of the produce they grew in the case of tobacco, turnips, peppers, vegetables, etc., but only one-third in the case of the maize crop. The fahs were the province of small proprietors, *métayers* (tenant farmers) or agricultural workers. The fahs averaged four to five hectares and on them were grown fig trees, olives and chestnuts, and usually had also a small area devoted to viniculture. In the oases, dates, bananas, etc. were grown and the cultivation was usually done by slave labour. The Mzab best illustrate this system. They themselves were extensively engaged in commerce and occupied an entrepreneurial role while their lands around their desert cities were worked by slave labour from the south. Within the Beylik, substantial stock-keeping was also practised, in particular by the nomadic tribes of the Saharan regions and on the high plains, as for example in the Sétif region.

Within this general picture, the Kabyle are especially interesting because their subsistence farming in their high, isolated hamlets of the

Djurdjura had led to a severe pressure on land availability which had begun to drive the rural population away from the land (Gallissot, 1971). As a result, they had become 'the labour force of the workshops and construction yards of the Dey, already the possessors of all the skills to be learnt outside of the corporations' (Gallissot, 1971: 155). This view of the Kabyle is supported by Boyer (1963) who records how the Kabyle were to be found squatting outside the gates of Algiers, waiting for employment. That employment might be porterage in the corn market; day-labouring on the country estates of the citizens of Algiers or in the brickworks and stoneworks of the suburbs; or as domestic servants for the consuls and Christian merchants. In the Kabyle region itself, it has been suggested, at least some kind of labour specialization had begun (Lord, 1855; Morell, 1854). Both these authors writing in the middle of the nineteenth century provide evidence of economic activity in the Kabyle region. They write that the Kabyle mined lead, copper and iron, from which they manufactured firearms, farming implements and domestic utensils as well as gunpowder, soap and coins. It is further noted that this entry into non-agricultural activity did not involve women, although women continued to work alongside men in the fields as well as being spinners and weavers.

France and Colonial Algeria: the French conquest and its legacy

Prior to the sending by France of its expeditionary force to Algiers in 1830, which began the process of colonization, French contact with the pre-colonial Beylik of Algiers was primarily as a result of the role which Marseilles played in commercial and political relations with the Beylik (Spencer, 1976). In addition, they had operated various small commercial operations at both Algiers and Bône,[17] and some even smaller operations at La Calle and Collo, run under the auspices of the Agence d'Afrique (the former Compagnie Royale d'Afrique). In 1808, Napoleon I had sent a reconnaissance expedition under a Commandant Boutin to draw up detailed plans of the environs of Algiers as a prelude to its conquest (Charles-Roux, 1932). Napoleon also calculated that it would require at least 30,000 and possibly as many as 80,000 troops to conquer the Beylik. However, Napoleon's interest was turned elsewhere and instead it was a French government, increasingly in debt to the Beylik, which finally in 1830 launched the attack which began the conquest of the Beylik of Algiers. The potential of the Beylik for self-development on the eve of the French conquest remains a question of the extent to which autonomous development outside western capitalism was possible. However, French conquest led to 132 years of French colonial rule, providing – as in Ibn Khaldūn's theoretical framework – a period of political stability.

Why, then, despite what was one of the longest periods of colonial domination in Africa, did French rule not realize the economic possibilities which its new colony offered? How this is answered is in many ways a reflection of the discourse which is chosen. For example, colonial discourse always argued that without colonization, the colonized country would have been in a substantially worse economic position. Post-independence discourse usually argued that colonial rule had destroyed all vestiges of the previous era and had therefore played an active role in the economic degradation of its colony. So what was the situation of France in 1830, and was its failure to realize some of the obvious economic opportunities presented by the new colony a unique consequence of the particular French situation or just another example of the relationship of colony and colonial power?

France's colonial venture into the Beylik took place in the wake of its own recovery from the effects of forty years of social and political upheaval, during which time the French king Louis XVI and much of the nobility had been executed or had gone into exile. 1830 itself signalled yet another political upheaval as one king – Charles X – was ousted by another – Louis-Philippe. Consequently, the France which undertook the conquest of the Beylik of Algiers in 1830 was not a strong, historically legitimated power but one which was still seeking legitimation. Furthermore, most sources attribute the conquest of Algiers to the failure by the French government to honour a debt contracted in 1800, the non-payment of which provoked the Dey of Algiers into striking the French consul in 1827, thus creating a debt of honour to be repaid.[18] However, it is also possible to argue that the occupation of the Beylik arose from a wider consideration of its strategic and political importance brought about at least in part by shifts which had taken place within the Beylik such as the realignment of corsair activity from the Mediterranean to the Atlantic and the beginnings of a network of commercial relations between the Beylik and northern Europe and the USA. Although it is possible to give a rationalist discourse to the conquest of the Beylik of Algiers, there is also evidence that it is an example of adventurist politics made possible by the political instability in France at the time. The evidence for this stems from the ambivalent attitudes of the French government which did not finally come down in favour of a full military conquest until 1840 when it sent General Bugeaud to crush the resistance of the Emir Abd el-Kader but which, despite a number of shifts in the composition of the French state during the period, allowed responsibility for the new colony to reside for most of the period up to 1870 in the hands of the Ministry of War.

The instability of the French regime in Algeria is indicated by the fact that until Bugeaud's appointment in 1840 as Governor-General, a post he held until 1847, there were five appointments to this the most senior post in the colony. In July 1834, responsibility for administration of the new colony had been transferred into the hands of the Ministry of War; and, although in 1845 Algeria was integrated into France and allowed to elect deputies to the French Assembly directly, this arrangement did not survive the seizure of power by the future Napoleon III in 1848 after the series of revolutions in Europe which had created the Second French Republic. The repression in France led to the reinstatement of the military administration in Algeria, although initially under the auspices of a Ministry of Algeria. This would survive until 1860 when central administration was once again transferred back to Algiers and a new Governor-General appointed.

Colonial dominance in the Beylik, now renamed Algeria, during the first forty years was therefore characterized by military occupation and a series of military campaigns aimed at establishing French control. However, from 1850 onwards that same military force began to come under constant pressure from the presence of a substantial and growing settler population, and the colony began to change its character from that of a military state to that of a colonial settler state. Whatever the actual form of the state, its goal remained the same – to establish French supremacy over the indigenous population. Establishing political control was, however, easier than establishing ideological control of the population or achieving the economic development of the colony.

Much has been written about the underdevelopment of the Algerian economy prior to its colonization by France; however, it has already been suggested that behind the initial conquest lay a series of debts incurred by the French revolutionary governments for grain imports, and grain was still an important export for the colony in 1831.[19] Furthermore, there were no large tracts of empty land waiting to be exploited by the new colonial power. On the contrary, land in parts of the Beylik was already under strain in the sense that its productive capacity was insufficient to feed the population which depended upon it.

Colonization therefore meant the forcible displacement of the indigenous cultivator and his replacement by a *colon* or settler usually of French origin, but also, depending on which region, by other European nationals (Bontems, 1976: 188): for example, immigrants of Italian origin were dominant in the Constantine area (Mekhaled, 1995). At the same time, the whole relation of land to people to government was changed because, in the process of their colonization, the French colonizers imposed their relations of land, of property, of government, of the individual and of the state. Thus, while those 132 years of French rule did not bring about substantial economic growth, except in the short period after World War II when the general pace of industrial and technical development increased dramatically, it did bring about major changes in the nature of the relationship of people to the state, to the economy and to society.

The nature and consequences of French rule in Algeria can be observed by examining this description of Algeria in 1954 which was published in 1962 in a book by Roger Le Tourneau.[20] According to Le Tourneau, one of the most noticeable features of Algeria in 1954 was the growth of the indigenous population. However, it was a growth in population which had not produced a corresponding growth in the administrative infrastructure and the economic resources of the colony. For example, his figures show that between 1936 and 1954 the Muslim population had grown from just over six million to around eight and a half million. However, that increase in population had not been matched by any increasing Muslim role in the colony's administration. Indeed the converse seemed true, that the numbers of Muslims in the administration had declined with the increase in Muslim population. He cites three reasons for this situation: first, the ossification of administrative areas to those set up in 1936 when the 'mixed communes'[21] disappeared; second, the actual non-recruitment of Muslims into the administration after 1946; and third, the fact that when recruitment did take place, it was at the lower levels of local government administration and into posts which were not only badly paid and insecure but also dependent upon local patronage, so that in consequence they did not necessarily attract anyone of either ability or quality.[22] Le Tourneau diagnosed the underdevelopment of the economic resources of the colony as the result of first the lack of initiative from official Government bodies such as the Secteur d'Amélioration Rurale (SAR) and then the widening gap between the European and Muslim sectors of agriculture which had resulted from the mechanization of the European sector in the post-World War II period.

If there were accumulating problems in the economy and the administration as a result of French colonial rule in Algeria, there were also other problems arising from their conduct of affairs in Algeria. In the first place, there was the lack of educational opportunities for Muslims. Secondly, there was the problem of the general lack of interest shown for Algerian affairs by the French Government in Paris. That lack of Government interest was accompanied by a lack of interest in general, both within France and in Algeria by the European expatriates, in the aspirations which had been developing among the Muslim population. These aspirations had received a boost after World War II as Muslim soldiers fought on the Allied side and encountered US troops (Mekhaled, 1995). Moreover, equal participation in the conflict had been accompanied by promises of changes in policy once the conflict was over, though these failed to materialize.[23] Furthermore, just before the ending of the war in Europe, the French authorities in Algeria committed one of the most notorious acts of their period of colonial domination: the May 1945 massacres at Sétif, Guelma and Kherrata.[24] This massacre illustrates the state of tension which had built up under French rule in Algeria and which had been exacerbated by the events of World War II in which North Africa became the site initially of Vichy control supported by the *colon* population and of the Allied counter-offensive of 1942 – a tension which even a writer such as Le Tourneau, firmly committed to the French presence in Algeria, had to acknowledge and express concern about, for it indicated the increasing instability of French rule and its failure to offer the prospect of viable solutions to the basic problems.

In order to explain this 'failure' of the French colonial administration in Algeria, it is necessary to look back at the history of that administration and the nature of the political entity it had tried to subsume. The state over which France had sought to impose colonial rule was one which owed allegiance to the Ottoman Turkish Empire based in Istanbul but nevertheless was also one which had known a considerable degree of independence derived from its corsair activities. There was a well-established system of central and regional government even if not all the regions which now comprise the Algerian state were fully incorporated within the administrative structures. In contrast, for much of the first seventy years of French colonial rule, this pattern of administration was disrupted by a process of pacification of the countryside carried out by the French army which would in practice effectively dislocate the basic infrastructure of economy and government in Algeria. There are then two recurring features of this period of French rule in Algeria: the military's attempts at pacification, and accompanying it, the gradual growth of a *colon* (settler) population. The process of pacification, or the attempt to gain at least the appearance of acceptance of French overlordship by the incumbent population, was to be a feature of practically the whole period of French rule in Algeria even though the widespread military resistance to this rule became less important after the 1880s.

However, early military resistance is not only important in the sense that it demonstrated the strengths and weaknesses of both parties in the struggle to establish and resist the establishment of a French colony, it also has a symbolic importance. Perhaps the most significant actual and subsequently symbolic act of resistance was the war fought by the French in the western region against the Emir Abd el-Kader. Abd el-Kader embodies different aspects of the Algerian trajectory in that he was, at one and the same time, a military leader but a military leader whose legitimacy was derived both from his family status and from his status as the head of the Qadiriyah *tariqa*.[25] His person was therefore representative of that particular union of the secular and the religious which lies at the core of the perception of the ordering of human affairs within the Muslim world. In this sense, he can be seen as the nineteenth-century manifestation of charismatic leaders and dynastic groups who are found throughout North African history.[26] The difficulty which this union causes can be illustrated by the ways in which the language used to describe Abd el-Kader immediately creates the image of a uniqueness of purpose different from that of previous rulers in the region. The practice of referring to him as a military and religious leader implies something quite different because, in nineteenth-century Europe as today, an individual will belong to one vocation or the other but not to both. There are similar problems with phrases such as 'he sought the establishment of a Muslim-based state' (*Historama*, June 1993: 118). At this time, in the context of existing forms of government in the region, he could have done nothing else. The strength of the oppositional forces which Abd el-Kader was able to muster is illustrated by the fact that it took the French army over ten years to defeat him. Furthermore, his defeat of the French army at Mascara in 1835 was so serious that it took the French army two years to recover sufficiently from it to be able to launch a major attack against him, at Oran in 1837. Even then, it was not until December 1847 that the French army finally succeeded in defeating him.

Abd el-Kader resisted French rule; this gives him a particular significance which as I have suggested is more than the fact of the military campaigns which he fought. To illustrate this, the issue of *Historama* (June 1993), dedicated to two thousand years of North African history, uses on its front cover a montage of four images. These consist of three passport-size pictures which depict Hannibal, Saint Augustine and Abd el-Kader, all in one way or another men of faith; and aligned with them is the picture of a man on horseback called the 'red horseman of Abd el-Kader' (*le cavalier rouge d'Abd el-Kader*). That this image occupies twice the space of the other three is illustrative of two competing western images of the Muslim world which is at one and the same time both an image of romanticism and one of threat.

Of course, Abd el-Kader was not the only local ruler to resist the establishment of French rule, but his struggle was perhaps the most prolonged of those struggles.[27] Another example of resistance is that maintained by the Beylik's regional governor in Constantine, the Bey Ahmad. In November 1836, he was able to repulse the first French attack on his Beylik and continued to resist for a year until finally defeated in October 1837. Bey Ahmad resisted for a year; Abd el-Kader fought the French army for almost seventeen years; and in Kabylia, the mountainous area immediately to the east of Algiers, pacification was not to be even nominally completed until 1857. In the Saharan regions, the Tuareg did not formally accept French rule until 1882, and the Oulad Sidi Cheikh (another desert nomadic group) not until 1884.

While the above remarks have been concerned with the length of time which it took to subdue or pacify various areas of the Algerian entity for the first time, it has also to be remembered that the French army was to be constantly faced with revolts in those areas which it had already considered to be pacified. There were major revolts against French rule in 1859 and 1865, and then in 1871 there was what is referred to in the literature as the rebellion led by Mokrani[28] when the major part of the eastern region rose in revolt against the French. Even when Mokrani's forces had been defeated and the subsequent repression endured, yet there were further revolts in Algeria – in 1876 among the Mzab; in 1879 again in the Aurès; and in 1881 in the southern Oran region. In the assessment of the effects of French colonization upon the social relations of the old Beylik of Algiers, a place must be reserved for taking account of this resistance by force to its establishment.

If the French army was engaged in conquest, it was also engaged in the administration of the territory over which it extended French rule. Thus until 1871 the main organ of French rule outside of the urban areas, the *Bureau arabe* (Arab Office) was the field representative of the *Direction des affaires arabes* (Department of Arab Affairs), the administrative arm of the army, whose director for many years was General Daumas (Yacono, 1953).[29] The declared aim of the Arab Office was to ensure a lasting pacification of the different tribes by means of a just and regular administration, and at the same time to prepare the way for French colonization and commerce. While their prime role was the maintenance of public security, they were also expected to play an academic role. This entailed them studying the country and making an attempt to appreciate the interests which motivated the indigenous population (Lorcin, 1995). Of course, the motivation behind such enquiries was the search for appropriate mechanisms for perceiving potential areas of conflict and, in cases where such conflict had already arisen, defusing it before it became the foundation of an actual revolt. While the role of the Arab Offices as repressive organs must never be forgotten, it was also true that because of their investigative role, the military personnel of the Arab Office gained at least some knowledge of the population among whom they lived. They also illustrate the significance, referred to in the opening section of this chapter, of the military in what would normally be seen as the civilian side of the colonial project.[30]

Furthermore, the duality of the role of the army in the colonial project is illustrated by the ways in which their administrative and representative role brought them into frequent conflict with the predominantly urban colons who saw in the personnel of the Arab Office native-sympathizing obstacles to their legitimate desires to expand into the Algerian heartland. However, although there was indeed a kind of sympathy which the Arab Offices might express for local culture, the direction of the policies which they were engaged in was designed to destroy the very rural fabric for which they expressed sympathy. In particular, it was the job of the Arab Offices to define property rights in terms of the individual and to create definitive tribal boundaries within which the movement of the nomadic or transhumant tribes would be severely restricted. Thus their activities indirectly increased the overall surveillance of the rural population. An additional feature of their policy in the rural areas was to be observed in their attempts to co-opt local chiefs and notables – the purpose of which was both to increase the local legitimacy of their rule and to ensure more effective control over the local population – a policy which in the end had only a limited success.

The period of pacification in Algeria was marked by the development by the French administration of legal policies which aimed at a different distribution of land and power within the countryside. The first major measure of this exercise was the Senatus Consulte of 1863. In this, over one million hectares of land were reserved for colon use (Nouschi, 1961); and land became subject to individual title. In pre-colonial Algeria, land had been held in a number of different ways but not generally under individual title. The introduction of strict rules of individual ownership profoundly upset the balance of forces within the countryside, as well as creating confusion in its initial stages. This confusion was caused by assumptions by tribal groupings that because they used the land, there could not be a question of ownership. As a result, they saw no obligation on their part to register their ownership and so cleared the way for the colon to register the land as his property and declare a right of ownership of it. Thus in many instances whole groups were displaced from their traditional land and agricultural habits by a formalization of property rights which was little understood. This dislocation caused by these changes in property rights also created secondary problems and most importantly it upset the rhythms of agricultural production which resulted in a loss of output from agriculture throughout much of the nineteenth century. Consequently when natural disasters occurred as they did during the 1860s – such as droughts, plagues of grasshoppers, etc. – famine was an almost inevitable consequence and in the wake of famine came epidemics of cholera and typhus.

It was this combination of events which fuelled the revolt led by Mokrani in 1871 but which, with his defeat, led to an acceleration of these same trends. Warnier's law of 1873 became the legal expression of the developments of the previous ten years. In it, the distinctions between Muslim property and French property were eliminated and all property became subject to French law. At the same time, there was an extensive sequestration of tribal lands so that it was possible to step up the whole pace of French colonization. This process was further aided by the tribes having to pay indemnities of 35 million francs and by the laying of the foundations of the policy of *regroupement* (forced resettlement).[31]

While the French authorities via the agency of the military were trying to establish some kind of authority over the rural population, there still remains the question of whether or not these attempts created a government which was more effective than the regional government structure employed by their predecessors, the Ottoman Turks, during the period of the Beylik. It is undoubtedly true that it is more difficult both to establish effective government over a rural population and to change radically whatever structures have previously been in force there. This is because the very diversity of geographical environment and space involved in the government of such areas means that government by default depends upon the informal links of persons and groups in order to maintain its authority. This makes it difficult to perceive what is the real structure of power and therefore also makes it more difficult actually to create or impose an authority which supersedes any previous authority. This forms a clear contrast with governing the towns where the dominance of formal government and economic structures makes it less difficult to introduce new systems of formal government.

Bontems (1976) shows how at a central level the system of government which had been operated by the Ottoman Turks was completely displaced, even though the system which replaced it was also a military one. However, he also argues that, at a local level, not only had this replacement not taken place and Ottoman Turkish institutions survived but also that they had actually consolidated, to the extent that they made it difficult for French institutions to gain a foothold at all. For example, the military used the local power structure to maintain their own authority. Furthermore, he argues, the administrative reforms of 1845 which officially integrated Algeria with France adopted a curiously hybrid tax system: in fact, a dual tax system which would basically continue to operate until 1919. In that system, the main taxes which were raised within the Muslim population were those of the Ottoman Turkish period, while a quite separate system was used for the European population. At the same time, the collection of taxes in the Muslim sector was carried out by designated *chefs indigènes* (indigenous chiefs). Thus one can see developing in the rural areas the basis of the rural elites who would prove difficult to shift after independence.

Although the French colonial government adopted Ottoman Turkish methods of taxation in the rural areas, in the area of justice, religion and schooling the picture was quite different. In particular, the judicial system which was imposed was based entirely on the French justice system. The main impact on the Muslims was that the system imposed was a secular judicial system which meant that for most Muslims it had little legitimacy. Thus the French system of law based primarily on civil statute and concepts of property ownership gained precedence over Muslim law, which was to create a complexity within the judicial system that independence would further complicate.[32] Although in theory, religious freedom was accorded to Muslims, there are a number of reasons for seeing this as restricted: Muslim institutions such as mosques and schools showed a dramatic decline after the establishment of colonial rule (Bontems, 1976).

In one final area must the impact of French colonial rule be considered, and this concerns the institution in 1838 of a system of what were called *corporations territoriales* (territorial corporations) (Bontems, 1976: 486). The territorial corporations divided the urban population into two categories: *hadars* (citizens) and *berranis* (floating population). The significance of the division was that it made compulsory the need for any Muslim who entered a town to be ascribed to one of these groups within 24 hours. Furthermore, ascription to a corporation was determined on ethnic or religious lines. For example, someone from Kabylia would belong to one corporation, a person from Biskra to another, a Mzab to another; and once a person had this ascription they could not easily leave town. This was because it was necessary to exchange membership of a corporation for a passport in order to travel. Such a system in practice made it very difficult for a Muslim to circulate freely. The other aspect of this policy was to focus on different regional origins and convert these origins into ethnic/racial differences largely absent within pre-colonial society. The importance of the development of this ethnic consciousness should not be underestimated because it would have a role to play in the changing perception of, and relations between, Muslims and Jews in Algeria.

To summarize, then, the consequences of the establishment of French rule in Algeria involved the removal of the old officers of government – the Oldjach – and more importantly of the institutions and relationship networks which had underlain that government. The life of the Algerian city, whether it is seen as Muslim or not, had not been structured on the same principles as those of a nineteenth-century European city. While this fact must preface one's conception of the effect of French government in Algeria, it is as important to remember that it was to the *cities* of Algeria that the initial flows of European migrants came.

In 1870, this population had risen to 250,000 (Laroui, 1970), and it was to increase rapidly in the succeeding years as refugees from the Alsace-Lorraine region emigrated to Algeria in the wake of the Franco-German conflict of 1870–71 and the demise of Napoleon III's empire. It also grew in the 1880s after attacks of phylloxera had devastated France's vineyards. Indeed it might be said that the history of European migration into Algeria follows the dates of the great traumas of the nineteenth-century French state. For example, the first major migration had been in 1848 following the 1848 revolutions, then came another after Prussia's acquisition of Alsace-Lorraine, and a third after the phylloxera outbreak. A further important feature of the migrations which occurred is that they contained a large proportion of Europe's dispossessed. These came to Algeria to seek a new future and it was this characteristic of *colon* migration which was to create a source of conflict and ambiguity in the political development of the European population in Algeria.[33]

Algeria is a particularly interesting example of the underlying problems within the colonization process itself. It shows how, in spite of the special relationship between the colony and the colonial power which were established, French colonial rule was unable in either the short term or the long term to create the conditions for a parallel industrial transformation within the Algerian economy to that taking place in the *metropole*. It is also true that industrial growth in France did not begin until the end of the nineteenth century (Silverman, 1992: 28). There is therefore a curious paradox incorporated within the French colonial adventure in Algeria, which is that while Algeria was a site for the settlement of a European population from the middle of the nineteenth century, industrial growth in France particularly after 1914 was dependent in part on a reverse migration of Algerian workers (Granotier, 1979; Trebous, 1970). The colonial adventure was a part of the process of the industrialization and economic development of Europe.

The most visible expression of French presence in Algeria was to be seen in the reorganization of agricultural production and in particular the spread of viniculture. The result was both the takeover of land already under agriculture, which was discussed above, accompanied by a change in its use, and also the incorporation of land which had previously been used for grazing. While there was a change in crop orientation, there was also a loss in the productivity of the land because the methods of cultivation with which the French colon had been acquainted proved not always appropriate to Algerian conditions, as well as occasionally quite disastrous (Dumont, 1957).[34] In addition, the conversion of land from growing grain and other foodstuffs to the production of wine led to the Algerian economy moving from a surplus-productive capacity in these areas to one where it was necessary to import grain and other foodstuffs, or to a condition of deficit in the food-producing arena. At the same time, the nature and provenance of colon recruits – the dispossessed of Europe's nineteenth-century political upheavals – meant that they were less able to provide the kind of stimulus which would generate industrial development within the economy than to provide the labour for that development which did take place.

Certain infrastructural develoments did take place, such as the founding of the Bank of Algeria in 1851 and the construction of a railway network between 1857 and 1881. However, although these infrastructural developments did take place, colonial Algeria's former ruling power – the Ottoman Turkish Empire – was promoting the same infrastructural developments (Lewis, 1995: 309). Thus it might be said that such developments would have taken place irrespective of French colonial policy. Consequently even though the colonial administration was active in developing some areas of infrastructure, it also neglected and even dismantled other areas, so that until the take-off in technical knowledge in the 1950s, a sustained and positive advance in infrastructural development within the colony could not occur. When industrial development did take place, it was based partly on food processing – flour milling and the like – and partly on the extractive industries. The benefit to the Algerian in terms of the creation of direct employment was conditioned by the particular composition of the *colon* population in Algeria which was itself dependent on such employment. This meant that the direct effects of such industrial enterprises upon the indigenous population would be limited. To illustrate how this operated in practice it is useful to look at a series of accounts of the development of the eastern town of Bône (Dumoulin, 1959; Lespès, 1930).

The city of Bône dates back to the Phoenicians and was the city of Saint Augustine; thus it has an ancient history.[35] Since that time, it had developed as a fishing port and had been one of the sites used by the Agence d'Afrique (Berbrugger, 1871) before colonial rule was established. However, not until the end of the nineteenth century when the French began to develop the mining potential of the hinterland did Bône come to be seen as a natural outlet for that hinterland – of iron ore mines at Ouenza; phosphate mines at Kouif; and copper, lead and zinc exploitations at Ain Babar – at which time it began a new phase of development. Consequently, Bône provides a very clear illustration that industrial development in Algeria was not undertaken until the same development had begun to take place within the metropolitan economy. Otherwise, its agricultural geography was typical of colonial Algeria in which agricultural production was dominated by export-orientated crops such as wine, cotton, citrus fruit and tobacco, of which only the last was grown in any substantial quantity by non-European-origin farmers. Agriculture was, however, the main employing sector for the majority of the local population, absorbing some 89 per cent of the Muslim working population. This was in contrast to the employment experience of the European population which was divided between the secondary (43.6 per cent), of whom over half were to be found in manufacturing industry, and the tertiary sectors (42 per cent), chiefly in commerce and the liberal professions. Numbers of Europeans and Muslims in the secondary sector were virtually the same, respectively 9,721 and 11,864; taking into account the total numbers of Muslims and of Europeans in the Algerian population, however, it is evident that Muslim representation in the secondary and tertiary sectors was negligible.

Bône was fortunate in that, once the technological capability was there, it was the access point for what were relatively easily exploitable mineral resources. This meant that the town was potentially less dependent on agriculture. However, the history of the exploitation of these mineral resources shows both how little they were used to promote local industrial development and how *laissez-faire* were the actual processes of extraction. For example, the iron ore which came from Ouenza was suitable for the manufacture of special steels as it was a high-grade ore but 75 per cent of local production was exported to the United Kingdom alone, with smaller proportions being exported to the United States, Germany and France. Consequently, little was left behind to develop a local iron and steel industry. This is important to remember because investment by the Algerian state iron and steel company SNS in the period after independence led to the growth of a vast iron and steel plant at Bône (renamed Annaba) called El-Hadjar employing over 9,000 people.[36]

To illustrate further the limited nature of industrial development prior to the commencement of the twentieth century and how little potential it had to impinge on the local economy, a look can be taken at each of the mining sectors. Mining of the iron ore at Ouenza was not begun until 1913 but by 1950, almost 98 per cent of total production was obtained by machine. In the phosphate mines at Kouif, mining had begun in 1893 and was run by a British firm until 1911. Mechanization did not even begin until the 1950s when a rapid mechanization programme was undertaken – in 1950, mechanization accounted for only 2 per cent of production but by 1955, it accounted for 43 per cent. As at Ouenza, however, most of the phosphate was exported, chiefly to France (28 per cent) but also to Spain, Germany, Portugal, Yugoslavia and Ireland, with only 12 per cent of total production being retained in Algeria. The exploitation of the copper, lead and zinc deposits at Ain Babar exhibits another aspect of the uncertainties of industrial development during the colonial period. The deposits were first discovered in 1850 but a mining concession was not granted until 1870; serious exploitation did not start until the mine was taken over by the Société de Caroute in 1904. However, they only controlled the mine until 1929 after which there were several changes of ownership, so that by the 1950s, production of the three metals totalled just over a thousand metric tons. As with Ain Babar, the company in charge began an expansion programme in the early 1950s which was then effectively stopped by the beginning of, and the lengthy nature of, the independence war.

Industrial activity in the Bône area itself was concentrated in four main fields: mechanical engineering, chemicals and textiles, building and construction, and food processing. Of these, the most important in terms of total value was building and construction. However, while the building industry was a large employer, it is not a sector noted for its use of new technologies. By contrast the mechanical engineering industry, concentrated largely in one plant whose main production effort was railway stock, did possess modern plant and machinery. However, even that was only set up in the years just before World War II and so was of relatively recent origin. World War II also helped the plant develop: its original purpose had been the maintenance and repair of machinery manufactured in France, but with this function impossible during the war, the plant's facilities were given over to the development of locally-produced rolling stock. However, having said that, employment was still for only 650 people, of whom no more than 50 per cent were Muslims. It cannot be said therefore to have made a substantial impact on the local employment market, and yet that company was the largest single industrial employer in the Bône area.

Within Algeria's colonial spectrum, Bône's pattern of industrial activity and its industrial growth were considerable and were exceeded only by those of the two urban conglomerations of Algiers and Oran. Both these towns had a substantial Muslim population which in 1954 was 379,000 in Algiers and 169,000 in Oran. However, half of this population lived in *baraques* (shanty towns). The growth of towns like Algiers, Oran and Bône outstripped the colonial state's ability to provide an adequate infrastructure particularly in the fields of housing and household services, such as water, and this was a legacy which the post-independence Algerian governments failed to resolve.

The pattern of industrial activity in such centres as Oran and Algiers followed the pattern already described for Bône. For example, the Algiers area which includes the suburbs of Hussein Dey and Maison Carrée was host to these industries: chemical products and fertilizers, cement, paper, textiles, flour-milling and other food-processing industries, mechanical engineering, tobacco, the manufacture of corks, etc. However, except for the tobacco and paper industries and cork manufacture, the greater part of the raw materials used in these industries were imported. In the textile industry, Algeria imported both wool and cotton; while in the paper industry, even though Algeria had long been a major exporter of esparto grass,[37] the first Algerian paper factory was not established until 1949 when the French firm Cellunaf began production. In the Oran area which also included the industrial township of La Senia, there were glassworks, textile factories, mechanical engineering, and food-processing industries.

The history of oil exploitation in Algeria follows a similar pattern to that of the general development of industry. Exploration had begun in 1915 but a suitable producing field was not found until 1948 when the technology of oil exploration had developed sufficiently to be able to drill the Algerian sub-soil (Schliephake, 1977). However the first franchises to commercial companies for exploration were not granted until 1952, when they went to the *Compagnie Française des Pétroles* (CFP) and the *Société Nationale de Recherche des Pétroles en Algérie* (SN Repal), to be followed a year later by similar franchises to the *Compagnie de Recherche et d'Exploitation du Pétrole du Sahara* (CREPS) and the *Compagnie des Pétroles d'Algérie* (CPA).[38] The importance of the advent of the technological ability to develop its oilfields is witnessed by the continuing exploration of Algeria's oil potential during the independence struggle.

Conclusion

It might be said that in the 1940s and 1950s, France rediscovered the economic potential of her Algerian colony and that this recognition formed part of the struggle for hegemony which took place during the Algerian war of independence. The recognition of Algeria's economic potential can be seen reflected in De Gaulle's Constantine Plan, which aimed to provide an economic development strategy for the years 1959 to 1964 even though 1959 marked the fifth year of armed struggle in the colony. The Constantine Plan made provision for the investment in the petroleum sector of over five and a half million francs with an additional provision of 2,700 million francs allocated as expenditure on replacements. The total net investment envisaged in this plan was 19,400 million francs (Norbye, 1968; Amin, 1965, 1970). This notion of rediscovery is also borne out by the various economic plans of both the war and the post-war period. For example, a plan for Algeria was put forward by General Weygaud in 1940–41; then the post-war French government introduced a modernization plan in 1946 which set up the *Fonds de modernisation et d'équipement métropolitain*. However, while France made some strenuous efforts in this post-war period to develop its North African colony, events elsewhere and within it had already overtaken them.

Notes

1. The different resonances of this title are discussed in Chapter 7.

2. The reform of education provision and its reconstruction within a military framework had profound implications for the structure of the state apparatus and in particular its organization within a 'strict disciplinary framework' (Weber in Gerth and Mills, 1948: 254). Furthermore, the idea and practice of military service, as part of a citizen's duty to the *patrie*, contributed towards the importance of the military in the colonial project (Lorcin, 1995). Brubaker (1992: 92) records that compulsory military service in the 1820s lasted from six to eight years.

3. The idea of *la francophonie* was originally put forward by the geographer Onésime Reclus (1837–1916) and was revived in the 1960s by the new national leaders such as Léopold Senghor (Senegal) and Habib Bourguiba (Tunisia). At a

conference held at the Institut Panafricain de Géopolitique in April 1987, it was suggested that *la francophonie* provided the opportunity for a new kind of cooperation in which the French language could also be used to encourage scientific and technical development (Mwayila, 1987).

4. Although he was born in Tunis in 1332, his family were of South Arabian origin and had migrated to Spain in the eighth century and settled within the Seville area. At the beginning of the Hafsid period (early thirteenth century), the family migrated to north-west Africa, settling first in Ceuta before moving to Tunis. Before he withdrew from public life to write his history, Ibn Khaldūn himself was active in the service of several Maghrebine dynasties and was even briefly Governor of Bougie. He travelled widely, including to the court of Pedro III (the Cruel) of Castile but from 1382 until his death in 1406 lived mainly in Mamluk Egypt. The interchange of ideas and people between Spain and North Africa illustrated by Ibn Khaldūn and his family forms part of a broader pattern of the period. The loss of Spain in 1492 has been described by Akbar S. Ahmed (1993: 70) as 'the Andalus Syndrome', an event which 'left a permanent scar in the Muslim psyche' as it meant not only 'physical expulsion' but also 'cultural annihilation'. See also chapter 3. For further details of Ibn Khaldūn's colourful life see Yves Lacoste (1966/1984) *Ibn Khaldoun: The Birth of History and the Past of the Third World*, London: Verso, translated by David Macey; and Franz Rosenthal's Introduction 'Ibn Khaldūn's Life' to his 1958/1967 translation of *The Muqaddimah*, London and Henley: Routledge & Kegan Paul.

5. Gellner's writing on North Africa and Islam was enormous, as is illustrated by the four pages of bibliographical listings at the end of his 1981 study *Muslim Society*, Cambridge: Cambridge University Press. The foundation of his work on North Africa was, however, his 1969 published doctoral thesis *Saints of the Atlas*, London: Weidenfeld & Nicolson.

6. Lorcin records that the first translation available in France of *The Muqaddimah* was de Slane's edition published in 1852 (1995: 105). However, in his Introduction to the English translation, Rosenthal records that de Slane's edition was not the first to appear. In fact, de Slane's three volumes were published in the period between 1862 and 1868. The earlier translation and publication was by Quatremère which came out posthumously in 1858 (1967: cviii).

7. Ibn Khaldūn here provides a link with the theories of nationalism in which the foundations for the national community are seen to be derived from the recognition of commonality of peoples through such mechanisms as the attribution of common descent. In the discourses on the origins of nationalism, authors may interpret these as real or imagined in the same way that the nationalist interprets them as of a real or an imagined nature. The diversity of literature on nationalism is illustrated by three authors – Benedict Anderson in *Imagined Communities*, London: Verso 1991; Ernest Gellner in *Nations and Nationalism*, Oxford: Basil Blackwell 1983; and Anthony Smith in *National Identity*, Harmondsworth: Penguin 1991. For a discussion of the use of genealogies

in the Spanish context see Pierre Guichard (1976) *Al-Andalús – estructura antropológica de una sociedad islámica en occidente*, Barcelona: Barral Editores – Breve Biblioteca de Reforma.

8. There is still a Spanish colonial presence in North Africa with its retention of the two enclaves of Ceuta and Melilla in Morocco, while it was Spanish withdrawal from its colony of Spanish Sahara in 1974 that led to a prolonged dispute between Algeria and Morocco over its status. Also worth remembering is that it was from Spanish bases in Morocco and with Moroccan troops that Franco launched his campaign against the Spanish Republic in 1936.

9. 'Dey' was the title given to the senior Ottoman official in the Beylik of Algiers.

10. Gallissot's remarks were made as part of the introductory document to a workshop entitled 'Problématique du féodalisme hors d'Europe: le Maghreb précolonial' held at the Centre d'Études et de Recherches Marxistes, Paris, on 27 April 1968 and published in 1971 as *Sur le féodalisme*, Paris: Éditions Sociales. Contributions to the session were made by André Nouschi, Jean Poncet, André Prenant, Lucette Valensi, Jean Suret-Canale, Albert Ayache and Catherine Coquery-Vidrovitch. Nouschi and Prenant with Lacoste were authors (1961) of *L'Algérie passée et présente*, Paris: Éditions Sociales; Nouschi (1961) *Enquête sur le niveau de vie des populations rurales constantinoises de la conquête jusqu'en 1919*, Paris: PUF; Valensi (1969) *Le Maghreb avant la prise d'Alger*, Paris: Flammarion; Poncet's work was on Tunisia and both Suret-Canale and Coquery-Vidrovitch wrote seminal works on Black Africa. Thus the group of delegates brought

together at this workshop represented some of the principal French academics writing on Africa.

11. This is land which was originally endowed by pious Muslims to the community, often a *tariqa* or a *zawiya*.

12. This was the collective name given to the Ottoman Turkish military community in Algiers.

13. Tribute payable by the local beys to the Dey of Algiers, and by him to the Ottoman administration in Istanbul.

14. The Ibadi represent a dissident group outside the four main schools of law. Their origins go back to the early days of the Caliphate and the emergence of internal divisions within the Muslim community over the nature of power and obedience. These struggles led to the emergence of a movement called the Kharijites which argued that if an imam did not protect your rights then you had no duty to obey him. They were involved in the assassination of the fourth Caliph, 'Ali, in AD 661, and in North Africa their policy of rebellion was found useful in the struggle which was taking place with the Umayyad governors. The initial Kharijite movement was crushed but the tradition of opposition through violence proved more durable. The original reasons for the Kharijite opposition form the basis of Ibadi beliefs although the Ibadi themselves maintained their dissidence by withdrawing into the area of these five towns (Mernissi, 1993: 27–32; Tritton, 1954: 70–1).

15. Historiography of the colonial period tends to impute a primordial hostility between Jews and Muslims in North Africa. This is irrespective of whether the authors are Christian or Jewish. However, much of this historiography dates from the end of the nineteenth century when

European and predominantly Ashkenazi Jewry was involved in the emergence of Zionism. This movement tended to perceive non-European-based Jewish communities as in need of modernization on a European model. Organizations such as the *Alliance Israélite* were founded with the express purpose of the reform of non-European-based Jewish communities after a European model. French historiography of the same period is reflective of anti-Semitic attitudes in France which culminate in the Dreyfus affair of 1894–1906. A particularly illustrative example is Vicomte Ch. de Foucauld (1888) in *Reconnaissance au Maroc, 1883–1884*. For a general introduction to the history of Jewish communities in the Muslim world, see Bernard Lewis (1984) *The Jews of Islam*, London: Routledge & Kegan Paul. Examples of Jews in significant positions in the Beylikal administrative hierarchy are the two Jewish merchants Busnach and Bachri who were also among the principal creditors of the French government and who were used by the French as their excuse for attacking Algiers in 1830.

16. Constantine's position as a centre of Muslim learning would survive colonization and form the basis in the 1930s for the development of the Muslim reformist movement, the Association of Reformist Ulama.

17. There have been a number of changes of names of towns since independence – for example, colonial Bône was renamed Annaba – but I have retained here the pre-independence names. Sources for the discussion of French commercial activity in the Beylik prior to colonization are 'La Régence d'Alger sous le consulat et l'empire', compiled from the papers of A. Berbrugger

(1871) *Revue Africaine*, 15, 241–70; L.-Ch. Féraud (1877) 'Causes de l'abandon du comptoir de Collo par la Compagnie française en 1795', *Revue Africaine*, 21, 124–40.

18. An example of the popular nature of this account is the article by François Maspero (1993) '1830: Un coup d'éventail historique! La conquête d'Alger', *Historama (Spécial)* 'Afrique du Nord: 2000 ans d'histoire", 33 (juin). Maspero was one of the leading French publishers of radical interpretations of economics, politics, sociology, etc. of the 1970s but has now turned to writing. *Historama* is a popular monthly history magazine. What is interesting about this issue is the episodes it has chosen to focus on as illustrative of North Africa's history.

19. See Administration des douanes 1827 à 1836 (1838) *Tableau décennal du commerce de la France avec ses colonies et les puissances étrangères*, Paris: Imprimerie royale.

20. A prominent French historian and political scientist whose principal work was on North Africa.

21. 'Mixed communes' were administrative areas where the European population was under civilian administration and the Muslim population subject to military administration through the medium of the 'Bureaux arabes'.

22. This putting in place in the administration of less qualified candidates raises issues around the calibre of the administration inherited in the post-independence period.

23. For a general discussion of these themes, see Michael Crowder (1984) 'The Impact of Two World Wars on Africa', *History Today*, 34, January, 11–18, which is a summary of his chapters in *The Cambridge History of Africa* and the *UNESCO General History of Africa*.

24. This massacre was of such importance that the writer Tahar Ben Jelloun in his Obituary of the Algerian poet Noureddine Aba (*Le Monde*, 25.9.96) refers to its influence on Aba and also another Algerian writer, Kateb Yacine, as 'le traumatisme vécu à Sétif en mai 1945'. For a study of the events leading up to the Sétif massacre, see Boucif Mekhaled (1995) *Chroniques d'un massacre, 8 mai 1945*, Paris: Syros/Au Nom de la Mémoire.

25. I have retained the spelling Abd el-Kader as it is the one most usually found in books on North Africa; see for example the English translation of Ageron (1991). The role of the *tariqa* in Muslim practice in Algeria and North Africa will be discussed more fully in the next chapter.

26. Two important examples of such dynastic groups are the Almoravids and the Almohads, who ruled over both North Africa and Spain from the eleventh to the thirteenth centuries, and who provide one of the sources of inspiration for Ibn Khaldūn's *Muqaddimah*.

27. Accounts of Algerian resistance to the extension of French rule are to be found in Gordon (1966); Lacheraf (1965); Lacoste, Nouschi and Prenant (1966).

28. A near contemporary account of this revolt is given in Louis Rinn (1891) *Histoire de l'insurrection de 1871 en Algérie*, Algiers: Adolphe Jourdan. Critical accounts are to be found in Ageron (1968) and Nouschi (1961).

29. General Daumas wrote a number of books on life in Algeria including a study of women's lives in *La Femme arabe*, Algiers: Adolphe Jourdan 1912 (posthumous). Daumas came to Algeria in the first period of conquest and served as a Consul at Mascara where he encountered the Emir Abd el-Kader. He was also a relative of de Slane, one of the first translators of the *Muqaddimah* into French. Such accounts as Lorcin's (1995) show that he had an important role to play in constructing discourses on the Algerian.

30. There is a very interesting discussion by Lorcin (1995) of the significance of the military in creating and projecting the character of the peoples of Algeria and the relations between them. She also points out that ideologically many of the military in Algeria were Saint-Simonians, and that this had an impact on the way in which they wrote about the country and its peoples.

31. *Regroupement* was a policy which involved the gathering together in secure villages of the rural inhabitants, and was introduced by General Chauzy after the 1871 uprising of Mokrani.

32. Ahmad (1992) discusses the impact of this 'layering' of different systems of law.

33. This characteristic of nineteenth-century migrations of European populations – in which revolution and counter-revolution/famine and disease at home forced politically radical populations to migrate but which often produced conservative and racist politics by the new migrants in their new home – is not unique to the Algerian experience. It also characterizes Irish emigration to the United States where from their labour market position they were in competition with African Americans, resulting in class polarization rather than class solidarity. For a discussion of this, see David Roediger (1991) *The Wages of Whiteness. Race and the Making of the American Working Class*, London: Verso.

34. Dumont (1957) particularly chapter 5: 'Sheep and cereals, trees and water in North Africa'.
35. The Phoenicians are the starting point for the *Historama*, June 1993 introduction to the history of North Africa, and a chapter (36–45) is consecrated to Saint Augustine under the title 'Saint Augustin assiégé par les Vandales' and with the sub-title '430: la fin de l'Afrique romaine et chrétienne'.
36. The El-Hadjar iron and steel plant is discussed in more detail in chapter 5.
37. Esparto grass was the principal raw material on which the Scottish paper industry was built.
38. Shell held a 35 per cent stake in CREPS, and had a similar stake in CPA.

3

The Changing Face of Islam in Algeria

The conquest of the Beylik of Algiers in 1830 by France was of a Muslim province of the Ottoman Turkish Empire which had in earlier centuries been instrumental in creating the Muslim empire in Spain. At the same time, it was perceived to be on the western fringes of the Muslim world but, for many Muslims, the culture which flourished in medieval Muslim Spain was one of the great cultures of the Muslim world (A.S. Ahmed, 1993). The Ottoman province of the Beylik of Algiers created by Aruj and Khayr ad-Din in the sixteenth century would dominate the southern seaways of the Mediterranean for the Ottoman Empire. The extended nature of the Ottoman Turkish Empire may have resulted in the gradual loosening of links between the Beylik and Istanbul but it had not changed the personal status of its inhabitants. The Beylik was a Muslim state within a Muslim world. The French conquest of 1830 was radically to alter its orientation. No longer was the Beylik on the western fringes of the Muslim world but on the southern fringes of Europe. It was not Istanbul from which laws would emanate and to which taxes would be paid, but Paris. The Janissary was replaced by the French soldier of the Republic who was inspired by the ideas of Saint-Simon (Lorcin, 1995) rather than the legacy of power invested in the Ottoman Sultan (Heper, 1985). The enormity of this change is symbolized by the fact that, throughout the 132 years of French colonial rule, the majority of the Muslim inhabitants of the new colony of Algeria would never hold formal citizenship of the French Republic. This was the direct result of the citizenship policy practised by the colonial state which effectively denied citizenship to those choosing to retain their personal status as Muslim. Thus it was not until independence in 1962 that the majority of Algeria's inhabitants would acquire citizenship and reestablish the link between personal status as a Muslim and the practice of a citizen within the contemporary state. However, reestablishing the link between personal status and citizenship was not sufficient to settle the question of the precise nature of this relationship. Thus the question which the 1991 elections provoked and which has dominated the political scene since 1992 is the question of what it means to be a Muslim in the Algerian state today.

At a general level the changes which were the result of the French conquest involved a shift from a time when civil and public life were integrated with personal and private life to one where the formal secularity of the state excluded from citizenship individuals whose religious beliefs were other than Christian. Consequently not only did the reality of the state change but so also did the discourses which surrounded it. The ideological dilemma today is the result of the attempted enactment of the switch from Algeria as a Muslim country to Algeria as a Muslim state, where the characterization of that new Muslim state is the site of contestation. That it is a site of contestation is largely due to the fact that the colonization of the Muslim world in the latter half of the nineteenth century and early twentieth century resulted in the dislocation of the natural lines of communication between the state, the polity and civil society. It is not a question of whether or not the environment within which the state will be enacted is Muslim, but of doubts over the form and content of the institutions and practices of the state within that environment that have become the focus of a debate over meanings. This absence of clarity in effect has left the delineation of the nature of the post-colonial Muslim state in the hands of those with the greatest certainty about the nature and meaning of their faith. Today's conflicts can be seen as concerned essentially with the form which the state should have and the nature of the relationship between the secular and the sacred within it.

To understand the processes which have been involved, it is necessary to explore the changing nature of the discourses which have been employed to describe Islam in the Algerian context and which have themselves played a role in the process of transforming the fact of being a Muslim in Algeria, an issue of individual faith, to an issue of whether or not the institutions and practices of the Algerian state conform to a discourse on the character of an Islamic state in the late twentieth century. This contestation illustrates the impact of modernity on the post-colonial Muslim world. The emphasis is on discourses both past and present because the relationship between the secular and the religious within the state was also the subject of a bitter debate in nineteenth-century France but from which Algeria was not excluded by the fact that some of the central actors in the debate were also involved in defining the parameters of the colonial state.[1] Consequently, a number of factors need to be taken into account when discussing the changing status of the Muslim in Algeria. These include a snapshot of the character of Islam in Algeria on the eve of colonization, and the subsequent impact of colonization; but these have to be contextualized within the wider discourses which have characterized the history of the re-emergence of avowedly Muslim states in the twentieth century. As a result, one is faced with not one but several discourses on Islam. The first of these is the colonial discourse on Islam; the second, the discourse of resistance to colonial rule through the medium of Islam; thirdly, the discourses which have developed since independence which include the discourse on the state within Islam, the discourse/s of the Islamic militants both within Algeria and within the discourse/s of the West in response to these phenomena; and finally, Muslim discourses in the wider world.

Islam on the eve of colonization

Constructing a picture of Islam on the eve of colonization involves bringing into focus not only local structures and practices but also the structures and practices associated with life within the Ottoman Turkish Empire. The need to take into account the impact of the latter is that, as a number of authors have pointed out (P. Anderson, 1974; Inalcik, 1973; Lewis, 1995), its long period of political dominance brought about a number of changes in the organization of urban Muslim practice. More particularly, it meant the development of an institutional structure in which there was 'a graded hierarchy of professional and academically trained men of religion, with territorial jurisdictions and defined functions and powers, under the headship of a supreme religious authority recognized as the highest instance of the Holy Law' (Lewis, 1995: 110). Lewis also argues that the Ottomans were the first actually to succeed in unifying Muslim law with state practice. As these innovations were concerned with the organization of the state, their impact on Muslim practice was most significant where the power of the state was greatest, which meant that in the Beylik of Algiers it affected the towns and therefore urban practice rather than the rural areas and rural practice. This was because, as the discussion in Chapter 2 has argued, it was in the towns that Ottoman control was primarily concentrated. Control of the rural areas was not a primary requirement for the maintenance of Ottoman control whose economic basis was commerce and more particularly the returns from the corsair trade. Without a real structure of power in the rural areas, Ottoman influence on the daily lives of the rural population was limited and consequently also its influence in matters of religious organization and practice. While this was primarily the result of the political and economic orientation of the Beylikal state it needs also to be remembered that the legal basis for the legitimation of the practices of the Ottoman Turkish state was through the Hanafi school of law whereas the dominant legal school in Spain and North Africa was

Maliki.[2] The impact of these differences is observable in the importance of *tariqa*[3] in Muslim practice in North Africa. Finally, religious and cultural life in North Africa had also been enriched by the continuous flow of Spanish exiles (of whom Ibn Khaldūn is perhaps one of the best known) from the eleventh to the sixteenth centuries which resulted from the reconquest of Muslim Spain by its Christian kings.

However, the Beyliks of Algiers and Tunis and the 'Alawi state of Morocco were, after the reconquest of Spain, the western limits of the Muslim world. This physical location on the edge is reflected in the adherence of the Maghreb to the Maliki school of jurisprudence. Indeed Ibn Khaldūn emphasizes the particular virtues of this adherence as a reflection of the continuance of a 'desert attitude' with its preference for 'simplicity' (1967: 13, III) while a contemporary Muslim writer on Islam, Fatima Mernissi,[4] says of the founder of the Maliki school that he should be remembered 'as one of the forgotten greats of the past' for his resistance to torture (1993: 19). Ibn Khaldūn's life also illustrates other aspects of the life of a Muslim in the Maghreb. The first aspect is mobility; in Ibn Khaldūn's case, this was partly a reflection of the political role he played in his early years when he travelled extensively throughout North Africa and Spain, but it is also a reflection of his religious life, for after he converted to Sufism he would become head of a Sufi foundation in Cairo as well as a Maliki judge (Lacoste, 1984: 185). Ibn Khaldūn also describes the ways in which new ideas were diffused as a result of the mobility which people had within the Muslim world at this time and cites both Bougie and Tunis as centres of dissemination (1967: 19, III). Other evidence of the degree of mobility which was possible within the Muslim world at this time is illustrated by the travels, a century earlier than Ibn Khaldūn, of Ibn Battuta.[5] Ibn Battuta's journeys after he left Tangiers included visiting Egypt, Syria, Iran, Istanbul, the Arabian peninsula, Central Asia, India and China. Although the extended nature of his travels may have been unusual, it was certainly not unusual for a Muslim to undertake the *hajj* to Mecca. Later, when the political centre of the Muslim world had moved to the Ottoman capital in Istanbul, it meant that representatives from the provincial regions which included the Beylik of Algiers were regularly required to travel to Istanbul to acknowledge the Sultan's suzerainty and to pay their taxes.

The life of Ibn Khaldūn has been used to illustrate the richness of Muslim life in the Beylik of Algiers on the eve of colonization. His life history also illustrates the intermingling of what are often seen as distinctly urban and distinctly rural practices, namely his position as a judge or *qadi* and his practice of Sufism. The image of division which this presents can be seen as a reflection of the impact of colonization which effectively cut off the town from the surrounding hinterland through the introduction in 1838 of the 'territorial corporations' (*corporations territoriales*).[6] As a result, urban religion appeared to adhere more to legal processes in which the *'ulama* (the teachers) and the *qadi* (the jurists) played key roles; while in rural areas popular practice was seen as focused on local charismatic leaders or *marabout* who were located in organized communities called *zawiya* (Gellner, 1981; 1969). The *marabout* of the pre-colonial period can be seen as the unofficial and unsalaried equivalent of the urban *'ulama*. Although *marabout* themselves were usually men, women were active members of the self-same brotherhoods (Rinn, 1884). Although *marabout* did not necessarily have much education, the absence of education would be compensated for by their reputation for pious living and behaviour. Although most *marabout* had a base – the *zawiya*, which acted as a physical focal point and was usually sited on land already religiously endowed – they spent much of their time travelling around the countryside. The size, standing and wealth of *zawiya* varied enormously, and the more wealthy a *zawiya* the more likely it was that it would be associated with one of the *tariqa*. However, in general, *marabout* obtained their income through their *zawiya* and from pious donations made by their adherents. These could take the form of land grants, local taxes or labour service. Piety was measured by both spirituality and generosity.[7]

It has already been mentioned that an important feature of both urban and rural Muslim practice in the Maghreb were the *tariqa* and Sufism. In order to illustrate the influence of the *tariqa*, it is possible to follow the history of one such *tariqa* founded towards the end of the eighteenth century called the Tijaniyah (Abun Nasr, 1965). In Abun Nasr's discussion of the life of the founder, he also shows how important the *tariqa* were in the daily lives of North African Muslims at the end of the eighteenth century. The founder of the Tijaniyah, Al-Tijani, came from the oasis of Ain Madi in what is now southern Algeria. Abun Nasr records that he learned the first principles of what it meant to be a Muslim from his father. Having obtained the fundamentals of his knowledge of Islam, he sought ways to deepen this knowledge. How he did this further illustrates the cosmopolitan nature of the Muslim world in the mid-eighteenth century. Al-Tijani began by travelling to Fez in Morocco, then both one of the major centres of Muslim learning in North Africa and host to a number of *tariqa*. In this early period and before his own revelation, Al-Tijani would become a member at least four *tariqa*.[8] His next step was to make the *hajj* or pilgrimage to Mecca. Such journeys were important in themselves as the relative slowness of transport meant that a pilgrimage journey could take many years and pilgrims both en route to Mecca and on their return would probably visit other parts of the Muslim world. They exemplify therefore another of the ways by which Muslims from different parts of the Muslim world met to exchange ideas and develop their own thinking. Al-Tijani's own journey included a visit to Algiers. According to Abun Nasr, after he arrived in Mecca he had a mystical experience which urged him to return to the Maghreb and to found his own *tariqa*. Al-Tijani returned and settled initially at Tlemçen in the Beylik of Algiers. However, he was discouraged by the attitudes of the people of Tlemçen who he felt did not have any real interest in his message; consequently he moved to Fez where the then sovereign, Mawlay Sulayman was more supportive because he viewed the new *tariqa* as a counterweight to the development of the anti-Sufi movement of the Wahhabi (OEMIW, 1995). Al-Tijani died in 1815 and the leadership of the *tariqa* was divided, but with the principal *zawiya* remaining at Al-Tijani's birthplace of Ain Madi.

Clearly, from this account, neither were Muslims in North Africa isolated from other Muslims nor was their Muslim practice static. Individuals moved to enhance their knowledge of their religion and to fulfil its basic duties. In so doing, they introduced new ideas and new organizations, and contributed to a fluidity and diversity which colonization would fundamentally disrupt. The colonization process would also dismantle the structures of organized religion in the urban areas and in so doing would create space for the development of a popularist rural-based Islam, primarily because rural practice did not depend in quite the same way on institutional reference points. It is these characteristics and developments of Islam in the Maghreb which form the basis of Ernest Gellner's configuration of *High* and *Low* Islam (Gellner, 1992). The problem with his configuration is that he sees one, *Low* Islam, as essentially anti-progressive. Furthermore, he argues, all societies have certain antecedents which as those societies develop are then superseded by new forms of social organization. Thus his schema requires that *Low* Islam is progressively replaced by *High* Islam as modernization takes place. While this is an attractive scenario, it does in many ways reduce the complexities of the processes at work to a linear progression and perhaps also denies the interactive nature of the processes which occur and which are necessary to each other. What is suggested here is that there were a variety of ways in which Islam was practised and that such differences were to a large extent suppressed during the colonial period and then denied by the nationalists. The notion of difference is also something which the leaders of the Islamist movements deny as they collude with the western discourse of a monolithic construction called Islam (Halliday, 1995).

The effects of colonization on Islam in Algeria

Colonization affected Muslim practice in Algeria in various ways: in the first place, it fractured the union of the secular and the religious with the result that not only did political activity in effect have to choose between operation in the secular sphere and operation within the religious sphere, but so also did the individual as, for the greater part of colonial rule, no law was passed which allowed a Muslim to be an Algerian citizen. The second major effect was on land tenure, an aspect of colonization which has already been explored in Chapter 2. Thus, the focus here is on the impact which colonization had on Muslim organization and practice and consequently on the structuring of political activity, in conjunction with its effects on the individual and on gender relations. In a sense, one of the questions which are at the centre of both the Islamist movements and those of their opponents is that of the most appropriate means by which the integrity of the secular and the religious, through the medium of the political, can be re-established. Both seek to make this reconnection, and the struggles today are partly about the choice of terrain on which this struggle should take place.

Studies of the evolution of nationalism and citizenship frequently attribute to the French Revolution the processes by which the formal delimitation of citizenry was made (Brubaker, 1992: 35). Brubaker argues that the Revolution through its articulation of the doctrine of national sovereignty linked the idea of citizenship with that of nationhood. However, the Revolution also saw itself as providing as gifts to the world Liberty, Equality and Fraternity (Brubaker, 1992: 44). However, in Algeria the majority of the population throughout the colonial period were not to possess citizenship, and without citizenship, they effectively had no political representation. The principal problem in acquiring citizenship was that it could only be obtained by naturalization. This meant that it was not an automatic right of birth but required the adult to make a declaration of intent to belong to the nation of France and to do this meant the abandonment of the personal religious status of Muslim.

The question of citizenship was to be articulated first among the indigenous Jewish community of Algeria where as early as the 1850s demands for collective naturalization became commonplace both in the press and at meetings of the Algiers Council (*Conseil d'Alger*) so that when Napoleon III visited Algeria in 1860 and again in 1864 he was presented with petitions asking for naturalization. The 1865 Sénatus-Consulte treated nationalization as a question of secondary importance with the result that only two hundred Jews were naturalized. It was not until 1870 and a series of measures of administrative reform sponsored by Adolphe Crémieux that collective naturalization for Jews was conceded.[9] However, opposition was immediate and the then Governor-General, Admiral de Gueydon, with the support of the French Minister of the Interior, Lambrecht, restricted Crémieux's decree. Furthermore, during the 1890s, anti-Jewish candidates held office in Constantine, Oran and Mostaganem; and Jewish communities were attacked in 1882 in Algiers and 1897 in Oran.[10] Jews in Algeria had the advantage of support from Jewish leaders in France and the different Jewish renaissance movements of the late nineteenth century; nevertheless both the demand for and the acquisition of citizenship were contentious. The experience of Algerian Jews in the search for citizenship, even with external pressure, helps to illustrate why similar demands by Muslims were never to be met.

In the history of the debate on citizenship for the Muslim Algerian, the project known as the Blum–Viollette project, which was proposed by the radical socialist government of Léon Blum elected in May 1936, is one of the most significant, particularly if it is seen in conjunction with the developments which were occurring as a result of the activities of Ben Badis's Association of Reformist Ulama.[11] Viollette had been Governor-General of Algeria from 1925 to 1927, after which he wrote a critical study (1931) of the French colonial project in Algeria, *L'Algérie vivra-t-elle?* Viollette argued, with some prescience, that there was a latent but fundamental disjuncture between ideologies in Algeria and those in the *metropole* and that a policy marked by the two categories, subject and citizen, in which the subject (the Muslim) was subordinated to the citizen, was in practice untenable. Consequently, he argued, Muslims should have the same rights and duties as those held by the colons but at the same time be able to maintain their personal status. He also argued that the size of colon properties should be limited and that there should be at least some redistribution of land in favour of Muslims. Viollette published his critique in 1931 and it can be seen as a response to the celebrations which had taken place in 1930 to mark one hundred years of French rule in Algeria. These proposals would form the basis of the proposal made by the Blum government finally to offer citizenship without loss of personal status to Muslims in Algeria, but as Lebovics (1992: 123) points out, this proved too much for the majority of the colon population and was withdrawn, thus fulfilling Viollette's warning that the colons would destroy Algeria unless the centre intervened.

If 1936 and the Blum–Viollette proposals marked the last stage of the failure of the Republic to accord equality to Muslims in Algeria, they highlighted the dualism which characterized the colonial project itself and which the earlier attempts at naturalization – the 1865 Sénatus-Consulte, and the 1873 Warnier Law – had also failed to resolve. Ageron (1968) argues that it was in order to pacify the colons that the Second Republic pursued a policy of assimilating Algeria to France. He summarizes this policy as 'political assimilation, civil government, land sales, the billeting of Arabs' (Ageron, 1968: 39) and identifies Warnier, Napoleon III, Duvernois and Jules Duval as responsible for a policy of staged assimilation. Furthermore, it was a policy which the Third Republic was not to change radically. Julien (1952) calculates that between 1865 and 1934, no more than 2,500 Muslims were naturalized.

In a fundamental sense the conflict engendered by the colons in Algeria which resisted any measure of collective naturalization of the Muslim population denied the basic rights of the Revolution of 1789. The policy of progressive assimilation was necessarily ambivalent in that, while it may have achieved its object of appeasing the colons, it did not offer tangible enough benefits to Muslims. Furthermore, even these were compromised by the fact that Muslims were nevertheless subject to conscription and the severe restrictions on movement imposed by the 1874 Law of the Indigénat. In this context, the 1933 statement by Tawfiq al-Madani, one of the leaders of the Association of Reformist Ulama, that 'Islam is my religion; Arabic, my language; Algeria, my country' (quoted in Nouschi, 1978) would fall on fertile ground. If the colonial project remained ambivalent about citizenship, and maintained essentially contradictory discourses between the colonial status of inferiority and the Revolutionary equality of peoples, it was to maintain equally contradictory discourses on the other symbolic confrontation, relations between men and women in Muslim society. The next section explores the elements of these opposing discourses.

Women and Islam and the colonial confrontation

In the struggle by modern Islamist movements over the nature of the state, one of the principal points of the struggle is over the position and role of women and girls. In the Algerian struggle, many of the victims are women and girls who have refused to wear the veil. In the recent victory of the Talibans in Afghanistan, a country where female literacy is low (*Le*

Monde, 2.10. 96), no girls are now permitted to attend schools. In the foundational texts of Islam and most notably in the Qur'an, women were not denied a place (L. Ahmed, 1992; Mernissi, 1991). It is therefore a curious reflection on movements which seek to create a new moral order that they should exclude women from their project. Consequently, in this section I want to explore the ways in which the colonial project helped create the conditions for this exclusion.

The effects of the colonization project on the lives of its colonial subjects were diverse and, although the principal effects were on public life, nevertheless by separating public and personal status, colonization made the personal political. Furthermore, in the case of Algeria, a key part in the trajectory of relations between the colonial power and its Muslim subjects was concerned with the perception of and interpretation by each, of relations between men and women. In exploring the dialectics of that relation, the following quotation from Floya Anthias and Nira Yuval-Davis, where they argue that within the majority of nationalist movements 'women are the *symbol* of the nation, men its *agents*, regardless of the role actually played in the movement' (1993), is helpful because it encapsulates several contradictions which are apparent in the colonial confrontation and the nationalist resistance. However, although this helps us to understand what happened in Algeria after the end of the independence struggle, at a more general level an understanding of the history of women in any individual Muslim country suffers from the same problems which feminist historians have encountered and explored within the west but these problems are compounded by the fact that many of the sources which are available from which to write this history were written by western men bringing with them exactly the same prejudices and perspectives from which they viewed women in their own societies. The effects of these on the nature of the accounts which have come down to us have been explored by writers such as Billie Melman (1992) and Judy Mabro (1991), while Lorcin (1995) highlights how colonial ethnology incorporated descriptions of women in their Manichaean opposition of types in colonial Algeria. Other writers, most notably Fatima Mernissi (1991, 1975) and Leila Ahmed (1992), have explored the ways in which a conservative tradition within Muslim thought has come to dominate the discussion of the relationship between men and women in Muslim societies. Marnia Lazreg (1994) in *The Eloquence of Silence* discusses how these issues have affected relations between men and women in Algeria.

It is perhaps impossible now to construct any undistorted image of women's lives before colonization. However, considerable use has already been made of Ibn Khaldūn's *Muqaddimah* as a means to an understanding of Maghrebine society prior to both colonization and the Beylikal state. It seems appropriate therefore that he should also provide some comment on women's lives. This is done in chapter V which is concerned with 'the various aspects of making a living, such as profit and the crafts'. After a general introduction, sections 23–31 are concerned with a description of what are referred to in section 22 (355, II) as necessary crafts which are 'agriculture, architecture, tailoring, carpentry, and weaving' and 'Crafts noble because of [their] object' where he places 'midwifery, the art of writing, book production, singing, and medicine'. In his individual treatment of each craft, some such as agriculture (s23, 356–7) are given a very cursory treatment; while others such as midwifery (s27, 368–72) are described in some detail. His description of the tasks of the midwife and the importance of her role is summarized in the words 'this craft is necessary to the human species in civilization. Without it, the individuals of the species could not, as a rule, come into being' (s27, 370). Although Ibn Khaldūn is also using his discussion of midwifery to refute certain premises of the Spanish philosophers of the time, particularly al-Farabi and Avicenna (Ibn Sina), nevertheless it is an extraordinarily sympathetic description of a profession which in Europe was often perceived as having links with witchcraft.

However, one of the more curious aspects of the French conquest of Algiers in 1830 is that there appears to have been relatively little interest in the life of the Beylik in the preceding years.[12] Even Lazreg (1994: 20–35) uses mainly post-conquest sources to draw a picture of the lives of women in pre-colonial Algeria; and Lorcin (1995), although concerned with the scientific and literary representation of Algerian society, has only a short section (64–7) entitled 'Domesticity and the family' which is concerned solely with the contribution made by studies of the lives of women to this history. Her focus is twofold, on the one hand using women as another category with which to draw the contrast between Arab and Kabyle; and on the other to condemn polygamy. In the contrast between Arab and Kabyle, attention is focused on the participation by Kabyle women in the military struggle against the French. However, Lazreg (1994: 20–1) implies that this image of the woman warrior draws on the much older tradition of the story of El Kahina who although betrayed and eventually defeated had resisted the advance of the Arab–Muslim armies of the seventh century. What both Lazreg and Lorcin illustrate is that in spite of the ideological importance of the condition of women in colonial discourse, remarkably little is actually known about their lives. The account which is given here draws primarily upon the colonial historical journal *Revue Africaine,* and the work of the early twentieth-century anthropologist Mathéa Gaudry.

While women's lives in the pre-colonial state were as varied as the lives of women in France and Britain in 1830, it is nevertheless possible to draw the broad distinction between the lives of women in the towns – where the social and economic influences of the Ottoman Turks was strongest – and the lives of women in the countryside – where Ottoman Turkish influence on social and economic relations was largely absent.

To consider the towns first, it was in the towns that two of the features of gender relations in Ottoman Turkish society were found. They were the separation of society into distinct female and male spheres in which the seclusion of women and its accompaniment, the *harem,* were both the practice as well as the two predominant elements in the image which the West has of women in Ottoman Turkish society. They were also the two main souvenirs of the incorporation of the Beylik into the Ottoman Turkish Empire. However, both these aspects of women's lives applied only to the urban society of the pre-colonial state and only to a particular stratum of that urban society. The reasons for the existence of two such distinct spheres – one female and one male – in Ottoman Turkish social organization arose from its political organization as a military oligarchy in which the power of the state depended upon the efficiency of its military forces and in particular its elite corps, the Janissaries. Their importance to the maintenance of political stability within the Ottoman state meant that they occupied a singular role within it. However, in order for them to maintain their privileged status, it was necessary for them to be seen to be outside of, and above, the normal constraints exercised on human behaviour and in particular, those of family and tribal allegiance. The original basis of recruitment of the Janissaries had been through the mechanism of the *devirshme* which entailed their separation from their immediate families and their countries of birth as small children to be then educated specifically for military service.[13] They were expected to be celibate so as to obviate problems of interest brought about by blood descendants. Penalties were imposed in the early years of the Empire to ensure that celibacy was maintained. As women had no place in this military hierarchy, it reinforced a number of existing currents towards the division of Muslim societies into male and female spheres.[14]

Requiring celibacy and dividing society into separate spheres tended to regulate relations between men and women via prostitution. Prostitution in Algiers was practised under the control of the state which operated a registry system for the licensing of both brothels and prostitutes. Prostitution itself is an ambiguous phenomenon because it acts as a means of restricting women in a global sense but, for any individual woman, it may become a method of evading particular social controls. For example, in Algiers, once a woman had had her name inscribed on the register of prostitutes, she became responsible to, and the responsibility of, the state, and in this way was freed from the control of parents and family. It was primarily the rank-and-file Janissaries who sought sexual release with the prostitutes; their commanders achieved theirs by the establishment of their own *harem*. For example, Hussein, the Dey at the time of the French conquest in 1830, was reported as maintaining an establishment in which there were 'more than sixty women and concubines' (Boyer, 1963: 110). The maintainenance of such large households was, however, dependent upon the parallel existence of slavery. Domestic slavery was common in the Ottoman Empire and, in the Beylik, sources were very diverse; for example, Lewis (1995: 175) records that the corsair ships acquired slaves from Iceland and Ireland as well as from Black Africa. With the economic needs of the urban household provided for by slaves, the lives of the women of the *harem* were also enclosed so that when they left its confines they did so heavily veiled and usually carried in some form of closed cart. The social constraints imposed on women by this tradition in urban culture were both exaggerated by colonization and extrapolated as general conditions.

Although in the early period of Ottoman Turkish rule the Janissaries were at least in theory celibate, once the prohibitions on celibacy were relaxed, Janissaries began to establish more permanent relations with local women. In general, once such an establishment with a local woman had been set up, he would adopt her status within society. Furthermore, any children of such a union would also take the mother's status. Although this particular act whereby children took their mother's status may have been as much a result of the Janissary interdiction against the recruitment of their offspring if they were Muslims, it was also true that such an attribution gave the Janissary a more solid position in local society as it brought him into a prevailing social network which was less dependent upon the favour of the Sultan in Istanbul.

In the rural economy, however, the social seclusion of women practised in the towns did not exist. Indeed, women were involved at all levels within the rural economy. Besides performing the tasks which occurred in relationship to the immediate environs of the domestic unit, such as the preparation of meals and childcare, women were equally active in the fields and in animal husbandry, although it is also true that there existed some gender separation of tasks. For example, amongst the Chaouia in eastern Algeria, the sowing of crops was done by men, but the reaping was done by women; sheep were sheared by men while women carded, spun and wove the wool. It was women who made pottery and who dried the various fruits and vegetables; however it was men who dried meat and who harvested and pressed the olives (Gaudry, 1929). The rural woman did not wear the veil. Marriage, while it was not generally a matter of decision between individuals but reflected the representation of the best interests of the families involved, generally included some prior acquaintance between the prospective bride and bridegroom.

Finally, while there is no specific evidence for such events to have occurred during the Ottoman Turkish period, both prior to it and during the first phase of French rule, local tradition, particularly among the Kabyle, speaks of a female involvement in military affairs. For example there are the traditions of Kahina, a woman of the Kabyle who took up arms in the fourteenth century against the government of the time. During the first phase of colonial rule, in 1836 a widow of a Cheikh in the Bejaia region led an attack on a French army column. In 1857, a woman called Lalla Fatma[15] led another attack on the French; and again in 1871 (the year of Mokrani's revolt), another woman also from the Bejaia region but from the Ait-Mimoun was found leading a rebel column against the French (Bugéja, 1929). This warrior tradition was of course at considerable odds to that of the passive restrictive urban tradition which had flourished under the Janissary regime of the Ottoman Turks and which the successor French rulers chose to re-emphasize.

To begin to understand the impact of French colonial rule, some discussion of the lives of women in the pre-colonial period was necessary simply because they so often seem invisible in the history of the colonization process itself. This is partly because much of the process of colonization was about conquest and conquest involves military action and therefore men. However, the new colonizers as with the Ottoman Turks before them also brought with them an existing pattern of gender relations, and like their Ottoman Turkish predecessors their impact on gender relations was felt most in the towns. This was because, like the Turks, the new colonizers concentrated their settlement in the same urban centres. However, there were important differences, not least of which was the absence of a shared religious code. This meant that the alliance-making social interaction which had taken place between the ruling population, the Ottoman Turks and the ruled population, the Moors representing the local landowners and traders, was lost. Thus there was no natural link between the French and their ruled population. The two populations were therefore divided from each other on a social as well as a political level, a division which was reinforced by the fact that the

French chose, for reasons of security as well as by preference, to construct new urban spaces leaving the original Muslim towns as external and enclosed space – one graphic example of this is the 'Casbah' in Algiers itself. This left Algiers as well as many of the other towns of the Ottoman Turkish period as physical and social museums which, devoid of their economic and political roles, had the effect of turning them in on themselves with the result that there was displayed a tendency to concentrate upon the maintenance of the social norms prevailing at the time of the conquest.

The primary impact of the French colonization was therefore one of withdrawal, characterized by an end to social contact between the rulers and the ruled, and accompanied by a retreat by the ruled into the physical confines of the old Muslim city. At the same time, economic relations were also taken over by the new colonizers so that even here the indigenous population found its spheres of activity severely restricted. For women, the withdrawal of the Algerian male from public life meant that her seclusion would be further reinforced. It has been argued that the public humiliation under colonial rule of the Algerian male led him to vent his humiliation internally by an equally violent repression of the Algerian woman (Charnay, 1965; Fanon, 1972). Certainly it would seem that the circumscribing of the Algerian male by colonization did lead to an intensification of pressure upon the Algerian domestic unit and in particular upon the women of that unit, of whom it was demanded that they perform the collective task of receiving and guarding tradition. Evidence for this process can be perceived whereby, as the political pressures within the colonial state built up, the response which was found among the indigenous population was through reference to Muslim reformist ideologies such as those of Al-Afghani and Muhammed Abduh.[16] In these there was an emphasis on 'tradition' and on women, as the authentic guardians of such 'traditions'.

While in general the Algerian woman retreated from public view during the period of French colonization, in two particular areas she did not. These two areas were prostitution and domestic service. In the first, the French continued the Ottoman Turkish tradition of state-registered brothels accompanied by regular health inspections of each prostitute. Prostitution also appears to have continued to be a means by which certain individual women could acquire relative economic freedom from their families (Gaudry, 1961). However, the Algerian woman who was a prostitute was in an ambiguous position both in relation to her own community and also in relation to the European community. To her own community, she appeared to have gained some kind of entrance to colonial society, in a way which was denied to her male compatriot. It was, however, a way which reinforced the image of women as had prevailed in the urban society of the Ottoman Turks – that is, of woman as a non-productive and purely sexual being. The image distorted the view of women held by both the colonial society and the colonized society.

The resulting ambiguity in women's position is illustrated by the fact that although women have not been much in evidence in the post-independence governments, they had not been absent from the independence struggle itself. The first major participation by women was a student strike in May 1956 when young women from the Algiers region were mobilized (Courrière, 1969). Many of the women who did become involved in the struggle were students, but others were secretaries and many joined because other family members were involved in the struggle. In the conflict, women were often employed tactically because they could more easily pass for Europeans and therefore enter without comment in areas which were virtual no-go areas for Algerian males. One such woman was Djamila Bouhired; others were Zohra Driff, Samia Lakhdari, Fatiha Bouhired, Hassiba Ben Bouali and Djamila Boupacha. It was these women who, when the FLN took the decision to bomb selected civilian targets such as cafés in September 1956, would plant the actual bombs (Courrière, 1969).

It is obvious that in order for the women to have intermingled without question in European society, they would necessarily have had to be dressed in the clothes of their opponents. One aspect of this dressing up was that it required, where it was worn, the removal of the veil. It is over the question of the veil that one of the modern symbolic struggles between the West and Muslim societies has been played out. The veil has come to assume a mirrored significance in the sense that the more important as a symbol of Muslim difference (and backwardness) it has become, the more important it has become as a symbol of Muslim piety for women. This has taken place even though, historically, its significance has varied over time and between different Muslim societies. That it played a symbolic role during the Algerian independence struggle is illustrated by the much publicized French organized removal of veils in May 1958 when a number of women, many reputed to be prostitutes, made a public and consequently symbolic ceremony out of removing their veils. An early interpretation of this event by Frantz Fanon (1972) argues that this attack on the veil was just another attempt by the colonial power to impose its own social and cultural values upon Muslim and Algerian society, a view shared by Leila Ahmed (1992) who argues that these kinds of display illustrated the ways in which the colonial powers used women to reinforce existing relationships between men and between men and women. However, a later commentator, Marnia Lazreg (1994), argues that this ceremony also had an actively negative effect on the constituting of women's position in the post-independence state. The Algerian war illustrates that the veil may have multiple uses and that these are constructed according to the political and ideological needs of the different parties. It can be donned or discarded to aid a struggle; it can be removed symbolically by a colonial or other oppressing power in order to express and reinforce its domination. The veil has then become – even if it has not always been so – more than an item of women's clothing.

The wider issue of the relationships between men and women which are revealed through this discussion of the veil is illustrated by the fact that until the arrival of General Massu[17] in 1958, the French authorities considered it unnecessary to search veiled women. However, after Massu's arrival, everyone was searched and some women fighters were tortured. The most well-known are Djamila Boupacha and Djamila Bouhired.[18] Some women joined male colleagues in the Maquis and fought alongside them, while others were attached to the medical units. However, in spite of this involvement there was no general programme which sought to examine social attitudes towards men and women, with the result that women simply disappeared after independence. In the First Algerian Assembly after independence, there were ten women members, and in the Second Assembly, two. Recently, it has been suggested (Amrane, 1992) that the whole experience of war for the women was too traumatic and they were just too tired at the end to continue fighting particularly while also believing that their interests would be safeguarded by the men beside whom they had fought. Such moves enabled Algerian male society to reject not only the actual symbols of female emancipation such as the veil but also the underlying principles of such an emancipation. In this context, it is perhaps significant that Algerian nationality law[19] categorically prohibits marriage between an Algerian woman and a non-Muslim, whereas there is no corresponding prohibition against an Algerian man marrying a non-Muslim woman.

The second area in which Algerian women appeared in colonial society was as domestic servants. In Ottoman Turkish society, domestic work was often carried out by slaves; consequently the transfer of what had been a task of slaves to one done by women in general impacted on the social perceptions of women. Furthermore, domestic service continued to be a significant sector of female employment after independence. For example, estimates of employment sectors and numbers available for work in 1969[20] divide the total numbers of women available for work as follows: 9,623 unemployed; 115,600 working in manufacturing industry; 23,000 working in agriculture; and 58,260 employed in the service sector. Thus some 55 per cent of female employment at this time was in the service sector.[21] If the 1977 Census figures are considered, one finds that the percentage of women in the service sector had risen to 73 per cent.

While in urban society during the colonial period, women were either not seen or they were present as prostitutes and domestic servants. In the countryside, a parallel process of exclusion was occurring. This was caused in the first place by the massive requisitioning of land by the colonial authority during the latter half of the nineteenth century, and in particular after the uprising by Mokrani in 1871. The result of these sequestrations was that the broad patterns of agricultural production and ownership were changed. In the place of small holdings, which had been farmed jointly by the male and female members of the domestic unit, were established colon-owned commercial estates specializing in export-orientated crops such as the vine and employing wage-labour. Once wage-labour was employed, it was usually male wage-labour. A second consequence of the concentration of land and agricultural production in the hands of the colon was that in certain areas it created an intense pressure on available land resources. This led to the indigenous population being forced not only off the land but also out of agricultural employment altogether. Furthermore, it served to accentuate the population pressures which had grown up in the pre-colonial period, in areas such as Kabylia, leading to the release of an itinerant population which had thus had to seek urban employment.

Colonization, however, restricted not only agricultural employment but also opportunities for urban employment. As a result, in those areas where such population pressures were particularly serious – as for example in Kabylia – the major effect of colonization in rural areas in the aftermath of World War I was the emigration of male labour to France. This emigration frequently left behind villages in which the only adult population were women, and men too old to emigrate. On their own, it was difficult for these two groups to continue village production in the old manner; and besides, the remittances that were received from the *émigré* husbands, sons or brothers further reduced the necessity to sustain agricultural production. The loss of an economic role, coupled to male absence, imposed severe restrictions on women's mobility and served to isolate them generally from the mainstream of social and political activity.

If in the long term the major test for the Islamist movements will be to resolve the political and economic forms of the state, in the short term the point of contestation, and the one which causes the most misunderstanding in the West, concerns the situation of women.

Nationalism, Islam and the State

In the interwar years, religion acted as one of the principal means through which the nationalist project could be expressed. The launch of an armed struggle in 1954 necessarily re-focused the nationalist project towards victory in that struggle. The concession of independence by France in 1962 and its aftermath – embodied in the departure of the majority of the colon population in conjunction with the effects of eight years of very bitter armed struggle, during which many of the leaders of the independence movement died – meant that the articulation of the form that the post-independence successor state would take had necessarily been schematic. Although two attempts, in 1956 at the Congress of Soummam and just before independence itself with the Tripoli Programme, were made to develop an idea of the shape that an independent national state would have, this had never been a priority of a nationalist movement preoccupied with the conditions of the actual armed struggle. Furthermore, the broader context within which this struggle took place was dominated by the accession to power of Gamal Abdel Nasser in Egypt and his essentially secular nationalist project, as well as by the enduring influence of the secular state project established in Turkey by Mustafa Kemal or Ataturk on the fall of the Ottoman Turkish Empire at the end of World War I. Finally, both the major powers – the United States and the Soviet Union – gave encouragement to the nationalist projects of the decolonization process set in train by the events of World War II.

A number of authors (Colonna, 1995; Gellner, 1981; Merad, 1967) have drawn attention to the importance in the 1930s of religion as a means for the articulation of the nationalist project. Furthermore, both Colonna (1995) and Gellner (1981) suggest that the character of the religious reforms advocated by the nationalist religious leaders through their organization – the Association of Reformist Ulama, founded in 1931 – and its leader Sheikh Ben Badis laid the basis of an interpretation of Muslim religious expression which formed the antecedents of the Islamist movements of the 1980s and 1990s. Gellner's argument is outlined in the chapter entitled 'The unknown Apollo of Biskra: the social base of Algerian puritanism' (1981: 149–73), and Colonna's in her 1995 in-depth study of religious practice in the Aurès, *Les Versets de l'invincibilité*.

Gellner uses Ali Merad's (1967) *Le Réformisme musulman* as the basis of his argument that the Muslim reform movement did not reach Algeria until the early part of the twentieth century but that its growth was the result of the impact of the defeat of Turkey and the accompanying discrediting of the *marabout* who had supported the western powers against Turkey (1981: 155). His focus is not Ben Badis himself but another *'ulama* called Tayyib Uqbi (1981: 156) who was born in the town of Biskra in the Constantine region on the northern edge of the desert, in 1888, and whose early life was spent in the Hijaz (Saudi Arabia) where perhaps not surprisingly he was influenced by the Wahhabis.[22] In Gellner's view, Tayyib Uqbi represents one of the two dominant styles of Muslim religious life, which is the 'puritanical, unitarian, individualist, scripturalist ideal of a single deity, which has disclosed its final message in a definitive Revelation available to all who care to read it' (1981: 159). Consequently it is opposed to mediation which is the feature of its alternative 'associationist' ideal, which Gellner argues was (and to some extent still is) the more characteristic form of religious organization in the rural areas, and is dependent on literacy. Gellner's evocation of the need for literacy is, however, also reflective of his argument that without literacy, nationalism is not possible (Gellner, 1983). Colonna (1995), although she agrees that the 1930s are the period when attitudes to and views about religion change (1995: 23), rejects Gellner's view that the reason why the Muslim reformists of the 1930s were able to take control of the religious field was that ideologically the movement appealed to a detribalized and atomized population living in small towns (Colonna, 1995: 300). She argues through a detailed study of religious practice in the Aurès that there were three principal factors involved in the success of the Reformists in the region (1995: 303). First of all, rather than poverty, there was actually a level of prosperity which made people demand education; but the colonial authorities' provision of schools left this demand unsatisfied, and she illustrates this by a comparison with the region of Kabylia where the Reformists were held in check by the counter-influences provided by the greater availability of *écoles françaises* (schools established by the French colonial government). Her second argument is that, rather than populations being atomized, there was actually 'strong social cohesion' which, combined with an unchallenged clerical control by the Reformists, provided the basis for the establishment of their Association. Again, she draws the comparison with Kabylia where the Reformists were challenged by powerful non-reformist *zawiya* (she uses the example of Sidi Mansour) which inhibited the growth of their influence. In her view, it was the limited range of options available which made the Reformist movement attractive to the young men of the Aurès who otherwise felt suffocated by 'a feeling of claustrophobia' (1995: 341). Finally, she argues, the Association provided an alternative to the 'anti-intellectualism' (1995: 361) of Messali Hadj's *Étoile* and its political inheritors, the PPA (Algerian People's Party) and the MTLD (Movement for the Triumph of Democratic Freedoms).

Colonna is, however, not only exploring the background to the reasons why it was possible for the Association of Reformist Ulama to become so powerful during what was a relatively short period of time. She is also concerned to explain how the modes of organization which it used had wider implications for the later development of the nationalist movement. Using the memoirs of some of the leaders of the movement which have recently become available – that is, of Cheikh Bachir Ibrahimi and Tawfiq al-Madani – she argues that the 1930s activists had an 'obsessive' desire for consensus (1995: 360) which had the effect of (and here she uses a term derived from Geertz (1968)) an *'idéologisation'* of religion (Colonna: 361). Among the means which they used were the provision of schools but also the publication of newspapers and journals. The most famous of the newspapers and journals was *Al-Chihāb* founded by Ben Badis himself. Apart from making use of the media, Ben Badis and the Association also emphasized the importance of education. In a speech to their 1935 Congress (Abdel-Malek, 1965) he argued that in Islam, the mosque forms the centre of educational provision, the evidence for this being visible in the existence of the great mosque/universities such as Al-Azhar (Cairo) and the Zaytuna Mosque in Tunis where Ben Badis himself had been a student. However, he also argued that if the Association were to develop a religious teaching institution in Algeria, it would achieve a major religious and scientific monument for the present and future nation (Abdel-Malek, 1965: 90).

The role of Ben Badis as a precursor of the post-war nationalist movement was perhaps underestimated even though members of the Association included such as Malek Bennabi (born in 1905) whose 1954 *Vocation de l'Islam* is both a statement of the debt owed by Islam to the colonial project because of the opportunity it offered to free Islam of outmoded thought and practice such as maraboutism, and a rejection of the western model as simultaneously in decay and corrupt. Bennabi also argued that the western world tended to marginalize the Muslim and, in a piece written in 1960, claims that in order to counter 'the ideological struggle against Muslim peoples', Muslims have to turn and reflect back to the West the negative view of Islam which the West seeks to impose, and he uses the analogy of the *'miroir de la paume'* (Abdel-Malek, 1965:

197–9). While Bennabi helped provide some of the intellectual credentials for the emergence of the Islamist movements, Ben Badis's co-founder of the Association, Tawfiq al-Madani, would hold office in the post-independence government, as Minister of Habous – that is, religious-endowed property. Madani was a key figure in arabization policies. Consequently, although Ben Badis died in 1940 and the Association was eclipsed by the converging of the different nationalist trends – partly in response to the changing political context engendered by the events of World War II which led to the creation of the PPA, the MTLD and the OS (*Organisation Secrète*) before the FLN itself was formed in 1954 – nevertheless the impact of the Association on Muslim practice particularly in the Aurès set in motion fundamental changes in Muslim thought and practice in Algeria which would ultimately affect post-independence government policy.

The general political climate of the 1950s and 1960s and the growth of nationalist movements throughout the colonial empires gave support to the idea that the modern state was a secular national state. In this sense, the FLN (National Liberation Front) was clearly part of a global process in which members of colonial states sought to articulate their demands for political and economic control through the medium of national liberation. With the benefit of over thirty years of such regimes in political control, it can be seen that the project which they undertook was in a number of ways flawed, as writers such as A. S. Ahmed (1992), Appiah (1992) and Davidson (1992) have pointed out. Nevertheless, the ideological role of nationalism appears to be even more important although the form in which it is expressed is often different. Nowhere is this more true than in the Islamist projects which, while they reject the secular nationalism of the nationalist elites of the independence era, themselves using the medium of Islam, utilize a rhetoric of universalism within the context of autonomous national development. Zubaida (1993: 55-62) illustrates graphically how intrinsic this was to Khomeini's vision of the future of the Iranian state.

Consequently, to understand the limitations of the FLN's state project, and in particular of the project undertaken by Boumediene between 1965 and 1978 which is the focus here, the discussion needs to be located within this broader context. Furthermore, while one of the roots of the modernization project which was undertaken by Boumediene can be traced to the economic models used to underpin the Soviet economic model, Boumediene himself was neither a Marxist nor a secularist on the Ataturk pattern. However, the fact of his preoccupation with economic matters effectively led him to cede control of the Ministries of Education, Justice and Religious Affairs and the cultural field in general to a section of the political elite which sought to arabize Algeria and reconstitute (on their terms) its Islamic character (Lamchichi, 1992; Reporters sans Frontières, 1994). Boumediene's attempts to regain control of this arena primarily took the form of Charters of which the most significant in the cultural field was that of 1976, entitled the *Charte nationale du peuple algérien* (National Charter of the Algerian People). This Charter enunciated three main ideological aims, which were: to assert and consolidate Algerian national identity and promote all forms of cultural development; to raise continuously the level of education and technical skills; to adopt a way of life which is in harmony with the principles of the Socialist Revolution as defined in the present charter. In practice, however, the main focus of the Socialist Revolution was on the development of Algerian industry accompanied by a raising of the level of education of the industrial labour force. Another major consequence of this secession of the fields of culture and ideology was the failure of the Boumediene government to enact a family law. Instead, the Islamist control of these fields sustained a protracted debate over family law, arguing that it should reflect the essence of Muslim character which was Algeria, and as a result succeeded in effectively blocking its passage during Boumediene's lifetime. However, the weaknesses in the ideological field which this revealed would result in the final passage of an Islamist version in 1984, despite mounting opposition by women who took to the streets to oppose it (Lazreg, 1994).

Economics and Islam

In analysing the failure of the Boumediene project, two issues of the relationship between economics and Islam are raised. The first concerns a debate over whether or not the Muslim world would have become capitalist without the intervention of colonization and therefore whether or not colonization had the effect of stifling the potential for the development of capitalism. The second concerns the ability of the Islamist movements to construct not simply an Islamist state but an Islamist economy. The question of what might be the features of a truly Muslim economy is an issue which confronts both the Islamists and existing Muslim states and has led to attempts to articulate what the shape of a Muslim economy might be (Naqvi, 1994). The problem which these authors face can be gauged from the debates which took place over the capacity or otherwise of the Muslim world on the eve of colonization to have been or have become capitalist. Central to that debate was Maxime Rodinson's *Islam and Capitalism*.[23]

Rodinson's argument is constructed essentially within the structure of orthodox Muslim exegesis; that is, the Qur'an is interrogated first and then the Sunna. This is done in order to verify whether or not it is theologically possible for capitalism to have developed within a Muslim state. He concludes that the basic tenets of Islam contain nothing which would have precluded or excluded the development of capitalist relations in the Muslim world. Instead, he argues, the actual manner of Muslim expansion in the Middle East and the associated growth of merchants actually provided the 'merchant capital' which was necessary to the development of capitalism in this period. To illustrate the argument that it was possible for a capitalist mentality to develop within the Muslim world he cites the case of the Mzab (Rodinson, 1966: 127). Another writer, Samir Amin in *The Arab Nation* (1978), also argues that it was merchant capital derived from the profits of the long-distance trade that provided the crucial surpluses in the Arab world which could have led to capitalist development. The Arab Muslim world's ability to trade rested on its strategic position between Europe and the Far East and between Europe and Africa. The size of the profits which were earned were then observable in the size of its great cities: Aleppo, Damascus, Baghdad, Basra, Antioch. However, Amin also argues that the process was aborted in the middle of the eleventh century because of the advent of the different Turkish groups and the disruption they subsequently caused. Amin like Rodinson concludes that while the conditions for capitalism did appear to exist in the Middle East at various times, they were never consolidated.

While this debate sought to explain the absence of the development of capitalism and used the techniques of exegesis to illustrate its arguments, those who reject capitalism utilize the same techniques of exegesis to conclude that there cannot be any form of capitalist development within the boundaries of Islam. In particular, these protagonists argue that within Islam there is an express prohibition on the practice of usury, that is, the creation of interest. Further support for these ideas comes from the declarations of the 'Islamic Revolution' in Iran as well as more generally in the public rhetoric of such countries as Pakistan and Libya. The essence of this position often referred to as 'fundamentalist' is that it calls upon the active employment of the country's Muslim heritage to create a new social and economic order. At the same time, such assertions are usually justified by reference to religious infallibility. However, as Marjorie Grice-Hutchinson (1978) argued, such prohibitions as there are in the religious texts have historically been quite effectively circumvented.

Conclusion

This chapter has sought to show how the colonial encounter affected the civil and religious life of Muslims in Algeria. The most important effect was undoubtedly the disconnection of civil and religious society, the unity of which is at the heart of the concept of *umma* or community that forms one of the guiding principles of Muslim society. In doing so, it both opened up and therefore left open the whole question of what it meant and means to be an Algerian Muslim. In a number of senses, the struggle for the constitution of a new societal community begins with conquest in 1830; and independence in 1962 can be seen not as a new beginning but as the start of a new series of struggles to decide what that community should be. That the colonial encounter should have been more than usually disruptive is partly a reflection of the historical moment of conquest. It involved an encounter between two states: the Beylik of Algiers, and France. The former, as a result of weakening ties with the Ottoman Turkish Empire, was engaged in a process of political and social change; the latter, despite the upheavals of the Revolutionary period, was still engaged in a struggle over whether the state should be a secular republic or a reformed monarchy. The encounter and the impact of a new colonial status for the Beylik arrested the process of internal political and social change in the Beylik but did not offer an alternative political model. At the same time, the struggle within and for the French state would continue until the end of the nineteenth century, when it was resolved in favour of the secular republic. However, even in the resolution of this central question of the French state, the colony of Algeria would play a role as the key players were Jules Ferry, who was at one and the same time responsible for the development of public education and colonial policy, and the head of the Catholic church in Algeria, Cardinal Lavigerie. It was Lavigerie, first appointed as Archbishop of Algiers in 1866 and who founded in 1868 the *Missionnaires d'Afrique,* better known as the 'White Fathers', who was chosen by Pope Leo XIII to provide the public affirmation of Ferry's secular French state at a dinner for naval officers in Algiers in 1890. The significance of the choice of Lavigerie and the alliance which it embodied between him and Ferry is that it shows once again how important Algeria has been in the development of the modern French state.

Notes

1. These were Cardinal Lavigerie, the Archbishop of Algiers from 1866, and Jules Ferry.

2. There are four 'schools' of Law in Islam which reflect considerable differences of both political and social origin and of practice. Historically, the majority of Muslims in Algeria were organized within the Maliki school whose founders had been merchants. By contrast, Ottoman Turkish government operated through the Hanifi school, the pre-eminent school of historical Muslim administrations from the Caliphate onwards. Present day Islamist movements operate under the aegis of the Hanbali school of law which historically had the most restricted geographical spread but was taken up by the eighteenth-century reformist movement originating from Saudi Arabia, the Wahhabbis. For discussion of the complexities of Muslim law, see Coulson (1971), Schacht (1964).

3. These are linked with the practice of Sufism and are discussed in more detail. A number of important figures in Maghrebine history were members of *tariqa* including the Emir Abd el-Kader and Ibn Khaldūn.

4. Fatima Mernissi is a Moroccan sociologist and writer who has written particularly about the role and position of women in Muslim thought and practice. She is a critical writer and, as she records in *Women and Islam*, has been attacked by some Muslim men (1991: 193–4) for her attempts to reclaim the Muslim women's past. For a positive review of her work, see the entry under 'Mernissi, Fatima' in the *Oxford Encyclopedia of the Modern Islamic World*, volume III.

5. The earliest translation of his travels which took place between 1325 and 1354 was made by C. Defrémery and B. R. Sanguinetti and was published in 4 volumes in Paris in 1854. It was republished with an Introduction by Vincent Monteil in 1969. The major English edition is an edited translation of Defrémery and Sanguinetti by H. A. R. Gibb first published in 1958. In addition there is an abridged account first published by Routledge & Kegan Paul in 1929 and reissued in 1983. The edition I have used is the Spanish translation by Serafín Fanjul and Federico Arbos (1987) *Ibn Battuta: A través del Islam*, Madrid: Alianza Editorial.

6. These are discussed on page 54. For a detailed account see Bontems (1976: 486).

7. As Lorcin (1995: 53–75) argues, much of the material which has been used to depict Muslim practice during the colonial period was intimately bound up with the legitimation of the colonial project itself. As a result the recent publication (1995) of Fanny Colonna's *Les Versets de l'invincibilité* helps provide a corrective to both the colonial description of rural Muslim practice and the later nationalist re-interpretations.

8. The entry on the Tijaniyah in the *Oxford Encyclopedia of the Modern Islamic World*, volume IV argues that by the nineteenth century, the *tariqa* have become associated with different occupational groupings. The author, John Ralph Willis, suggests that the orders which al-Tijani joined were the Wazzaniyah, Darqawiyah, Nasiriyah and the Khalwatiyah and that he was in the Shadhili–Jazuli tradition in the sense that his order employed charismatic power. The history of the Tijaniyah during the last quarter of the nineteenth century

and the early twentieth century was controversial, as it was accused of collaboration with the colonial authorities, but Willis suggests that although this was true of the main *zawiya* at Ain Madi, the picture in other centres was different.

9. These are the decrees of 24 October 1870. The decree which provided for the naturalization of Jews was the seventh of the nine decrees (Ansky, 1950).

10. The appearance of anti-semitism in Algeria in the late 1880s and 1890s coincides with similar developments in France which were to come to a head with the conviction of Alfred Dreyfus for spying in 1894. The conviction was quashed in 1899 but, as Lorcin (1995) shows, the ideological basis for the racist constructions used to convict Dreyfus had been developing throughout the nineteenth century.

11. The space granted to and the impact of the Association of Reformist Ulama is discussed on pages 101–5.

12. This provides a marked contrast to the availability of a popular literature in English on the lives of women in the Muslim world. For example both Lady Mary Wortley Montagu's and Lady Elizabeth Craven's studies of women in the Ottoman Turkish capital were published in the eighteenth century: Montagu's 'Turkish letters' posthumously in 1763 and Craven's *Journey through the Crimea to Constantinople* in 1789 (Melman 1992: 77–98). While in general sympathetic accounts of the women's lives, Melman also suggests that both of these authors succeed in turning their description of the *harem* into a reflection of the English aristocratic household (Melman 1992: 97).

13. This method of recruitment had largely broken down by the end of the sixteenth century and, as illustrated by local practice in the Beylik, became staffed mainly by the sons of Janissaries (Lewis 1995: 125).

14. As Melman (1992: 59) points out, seclusion of women had been an aspect of aristocratic society in the Mediterranean region before the creation of the Ottoman Turkish Empire. Leila Ahmed (1992: 26–7) refers to practices of strict seclusion within the Byzantine Empire to which the Ottomans were the successors. Leila Ahmed also argues that the misogynist tradition has its historical origins in Greece and Mesopotamia and that such practices had become widespread throughout the Mediterranean region by the time of the Muslim conquests in the seventh century AD (1992: 33). Fatima Mernissi (1991: 195) argues that it was during the Abbasid period that the combination of international conquest and the arrival of women slaves from the conquered countries led to the retreat of the free woman 'behind locked doors and windows'.

15. Hocine Ait Ahmed (1983:14) recalls that his mother claimed direct descent from Lalla Fatma and would frequently draw her children's attention to it.

16. For an account of the life and traditions of Afghani and Abduh, see Hourani (1962) and Kedouri (1966).

17. Paratroop commander sent to Algiers in 1958 to crush resistance. Famously depicted in Pontecorvo's 1966 film *The Battle of Algiers* under the name of Mathieu, he largely succeeded. French withdrawal in the end came about not because they had lost but because they chose not to pursue the war. Massu later wrote his own account of the Battle of Algiers.

18. Simone de Beauvoir and Giselle Halimi were among those who campaigned on behalf of the women,

drawing the attention of the French in France to the nature of France's war in Algeria.

19. 27 March 1963. See also discussion in Borrmans (1977); and for a personal account of its impact, see T. M. Maschino and Fadéla M'rabet (1972).

20. Earliest post-independence date for which appropriate data available. Statistical sources are the *Annuaire statistique de l'Algérie* for the years 1970 and 1977–78.

21. For further examples of this pattern of the continuation of previously oppressive forms of female employment, the experience of African American women in the period immediately after slave emancipation in 1865 is instructive (Amott and Matthaei, 1991).

22. The Muslim reformist movement in the Hijaz held beliefs which were derived from Muhammad ibn 'Abd al-Wahhab (1703–87), whose own inspiration was the Hanbali school of thought. It was later adopted by the House of Saud who became the Kings of Saudi Arabia after the division of the Ottoman Empire in the aftermath of World War I. As a result, they elevated a previously minor school of Muslim thought to the world stage. Most contemporary Islamist movements have Hanbali/Wahhabi roots. See also note 2.

23. English edition, Allen Lane, 1974. However, references are to the French edition, *Islam et Capitalisme*, Paris, Éditions du Seuil, 1966.

4

The Post-Independence Algerian State
1962–78

The problems which the Algerian state faced in 1962 were constituted from the character of the state in 1830 and the impact upon it of the French colonial project. However, the state which was constructed in the period between 1962 and 1978, after independence was achieved, would add new problems. A key element in the construction of this state was Algeria's second President, Houari Boumediene, and the years 1965 to 1978 when he was the Head of State. Although Boumediene died in office in 1978, it was his Presidency that put in place the principal structures of state and economy which helped create the conditions from which emanated the crisis that developed during the 1980s. This chapter examines the attempt to construct the post-independence national state.

A key factor in this process was the character of the struggle for independence, and the fact that it was not simply a war of national independence fought against a colonial power – France – but also an internal war in which the conflicts resolved and unresolved would affect the character of politics after independence. The violence of the conflict which has followed the aborting of the 1991 elections has deeper historical roots that are both specific to the Algerian situation and also illustrate some more general problems which have arisen from the attempts to construct nationally-based states within the ex-colonial Muslim world. The violence which has formed part of the experience of the last five years is therefore an expression both of the particular limitations of the Algerian state project and of the wider difficulties which former colonies have had in reshaping their political, social and economic character after the achievement of independence.

The independence struggle: 1954–62[1]

The battle for Algerian independence was a long and bitter struggle which was costly in both human and economic terms. De Gaulle remarked at his press conference on 11 April 1961 that *l'Algérie nous coûte* ('Algeria costs us') (quoted in Stora, 1993: 87). De Gaulle was talking in terms of the impact of the war on the economic reconstruction of France but the war also claimed human lives. At the June 1962 Tripoli Congress, the FLN claimed that the war had cost over a million Muslim lives (Algiers Charter: FLN, 1964) whereas other estimates suggest that the loss of life was around 500,000 (Stora, 1993: 91). For what was for much of its history an undeclared war, this is a not insignificant figure and its casualties include many of the original leadership of the FLN. Thus the war was fought, and it affected the lives of most Algerian families. How people were affected varied, but there was both a sense of relief and also even of euphoria that the period of fighting was over and people could get back to living their lives.[2] However, if De Gaulle was concerned about the costs in respect of the reconstruction of France, the costs in terms of the reconstruction of Algeria were even greater. They included not only the creation of a new political structure but also the costs of the reconstruction of the economy, as much of the economic infrastructure was to be destroyed in the last days of the war through the actions of the OAS (*Organisation Armée Secrète*).[3] Thus even at the end, there was no smooth transition to independence but, rather, further chaos as the intensity of struggle in these final stages precipitated a mass departure of the colon population.

However, it was not only the successful nature of the French military campaign both official and unofficial that won the day, but also the fact that at the ideological level, the FLN was less organized and less unified than might have been expected from an organization which had just fought an eight-year war for independence. This was also in strong contrast to the circumstances of France's previous anti-colonial opponents – the Vietminh. Part of the reason for this lack of coherence stems from the fact that the original declaration in favour of armed struggle in 1954 split the nationalist movement in Algeria. In particular, it took the initiative within the nationalist leadership away from the veteran nationalist leader, Messali Hadj[4], which led to the formation of a counter-movement by Messali Hadj and his remaining supporters, with the result that the FLN could never fully claim to represent all of the population, nor was it ever able to gain a real foothold in certain of the Messalist strongholds. Consequently, not only were the FLN fighting the French colonial forces but they were also in places engaged in a virtual civil war. The difficulties which the FLN had in exercising total control of the nationalist struggle can be observed in the uneven distribution of the wilayate command structure, with its concentration of command districts in the eastern region. In addition, the nature of the war which was fought necessitated a command structure which used a hierarchical cell group structure dependent on secrecy for its success.

The FLN (*Front de Libération Nationale*) was founded by six men in 1954 with the single objective of national liberation. These six men were Mohammed Boudiaf, Mostefa Ben Boulaïd, Rabah Bitat, Belkacem Krim, Mourad Didouche and Larbi Ben M'Hidi. In March 1954, they formed the CRUA (Revolutionary Committee for Unity and Action) and it was CRUA which was the basis of the initial command structure of the FLN. Under this command structure, Algeria was divided into five initial regional command areas or wilaya as follows: Wilaya I (the Aurès region) was under the command of Ben Boulaïd; Wilaya II (north Constantine) was under Mourad Didouche; Wilaya III (Kabylia) was under Belkacem Krim; Wilaya IV (Algiers) was under Amar Ouamrane (August 1956); and Wilaya V (Oran) was under Larbi Ben M'Hidi. A sixth was added later to cover the South which was under Ali Mellah (or Si Cherif as he was called). This left Mohammed Boudiaf as general co-ordinator. It has already been pointed out that this division heavily favoured the eastern half of the country; if, then, it is also recognized that three of the above – Boudiaf, Ben Boulaïd and Ben M'Hidi – were from the Constantine region, this bias in favour of the eastern region becomes more strongly marked. Although six men formed the inner core of the CRUA inside Algeria, they were externally represented in Cairo by Hocine Aït Ahmed, Ahmed Ben Bella and Mohammed Ben Youssef Khider. Although these nine men were the principals, the final leadership group counted twenty-two members.

While there was a strong regional bias in favour of the east of Algeria, particularly the Constantinois area and Greater Kabylia, social origins of members of the leadership group were more diverse. These are described by Harbi (1975)[5] and Stora (1993) in the following terms: Boudiaf's as 'grande tente', that is, from a lineage of superior social status (Harbi) whose social status had declined under colonization (Stora); Ben Boulaïd, who was one of the oldest, is described as of peasant origin (Harbi) but from a family of small landowners (Stora). He had followed his father into flour-milling and, after service in the French army during World War II from which he was invalided out and then remobilized, had in civilian life become sufficiently prosperous to head the guild of cloth merchants in the Aurès, to set up his own flour-mill and to have just obtained a licence to operate his own bus line. Krim was the son of a local policeman (Stora) who had been appointed a *petit caïd* (local administrator) and had been himself in the colonial adminstration as an employee of one of the 'mixed communes'[6] (Harbi). Mourad Didouche is described as from a *famille aisée* – that is, comfortably well-off (Harbi); and Ben M'Hidi from a family of *paysans aisés* or well-to-do peasants (Harbi) whose family were also marabouts and respected in the high plains of the Constantinois (Stora). All were in their thirties and had become involved in politics in the period after the end of World War II with the result that, by the early 1950s, all had either served a prison sentence for political activities or were under attainder for them. In addition, Aït Ahmed came from a distinguished marabout family in Kabylia (Harbi, Stora) but both Ben Bella and Khider, who was both the oldest member and the only one to have been a member of *Étoile Nord-Africaine*, came from poorer backgrounds. Ben Bella's family is described as that of 'poor peasants'; and Khider is described as coming from a poor family in Biskra (Harbi). Others such as Abdelhafid Boussouf, who is described by Harbi as a 'remarkable organizer' responsible for the communication system which enabled contact to be retained between the organizational heads and the wilaya, belonged to the poor branch of a 'grande tente' family (Harbi). However, he was also an opponent of Abane Ramdane, one of the early victims of assassination, who was from a *famille modeste* (Harbi).

While the main external opposition to the FLN as leaders of Algerian nationalism were the Messalists, internally the FLN never achieved the unity which was depicted in Pontecorvo's film and in much of the early post-independence writing.[7] In particular, early divisions in the leadership and in particular between Ben Bella and Boudiaf on the one hand and Abane Ramdane on the other, were probably responsible for the assassination of the latter in 1958. After Abane Ramdane's assassination, there was yet a further internal power struggle as three men – Krim, Bentobbal and Boussouf (Lebjaoui, 1970)[8] – attempted to concentrate the leadership of the FLN in their hands. At the same time, both Bentobbal and Boussouf were united in an attempt to deny to Krim, as one of the few survivors of the 1954 declaration, actual leadership of the liberation struggle. These power struggles were also reflected in the fates of the various wilaya commanders. For example, of the original wilaya commanders, three were killed in one way or another by the French forces. They included Ben M'Hidi, originally in command of Wilaya V but in Algiers during the Battle of Algiers, where he was arrested in February 1957 and soon afterwards died in custody; Mourad Didouche (Wilaya IV) killed by French troops in January 1955 as was his successor Youssef Zighoud; and Ben Boulaïd (Wilaya I) who first arrested in February 1955 and escaped in the November only to be killed in the following March. In addition Ben Boulaïd's deputy, Bachir Chihani was assassinated by two of his assistants in October 1955; and the commander of Wilaya VI, Ali Mellah was also assassinated in 1957. Ahmed Mahsas, a member of the group of 22, was forced to seek exile in Germany after his arrest in Tunisia had been ordered by another member of the group of 22, Amar Ouamrane (Harbi). Nine members of the group of 22 died during the independence struggle but a further six – Hocine Aït Ahmed, Ben Bella, Boudiaf, Lamine Debaghine, Khider and Bitat – spent the greater part of the war in French prisons.

This decimation of the original leadership of the liberation struggle meant that, in terms of the conduct of the actual struggle on the ground, a certain fragmentation of the leadership was inevitable. Similarly, the percentage of the leadership in exile meant that when independence did come and they were released and able to return to Algeria, there were conflicting interests between the internal commanders and the GPRA (Provisional Government of the Algerian Republic), hence the power struggle which took place on the very eve of independence from which Ben Bella emerged, significantly with the support of Boumediene, as the leader. Thus the actual exigencies of return were an additional factor in the continuing struggle for power which had characterized the entire period of the armed struggle. It can be seen therefore that the period 1954–62 involved a series of power struggles which, while they may have resolved immediate difficulties, left a complex and difficult legacy for the construction of a workable political system after independence.

The absence of unity within the original leadership and its main figures is illustrated by the changes in personnel which took place and which led to the emergence of new leaders. The most significant of these was Houari Boumediene who had succeeded Boussouf as the Head of Wilaya V and would end the war as Head of the unified General Staff of the ALN (Army of National Liberation) (Ottaways, 1970). Boumediene and several of his principal supporters – namely, Abdelaziz Bouteflika, Ahmed Kaid and Ahmed Medeghri – were all much younger than the original leaders of the FLN. In 1954, Boumediene had been 22, Bouteflika 17, Kaid Ahmed 24, and Medeghri 20 and were therefore in their early thirties or late twenties at the end of the war. This meant that neither had they been leading figures in the earlier phase of the resistance struggle nor had they been party to the political dissensions of the 1940s and the early 1950s which had lain behind the formation of the FLN in 1954. Consequently, although key figures in the post-independence struggle, they were less involved in the power struggles during the independence war.

To sum up, until the creation of the FLN and its declaration of armed struggle in 1954, each previous attempt including that of the OS

(*Organisation Secrète*) had been effectively neutralized by French forces. In spite of the fact that the French armed forces eventually did largely succeed in winning the military struggle, the political climate at the end of the 1950s had changed, as De Gaulle was to recognize, and it became no longer a politically viable struggle to continue. Furthermore, De Gaulle was also anxious to maintain French access to the now valuable petroleum and natural gas resources of the Sahara which might have been more difficult if the war had continued. Certainly France went on to exploit these resources for almost ten years after the war ended. However, although the FLN leaders finally gained their objective of independence, it was at considerable cost to themselves. In this context, it cannot be said to have been unexpected that independence would pose formidable practical problems of organization and direction for the survivors of the struggle and that, in practice, the power struggles which had been taking place were not themselves completed with the war's end. The declaration of independence precipitated a further power struggle from which Ben Bella, one of the exiles supported by Boumediene, emerged victorious, only to be ousted three years later in a *coup d'état* by Boumediene himself.

The struggle over leadership on the eve of independence meant that the policies which would be pursued by the newly independent state were also a site of struggle. After all, the foundation of the FLN in 1954 with its principal aim the fight for independence meant that, by virtue of its origins, it had no previous history as an organization within which its members could have the opportunity to develop coherent programmes. Its membership had been drawn from a variety of sources including the PCA (Algerian Communist Party) and the earlier nationalist movements. Consequently, there were a variety of tendencies represented within the FLN and which the exigencies of struggle and the dispersal and loss of many of its leading cadres did not erase. In addition, as the FLN and the ALN had evolved, different tendencies developed within them including a strong current opposed to questions of ideology and debate over the type of state which might be enacted. In spite of this, there were two main attempts made to outline a post-independence strategy for the FLN: at the Congress of Soummam in August 1956; and then, in the immediate pre-independence period, the discussions which led to the drawing up in May 1962 of what was called the 'Projet de Programme pour la Réalisation de la Révolution Démocratique' or, more shortly, the 'Tripoli Programme'. The Tripoli Programme was prepared by six men: M'Hammed Yazid, Mohammed Ben Yahyia, Reda Malek, Mohammed Harbi, Mostefa Lacheraf and Abdelmalek Temnan,[9] ostensibly under the aegis of Ben Bella. The 1956 Congress of Soummam had been organized by Abane Ramdane and Belkacem Krim,[10] although its published programme was largely written by Amar Ouzegane, a former secretary-general of the PCA.[11]

Both these programmes can be taken to illustrate the nature of thinking within the FLN on the shape they expected their future state to take. In terms of its timing and the context of its publication just before independence was achieved, the Tripoli Programme is of most concern because it was specifically concerned with what would be the shape of post-independence Algeria. However, the Congress of Soummam serves to indicate some of the difficulties which confronted the Algerian armed struggle and how these problems were still unresolved when the Tripoli Programme was drawn up. In Harbi's view (1980), the themes which emerge from the Congress of Soummam were nationalism, within which was incorporated a denial of class difference as long as the person concerned was an Algerian Muslim; and the concept of the FLN as a counter-state rather than the source of the creation of a counter-society.[12] Other themes to be expressed were populism, where society would be led by the collectivity composed of good, honest, incorruptible and courageous men with the peasantry taken to be the 'shock troops against colonialism' (Harbi, 1980: 178–9); and social conservatism in that nothing was said about the role women would have in the new state.

The Tripoli Programme very clearly indicates that Algeria's eight-year struggle for independence had been a national liberation struggle – that the central purpose behind the organization of the CRUA and the launching of the armed independence struggle under the aegis of the FLN had been for the purpose of obtaining *national* independence. It is also significant that one of the authors of the programme, Mostefa Lacheraf, would publish in 1965 a study entitled *L'Algérie: nation et société*.[13] In other words, there was a concern about the nature of meanings particularly as independence approached. Lacheraf argued that when the French conquest began in 1830, the country it was about to conquer had a well-organized society and its own civilization, with the result that colonization's principal aim had been to substitute one population group for another people. In his view, national sentiment in Algeria was well developed by 1947; and that by 1959, the FLN had reached the second stage of nation-building which entailed the transformation of nationalist sentiment into the processes which would construct the Algerian nation.

Harbi for his part argues (1980: 305) that the particular view of the nation-state which was adopted was the consequence of a colonial history in which 'Islam had become the substitute for the state before it had become its soul'. As a result, the view of the nation-state which was presented only made sense if it was equated with the Muslim community. In part, the use of the term 'Muslim' was derived from the practice of the French administration in Algeria which used the word as the means of distinguishing between different categories of citizen. As late as 1947, the French administration would introduce laws which established separate voting structures, effectively on the basis of religion, for the different members of its Algerian *département*. Consequently, persons who declared themselves to be Muslim could not also obtain full citizenship. The FLN leaders in their use of the word 'Muslim' were in a sense employing an identifier which had already been used imprecisely by the colonial administration to identify that section of the population which was not considered to be European. The FLN leaders were therefore faced with an identifier which, while vague in origin, had acquired a meaning through the process of the struggle for independence, and therefore were also faced with the problem that no other identifier would have sufficient currency to encompass all the differences which were contained by the borders of Algeria. However, even at the level of the 'imagined' (Anderson 1991),[14] the FLN leaders faced a formidable task in transforming the 'community' of their imagination into a reality. The measure of their difficulty can be assessed from the discussion which has already taken place on the internal divisions within the FLN itself and the divisions which existed between the FLN and other organizations.

The combination of the manner of the FLN's formation and the different political currents contained within it – including nationalist, Muslim, socialist and communist – with the effort that eight years of armed struggle had required meant that the development of an idea, no less than a programme, of the shape which the post-independence state would take had tended to be seen as a secondary-order task. Furthermore, the geographic separation of the FLN, the ALN, the GPRA and the internal divisions within the FLN, and between them and in particular the Messalists, also made the task of bringing together some kind of coherent strategy all the more difficult.

The Tripoli Programme is therefore especially interesting because it is both an attempt to sketch the broad outlines of a political and economic policy for the post-independence state, and an attempt to assert the development of national unity. Implicit throughout the Tripoli Programme is a belief that, despite the political weaknesses of the FLN attributed to its founders' – the 1 November 1954 clan – sole focus on national liberation, the seven and a half years of struggle had been able to achieve 'national unity, national renaissance, all within the perspective of a radical transformation of society' (Tripoli Programme, 7). As witness to the different political ideologies which were present within the FLN, the Programme also argues that as an organization the FLN had displayed problems of paternalism, feudalism, petit bourgeois sentiments and, as a direct result of the exile of many of the FLN's leaders, internal depoliticization. Therefore: 'The Revolution has amongst its tasks to consolidate the newly independent nation by restoring within it all the values which have been frustrated by or destroyed by colonialism and so create a sovereign state and a national economy and culture.' (TP, 28) The contradictions which lay at the the heart of the FLN project are quite apparent here, as it is difficult to reconcile the first statement with the observations by the authors about the state of politics in Algeria on the eve of independence and the tasks they envisage as being necessary afterwards. This same division is also observable in the very short section devoted to the proposed post-independence economic programme which is contained in six pages of a pamphlet totalling sixty.

The basic economic development strategy envisaged by the Tripoli Programme's authors was that 'it would be rapid, correspond with and be directed towards the satisfaction of the needs of all, within a framework of collectivization. Of necessity, it must therefore be understood in a social-ist perspective' (TP, 28); and that such development should further aim to develop 'the democratic spirit' which would be best achieved 'in clearly defined state-sponsored institutions'. In planning for this future, the authors argued that they wished to avoid what they refer to as the 'liberal' approach to economic development because it did not permit 'a real transformation of society'. In their view, the effect of such economic measures on newly independent countries was that 'They aggravate the anarchy of the market, reinforce economic dependence with regard to imperialism, make the State an organism for the transfer of wealth into the hands of the already rich, and nourish the activities of the parasital classes allied to imperialism.' (TP, 37) They saw the consequences of these processes as involving the substitution of a local bourgeoisie for the old alien bourgeoisie of the colonial period and the promotion of the development of the unproductive sectors of the economy, because it was those sectors of the economy which allowed for the development of personal wealth but at the expense of the mass of the people. If the danger of the creation of a local bourgeoisie was not enough, the authors of the Programme also argued that Algeria's particular circumstances – the weakness of its national income; the poor level of private savings generally coupled to the practice, where they did exist, of their being transferred abroad; and the tendency to engage what local capital there was in activities such as rent and usury – meant that a capitalist road to development was impracticable.

Taking these factors into consideration, the authors of the Tripoli Programme preferred the adoption of 'a planning policy which incorporated the democratic participation of workers in economic decision-making' (TP, 38). They argued that planning alone would allow for the accumulation of the necessary capital to achieve the industrialization of the Algerian economy within a relatively short time-span. They also felt that nationalization and centralization would help to suppress local-level corruption and waste. However, they acknowledged that following the planning road would be accompanied by certain problems. The problems they envisaged were associated with the lack of capital resources and an absence of qualified manpower, but they also identified as a problem something which they referred to as a certain degree of cultural backwardness. Nevertheless, in spite of these problems, they felt that the choice of the centrally-planned economy would in practice be a better risk than the uneven development the economy would experience if it followed 'liberal' economic precepts. Having set out the theoretical issues, the authors then identified what they saw as the steps which it would be necessary to take first in order to make this system of central planning process possible. The measures envisaged were the nationalization of banks and insurance companies and foreign commerce. While bank and insurance nationalization were seen simply in terms of ending the 'financial extortion of imperialism' in general, the nationaliza-tion of foreign trade was seen as providing the means for suppressing specifically the dominance of France in Algeria's commercial exchanges. As such it would provide the basis for the development of a more equal system of foreign trade in which new trade partners would be sought among countries who would be prepared to offer fixed prices and long-term markets. Somewhat curiously, the control of prices in rural areas in order to eradicate speculation and usury was seen as another part of the process of nationalizing foreign trade.

Significantly, given the structure of economic activity, the longest section in the economic policy section of the programme is devoted to agriculture. There they argue that the actual basis for industrialization as well as the creation of an internal market is determined by an actual revolution in the structure of rural life. However, they argue, in order to revolutionize agriculture there would have to be agrarian reform alongside the modernization and the conservation of national land assets. The principal theme of the agrarian reform programme would, however, be 'the land to those who work it' (TP, 40).[15] The policy itself would require an immediate embargo on the sale of land and agricultural equipment; the limitation of the size of holdings on the basis of the type of farming and profits; the expropriation of holdings exceeding a fixed optimum; free transfer of recovered land (that is, land which had previously been colonial property) to those peasants with insufficient land or income; the democratic organization of peasants in production cooperatives; an embargo on the sale or renting of redistributed land, in order to prevent it being amalgamated into large land-holdings; write-off of debts of the peasants, the *khammès* workers and the *métayers* workers; and material and financial aid from the State. Accompanying this redistribution of landed property, there would also be agricultural modernization. Agricultural modernization was to be achieved by a unified land-holding system; increased productivity of the land as a result of a massive diffusion of modern agricultural techniques; a diversification into higher-yielding varieties and their substitution for poorer-yielding varieties; and the rebuilding of livestock numbers accompanied by better methods of raising livestock. Finally, there was to be an attempt to conserve national land resources, considered at the time particularly necessary because of an acknowledged deterioration of soils and loss of agricultural land. Consequently, independent Algeria would attempt to reclaim eroded land; follow a programme of reafforestation; and extend irrigable areas and clear new land for cultivation. It also argued that a relative overpopulation in agricultural areas meant that there was a large underemployed population which was immediately available for putting into effect this agricultural programme. It was also felt that such a mobilization was a major way of absorbing unemployment and reclaiming large tracts of territory.

This is an extremely ambitious programme and in practice went far beyond what was ever attempted by succeeding regimes. At the same time, it should be noted that the actual institutional organization of agriculture was scarcely mentioned, apart from the two phrases which speak of the 'democratic organization of peasants in production cooperatives' and '. . . state farms with worker participation in the management of surpluses' (TP, 40), and that the Programme is silent on this issue. It certainly did not anticipate nor did it have in mind a system of agricultural organization of the autogestion type.[16] This is important to remember when considering the later history of autogestion in Algeria as well as the relationship between the future of agriculture as envisaged here and the realities of post-independence agricultural organization and production.

This discussion of the Tripoli Programme, the clearest statement there is of the type of social order which was envisaged by at least some of those engaged in the independence struggle, illustrates that considerable changes were thought necessary if Algerian society was to be rebuilt after the colonial experience. In these processes of rebuilding, changes at an ideological level were required and were envisaged as taking place in both the educational and cultural fields. A particular medium of such transfer were the 'free medersas'.[17] Cultural and educational efforts of the post-independence period were seen to entail such measures as the restoration of national culture by a progressive arabization of education; the preservation of the national heritage of popular culture; an expansion of the education system to give universal access; 'algerianize' programmes through their adaptation to the local realities; mass mobilization in order to eradicate illiteracy. The major problem of all these programmes lay in the difficulty in defining what their content should be – for example, what constitutes national culture. In fact, the authors of the Tripoli Programme side-stepped such questions by arguing that the need for rapid expansion of education stemmed from the need to produce in the shortest time possible technical cadres, administrators and teachers without whom it would be impossible to achieve control of the national economy.

The Tripoli Programme illustrates the difficulties, which not only the authors of this Programme but also nationalist movements in Africa in the 1960s generally faced, in finding an appropriate discourse with which to articulate the character of state and society that they hoped to create in the post-colonial world. The limitations of the nationalist projects in Africa and elsewhere have in recent years been subjected to more general scrutiny and, in an attempt to understand the wider context within which the Algerian authors of the Tripoli Programme worked, it is useful to consider two critiques of the national project in Africa, both published in 1992. The first is Basil Davidson's *The Black Man's Burden: Africa and the Curse of the Nation-State*; and the second, Anthony Appiah's *In My Father's House: Africa in the Philosophy of Culture*. Davidson has written extensively about Africa but from outside the Academy, and often critically of it. In *The Black Man's Burden*, one of his aims is to regard reflexively both the nature of his encounter with the African continent and the nature of his work about it. Essentially he is arguing that the crisis of today's African states is the result of 'the nationalism that became nation-statism' (1992: 10). Appiah is also working reflexively and writes that he grew up 'believing in constitutional democracy . . . . And by the time I was old enough to be *for* democracy, I knew we were also *for* development and modernisation' (1992: 256). He goes on to argue that further characteristics of this environment were sets of 'paired adherences' where 'the first member of the pair was something we took to belong to the sphere of the state . . . ; while the second belonged to a sphere that we could call society' (1992: 257). This notion of 'paired adherences' goes some way to explaining the pre-independence and post-independence discourses on Islam, in which the issue of faith had been allocated to this second category by a colonial project which did not acknowledge the right of a Muslim to be a citizen. Commenting on the collapse of unity once independence was achieved, Appiah writes 'If the history of metropolitan Europe in the last century and a half has been a struggle to establish statehood for nationalities, Europe left Africa at independence with states looking for nations.' (1992: 262) The search for the 'nation' in Algeria had begun in the 1930s with the speeches and writings of the Association of Reformist Ulama, and where and when it could be said to exist occupied some of the leading intellectuals of the independence struggle, such as Mostefa Lacheraf.[18] Algeria provides a clear example of the consequences which were the result of a conscious effort to find and constitute a 'nation' in the absence of unity.

The Algerian nationalists were heirs to two concepts of community, the universal community or *umma* of Muslims, and the notion of community derived from the French Revolution, where it was projected as a means of emancipation for the oppressed. Furthermore, even though in the debates which took place within the Communist Third International, colonial nationalisms were consistently seen as limited projects (Lenin, 1966), and Lenin's formula of 'the right of nations to self-determination' (1964) was written in the context of revolution in Europe, it would nevertheless become an inspiration to many colonial nationalists in their struggles for independence. However, as Davidson points out, the idea of nationalism owes as much to the encounter with the west as the need for it as a goal of the anti-colonial struggles. Finally, Appiah points out the limited nature of the colonial project in which the central aim was 'raising – not spending – government revenues' (1992: 265), with the result that on independence 'the formal agencies transferred to African hands were . . . alien in derivation, functionally conceived, bureaucratically designed, authoritarian in nature and primarily concerned with issues of domination rather than legitimacy'(1992: 265).[19] It is ironic that in the nationalist movements of Africa, the ideational base was essentially supplied by the two opposing political systems of the day.

Algeria's economic base in 1962

By the eve of independence in 1962, the Algerian economy – despite the absence of development which had characterized the greater part of French rule – appeared to possess considerable economic potential.

Central to this view of its economic potential lay the question of oil. In 1962, oil had become an increasingly important commodity in international markets with world production having doubled between 1950 and 1960 (Odell, 1975), and the implications of its particular pattern of exploitation for producer countries was not so evident. Secondly, although the major profitable sector in agriculture in 1960 was viniculture, Algeria had until the French conquest produced surpluses in both grain and livestock, which led to a general optimism that it would be possible after independence to develop a productive agricultural sector. Algeria was seen to be different from many of the other states of Africa who gained their independence in the 1960s in that its economy, though acknowleged to be both undercapitalized and underdeveloped, was not viewed as without resources.

However, in reality the problems which the new Algerian government faced in 1962 were both serious and fundamental. There was not only a problem of dealing with an economy and a society which had been disrupted and devastated by eight years of war, during which policies for the better management of the military campaign in the rural areas had led to the uprooting and resettlement of agricultural populations; but also the dilemma on the very eve of independence, of Algeria losing the greater part of its technical and management cadres. This final shock was caused by a colonial economy in which the modern sectors had been dominated by the foreign/European population who, once it became clear that national independence would indeed be the result of the war, deserted Algeria. As a result, in the period immediately before the GPRA took over, approximately 800,000 Europeans, or the greater part of the foreign/European population, left Algeria.

In preparing a balance sheet of the state of Algeria's industry in 1962, there are certain problems. These arise from the fact that, because of the liberation struggle, the various statistical services virtually ceased to operate; so the figures which are used to describe Algerian industry in 1962 are in practice figures from 1954, the last year before the liberation struggle began. Nevertheless, what these figures can illustrate are the economic parameters within which the colonial government had been working. They allow one to see exactly what kind of economic structure was bequeathed and with what problems. Those economists who have worked on this period, such as René Gendarme (1959), describe an economy where the most important industry in 1954 was the food industry (which also included matches and tobacco, and soap). Second in importance was building and public works; and third: mines, electricity, gas and petrol; and fourth came heavy engineering. These four sectors together accounted for about 78.2 per cent of Algeria's GDP. Principal imports were consumer goods (16 per cent) and energy (6 per cent), while principal exports were consumer goods (72 per cent) and raw materials and semi-finished goods (25.4 per cent). Algeria's consumer goods exports were essentially composed of agricultural products such as wine, fruit and vegetables; while its raw material exports were principally iron ore, phosphates, esparto grass (*alfa*) and cork. Furthermore, it was France who took the greater part of Algeria's exports (either 73 per cent or 81 per cent depending on whether exports to other French colonies are included) and provided most of its imports (79 per cent, or 88.5 per cent inclusive of imports from other French colonies).

Thus the industrial base which Algeria had in 1962 consisted of a small paper industry based on esparto grass; some iron- and steel-producing capacity; mining; textiles; food and tobacco. The exploitation of its oil resources had in fact barely begun. This was partly because it had only become economically viable to exploit Algerian reserves in the early 1950s, so that the almost immediate launching of the independence struggle served to exacerbate the difficulties of this take-off period. However, the war did not prevent the French governments, and more particularly De Gaulle's government, from building up a structure of oil exploitation which would continue until the Algerian oil nationalizations of 1971. This structure used a system of ownership of the oilfields based on franchises whose owners were French-controlled ELF-ERAP and CFPA; with the result that Algeria's revenue expectations from its oil resources in 1962 were confined to the receipts of oil royalties. In 1962, this system of oil royalties operated by the major oil companies in the Middle East was highly discriminatory against the producing countries, even though the oil companies themselves were reaping very high profits. Such profits were possible because the costs of extraction and the royalty payments and transport costs did not in any way match the price which the oil companies were able to obtain for their oil on world markets (Odell, 1975; Tanzer, 1970).

Some further indications of the structure of the Algerian economy in 1962 can be learned from an examination of the occupied population for the year 1960 (Table 4.1). Table 4.1 shows that out of an active labour force (Algerians and Europeans) of just under two million, there were 34 per cent employed in the industrially orientated categories; and a further 15.7 per cent employed as artisans, tradesmen and members of the liberal professions. The last category covered teachers, lawyers, pharmacists and doctors; and it is worth noting that a relatively high proportion of those Algerians who penetrated the European sector of the labour market were employed within the liberal professions category. However, Table 4.1 also illustrates that in general the distribution of Algerians and Europeans across job categories presented two very different pictures. Most importantly, the European population was disproportionately represented in the managerial categories whereas the Algerian population fell predominantly into the unskilled categories. The presence of such high numbers of Europeans in the managerial, middle-management and skilled-labour categories provides an illustration of the dominance and the control which the colon population exercised over the Algerian economy. The only labour categories in which Algerian Muslims were in a majority were the manual- or unskilled-labour category, shopkeepers and traders, and the agricultural sector.

To illustrate the structural nature of the deficit in the Algerian working population which these statistics imply, and the effects of the economic policies undertaken during the Boumediene Presidency, they can be

Table 4.1 Occupied population in 1960 (using socio-professional categories)

Socio-professional category	Algerians	%	Europeans	%	Total
1 Farmers	442,800	99.4	2,700	0.6	445,500
2 Agricultural workers	324,400	99.0	3,300	1.0	327,700
3 Artisans	79,200	64.5	43,500	35.5	122,700
4 Shopkeepers, traders	135,600	81.0	31,800	19.0	167,400
5 Liberal professions	12,800	54.9	10,500	45.1	23,300
6 Managers, etc.	2,400	18.2	10,800	81.8	13,200
7 Middle management	38,800	33.6	76,800	56.4	115,600
8 Skilled labour (*employés*)	65,200	49.5	66,600	50.5	131,800
9 Manual, unskilled	372,400	87.3	54,300	12.7	426,700
10 Domestic & similar	60,000	74.3	20,700	25.7	80,700
11 Army, police	69,200	68.3	32,100	31.7	101,300
Total	1,642,800	82.3	353,100	17.7	1,995,900

Source: RADP (no date), *Note rapide sur la situation de l'emploi avant et après l'indépendance (1960–1966)*, P.I.T. No 17.

Table 4.2 Occupied population in 1977 (using socio-professional categories)

Socio-professional category[1]	Numbers	%	% in 1960[2]
Farmers	295,545	10.8	26.9
Agricultural workers	359,810	15.2	19.7
Artisans, shopkeepers and traders	224,861	9.5	13.1
Liberal professions	4,936	0.2	0.8
Managers	42,204	1.8	0.1
Middle management	191,877	8.1	2.4
Skilled labour	871,207	36.8	4.0
Manual, unskilled	246,570	10.4	22.7
Domestic and similar services	112,455	4.7	3.6
Other	57,770	2.4	–
Total	2,367,325	100	100

Notes: [1] These categories have been amalgamated to equate to the categories in Table 4.1; [2] These percentages are derived from Table 4.1 and refer to 'Algerian' workers only.

Source: RADP (1979), Recensement général de la population et de l'habitat 1977–78, données abrégées. Résultat du sondage, Algiers.

compared with Table 4.2 taken from the 1977 Census and consequently illustrative of the employment situation at the end of his Presidency. Table 4.2 shows that the total occupied population had risen to 2.4 million which represents a rise of +44 per cent. However, the effects of this rise in the occupied population have to be offset against a much greater rise in the total population which in the same period had grown from ten million to seventeen million, giving a rise of +70 per cent. Table 4.2 illustrates just how difficult it proved in practice to overcome the inherited unevenness of the labour market structure. Other trends in the distribution of the occupied population (which will be considered in more detail in Chapter 6) are that the proportion of workers in the agricultural sector had dropped significantly, from 47 per cent in 1960 to 27 per cent in 1977; and that total numbers had also dropped. By contrast, for the category of artisans, shopkeepers and traders, while the proportion of workers had dropped, overall numbers had increased. In the liberal professions, the overall number as well as the proportion involved appeared to have declined but that decline can be counteracted by a much higher total number of workers in the *cadres supérieurs* (managerial category) where the number in 1977 was just over 42,000 compared with a figure of under 2,500 in 1960. The numbers in the middle-management category had also risen from just under 40,000 in 1960 to almost 192,000 in 1977. However, the most spectacular rise had been in the skilled-labour category which accounted for only 4 per cent of the total in 1960 with 65,200 workers to 37 per cent of the total in 1977 with 871,207 workers. This did represent a shift in the structure of the labour market from the colonial period where Algerian workers tended to be classified within the unskilled category.

These two tables provide a means of understanding what the labour market problems of the new Algerian government were going to be. However, they omit one key area of labour market activity, namely the number of people employed in the armed forces. Given that at the end of the war the government now had a standing army, and given that all the long-term leaders of the republic have been military commanders,[20] the size of the armed forces and the amount of GDP it has absorbed has been a matter of continuous speculation since independence even if its impact on political affairs has, since the events of 1991, come increasingly into the public domain.

It has already been suggested that even in 1962 Algerians were only just beginning to penetrate the industrial labour market, and that after independence there was a marked shift in employment from agriculture to industry. While such a trend is clearly observable, estimating the actual size of the agricultural sector in 1962 is more difficult. This is, as Raymond Barbé (1959) shows, because different statistical sources used different bases for estimating the size of the agricultural population. To illustrate the problems which this poses, he gives examples from the main sources. In an agricultural census of 1950–51, the numbers of workers engaged under the khammès system was given as 154,692; however, the 1948 Census had assessed the numbers of khammès workers as 132,913 and the 1954 Census assessed them at 60,563. Barbé suggests that such differences were probably caused by difficulties in assessing different types of dependence on agriculture, so that the smaller number could represent a number wholly dependent on the system while the larger figure might represent those who were dependent for part of their income on the same system. Assessing the size of an agricultural population is always difficult, and Barbé goes on to argue (1959: 21) that agriculture in fact covered some 5.8 million people or 69 per cent of the total population, with an active population of 2.6 million (1959: 10) of whom 0.6 million (or 22 per cent) might be classified as wage earners but with only around a fifth of these in permanent paid work. An additional 0.6 million could be classified as self-employed agriculturalists (that is, owning or renting land) but the majority of around 1.4 million being persons within the family unit dependent on agriculture but not necessarily wage-earning.

In spite of the size of the Muslim agricultural population, total landholding and disposable income in the agricultural sector were dominated by the *gros* (large) colons, of whom there were about 6,385, who held estates of 100+ hectares. It was this group that controlled around 87 per cent of landholdings and over 70 per cent of gross revenues (Barbé, 1959: 12). This control of agricultural land and revenues by the large colons effectively excluded the Muslim agriculturalist from the capitalized sector of agriculture, even if the earlier marginalization and retreat to the less productive agricultural areas during the different periods of colonial expansion are ignored. Furthermore these Muslim agriculturalists had access neither to agricultural machinery nor to the use of fertilizers. At the same time, the size of their landholdings was generally small – that is, around 70 per cent of their holdings were of under 10 hectares (Barbé, 1959: 17); and a further 17 per cent were actually of less than one hectare. Consequently, the greater part of the Muslim agricultural population was poor, with access to neither education nor credit. To emphasize this, a study by Jean-Jacques Perennes (1979) of date-growing areas in the Touggourt region shows how a small European population, through its access to state credits and its monopolies on processing and export, was able to dominate a region otherwise relatively inhospitable to the European. This study of date-production illustrates not only that the colon population controlled supplies of water and machinery, but also that production was organized via small companies who were controlled by large processing warehouses in Marseilles. Consequently, it was the processing warehouses in Marseilles who dictated what kinds of date should be grown – dominance which survived independence.

Outside the agricultural sector, the names of several well-known European companies are found, such as Lessieur (fats), Unilever and Ripolin (chemicals), Cellunaf and Solvay (paper), Lafarge (construction materials), Durafour (mechanical engineering), Acilor (iron and steel). All of these companies would remain in operation in Algeria until the major nationalizations of 1968. In other words, in the immediate post-independence period, the ownership and control of industry changed very little as foreign capital investment continued as before. Similarly, if one looks at private commerce[21] in the period up to 1970, it can be seen that the private sector was of particular importance in the food industry where it accounted for over one billion dinars in turnover.[22] Consequently, while individual colons particularly in the agricultural sector fled Algeria on independence, much of their investment remained, especially in the urban areas around Algiers, Oran and Constantine where, as late as 1969, they accounted for as much as 69 per cent of commercial activity.

Finally, 1962 can be described as a period in Algeria in which contradictory tendencies were in evidence. Those of the liberation movement had come to power with many of the differences among themselves still unresolved. The actual economic and social policies of the post-independence government had barely been enunciated and, in many ways, the colons – despite their physical departure – still retained control of the greater part of industrial activity; while in the countryside the autogestion movement ensured to some extent the continuation of their methods of production. It is the presence of these many unresolved contradictions that forms the background of the political and economic conflicts of the early years of independence.

Political and economic conflicts in post-independence Algeria: 1962–65

The period 1962 to 1965 has been variously characterized by writers according to their political orientation and the importance which they have ascribed to autogestion. Once Algerian independence was achieved in 1962, writers could take clear stances, and the principal point of division centred on those writers who considered that autogestion was the authentic expression of socialism in Algeria and who argued that the whole subsequent history of Algeria was marked by a progressive retreat from socialism. Examples of this positioning are to be found in the work of Chaliand (1964) in France and Clegg (1971) in the UK. In part the stance of these authors was also a reflection of the political position which the FLN claimed for itself and the belief shared by both actors and commentators at the time that the struggle for national independence was sufficient in itself to enable the construction of a new society on the ruins of colonialism. The limitations of the nationalist ideal, whatever the colour of the ideology espoused, were less apparent in 1962 when Algerian independence was achieved than they appear today.

However, the limitations of the nationalist project are only a part of the story. The other part concerns the actual models for economic and political development which existed and persist to this day. How does an economy emerge from the shadow of subordination, how does it achieve its own authentic development within the dominant economic paradigmatic framework of a world in which capitalism has achieved or appeared to achieve total dominance? In the 1960s and 1970s, it appeared that there were different models and it was possible to argue that there might be other models. Western socialists in particular sought alternative models to communist/Soviet-style central planning and they looked to the newly emerging post-colonial societies to provide the answers. Algeria was attractive because it appeared to have found a means to independently manage its human and material resources. Central to this perception was the fact but also the interpretation of the meaning of autogestion. How writers saw this profoundly influenced their whole analysis of the post-independence Algerian state. What hindsight allows us now to do is to question the bases on which their optimism was founded and to re-open the question of the structural relationship of the colony within the metropole and the range of possibilities which existed and exist for it.

In the 1960s and 1970s, the models available were principally the body of writing associated with 'underdevelopment' and which owed many of its basic precepts to Marxist constructs. These will be examined in more detail in the following chapters. Here we only wish to note that the different trajectories of the different critiques of the post-independence Algerian state's political and economic strategies are a reflection of perceptions of meaning for the realization of a socialist state. They are therefore interesting not only for what they say about Algeria but also for what they say about western socialists' perceptions of socialism. In this context, the ideological role of Islam was largely ignored. Having said that, the critiques which were made did highlight certain tendencies which have implications for the later development of the state. Perhaps the most important of these is that which draws attention to the processes which led to the establishment of the administrative and bureaucratic apparatus which came to dominate the political process and which forms the counterpoint to the intensification of the struggle with religion.

The critical period in this analysis is held to be 1962–65, with its impact on the development of autogestion as a new form of ownership of productive forces. As in the view of these authors the progressive bureaucratization of autogestion marks the failure of the post-independence government to fulfil its promise of a new radically different society, thus the authors have an ambiguous attitude towards Ben Bella, whose government is seen as both responsible (through the enacting of the March 1963 decrees) for the institutionalizing of the administrative and bureaucratic procedures that fettered autogestion and, however, also more democratic than the government of his successor, Boumediene, whose seizure of power by *coup d'état* fundamentally compromised autogestion.

Another aspect of analyses at this time is that they utilized a much more unitary view of the FLN than was the case in practice. Similarly, while there were men of avowedly radical intentions employed by the Ben Bella government – Algerians like Mohammed Harbi, and foreigners such as Michel Raptis and Chaliand himself – these represented only one aspect of the liberation movement. Moreover, as the discussion of the Tripoli Programme showed earlier, Algerian thinking about the form and content of the post-independent state was still fairly inchoate. In addition, Ben Bella's assumption of the office of President in 1962 had not been without challenge. He had in fact only finally been able to gain and to hold on to the office of President through the support of Boumediene, who could call upon his previous roles as the successor to Boussouf as commander of Wilaya V and then after 1960 as Head of the unified General staff of the ALN.

The period 1962–65 is also characterized by internal discontent. For example, there was a revolt in Kabylia led by Hocine Aït Ahmed, and an army uprising just before Boumediene's own coup, led by Colonel Chaabani (the former commnader of Wilaya VI). It is during this same period that Mohammed Boudiaf was arrested as well as condemned to death, even though as one of the original members of the group of six, and the co-ordinator of the founding wilaya commanders, he represented a major figure of the independence struggle. His sentence was in the end commuted and he went into exile, not to return until January 1992.

The whole period 1962–65 represents a further example of the confusion and uncertainty that were perhaps inevitable given the limitations of the FLN's project of national independence. While it had been discussed and to some extent promised that independent Algeria would be different from colonial Algeria, French withdrawal forced into the open the question of the identity which the new state would assume, but posed it in conjunction with the practical effects of the sabotage of the economy and state machinery which accompanied the French army's retreat. These had been effected in the certainty of the knowledge that Algeria was possessed of considerable natural resources which had only been very partially exploited under colonialism. It was in a sense inconceivable that an avowedly nationalist movement such as the FLN would not seek to exploit these resources for its own benefit.

The economic development model which Algeria adopted was based on the premiss that the possession of strategic raw materials first of all provided an entry into the world market and, secondly, supplied the purchasing power which would enable Algeria to obtain the heavy industrial goods and machinery which were seen to be necessary for the transformation of its 'backward' economy – that is, one dependent on agriculture – to a modern industrialized economy able to provide the material base from which to improve standards of living. The origins of this model are diverse but some of its ancestry can be traced via G. Destanne de Bernis to one of the leading French economists, François Perroux.[23]

The post-independent Algerian state

In constructing the archaeology of the post-independent Algerian state, the following formations need to be taken into account: a modified relationship between the secular and the religious character of the state caused by the impact of the centralized and elitist nature of the Ottoman Turkish state, counterbalanced by the societal organizations derived from the pre-Ottoman Turkish period where power was decentralized and fragmented; and a French colonial power which had come to Algeria with a Napoleonic tradition of centralization that encouraged the formation of a highly educated elite prepared at the same time for controlling and to control not only the functioning of government but also the economy. The conception and practice of the independence struggle had given rise to a dual structure which combined a highly centralized centre with a fragmented base where no single member knew more than any one other member. While it had helped to preserve the effectiveness of the FLN as a fighting force, this pattern of organization was less useful once independence was achieved.

While the *coup d'état* of 19 June 1965 by Houari Boumediene did not end the debate on the direction which the post-independent Algerian economy and polity should be taking, it did in practice both introduce and institutionalize new practices in its organization. In particular, it inaugurated the era of the national plan with the presentation of the 1967–69 *Plan Triennal* (Three-Year Plan) in which the broad directions of Algeria's industrial strategy under Boumediene were to be established and the infrastructure for its implementation set up. His second plan, 1970–73, the first of the *Plans Quadriennals* (Four-Year Plans), was also still primarily concerned with the establishment of the infrastructure of industrial development. The third plan or Second Four-Year Plan of 1974–77, however, began to turn its attention to broader questions of the nature of the development strategy itself. This was possible and also made necessary by the integration into the economy of the petroleum sector which had been nationalized in February 1971. Planning was an important element of the post-1965 economic strategy while the primary means for achieving these strategic industrial aims were the *sociétés nationales* (SNs – state enterprises).

The period 1965–78 is then characterized by the growth of a powerful state machine which directed both political and industrial affairs. The instruments it used for the direction of industrial affairs were the Plans and, for political affairs, Charters (*Chartes*). In order to elaborate its industrial policies, reliance was placed not only upon a Ministry of Planning but also on a series of specialized industrial Ministries. These began simply enough with the Ministry of Industry and Energy but were later divided into three separate Ministries: the Ministry of Energy and Petrochemical Industries, the Ministry of Heavy Industry and the Ministry of Light Industry. Besides the industrial Ministries and the Planning Ministry, an important role was also played by the Ministry of Finance. This whole development of specialized Ministries in charge of different aspects of industrial development can be seen to represent part of the bureaucratization process which the state underwent.[24]

Although an economy becoming increasingly complex requires more complex structures within which to operate, the elaboration of the ministerial structure as the mechanism with which to handle the process of industrialization illustrates two slightly separate developments. One is organizational and concerns the role which the ministries have played in determining what was produced – in other words, they imagined the market and production was then administered. The second is structural and concerns the role of bureaucracy in industrializing and complex industrial societies. Weber (Gerth and Mills, 1948) argued that the industrial economy was dependent on bureaucratic modes of organization because of society's need for 'calculative precision in the administration of its various institutions' (Giddens, 1971: 236). However, while Weber saw bureaucratization as an inevitable consequence of increasing complexity in society, writers on industrialization have also seen it as a specific legacy of colonization and 'the need of the colonial powers for various resources and for the maintenance of law and order' (Eisenbeth, 1970: 160). However, in the 1960s and 1970s, planning was also seen as offering a positive alternative to the uncertainties of the market (Nove, 1986: viii). Consequently, the adoption of the planning model in Algerian economic strategy during the Boumediene period needs to be seen within both of these discourses.

The formal structure of planning under Boumediene was organized initially through the medium of the State Planning Secretariat (*Secrétariat d'État au Plan*) whose structure and functions were extended for it then to become the Ministry of Planning and Town and Country Planning

(*Ministère de la Planification et de l'Aménagement du Territoire*). It has been suggested above that in the 1960s views on the efficacy of planning were generally more positive than they are in an economic climate today where most states have been dismantling their planning apparatuses. The post-independence Algerian government's adoption of planning had two distinct ideological roots. The first and, in the view here, the most important were the experiences of the French state in the planning field, particularly during the immediate post-World War II period when the French state was active in nationalizing key economic sectors. Since then the French state has both developed and encouraged the development of strategic cooperation between the policy interests of the state in the industrial field and the interests of private capital.[25] This was the model that the Algerian planners actually had real knowledge of, not only because of having France as the former colonial power but also because of their being educated within the French tradition. Furthermore, Algerian planners made use of key concepts from the discourses of two French economists, François Perroux and G. Destanne de Bernis – most notably the discourse of 'industrializing industries' (Perroux 1965; de Bernis 1963, 1971b, 1975). The second ideological root was derived from the Soviet Union's experience of both rapid industrialization and the planning process,[26] in which a primary emphasis was laid on the need to develop self-sufficiency in the base industries, such as iron and steel, and mechanical engineering.

The attractiveness of planning was that it appeared to be a means by which economic control of the market was possible. However, the longest experiment in planning – the experience of the Soviet Union – illustrates that planning has its own problems. In particular, there is the slow pace of decision-making as the size of the planning apparatus grows in order to accommodate all the data it requires from which to make its decisions. At the same time, despite the growth in size of the planning apparatus, it still has difficulty in acquiring all the information it needs in order to make rational decisions about an industry or an enterprise. Furthermore, planning tends to be controlled from the centre so that it frequently finds itself remote from those whose lives it is aiming to plan. Thus it suffers both from inefficiencies associated with size and remoteness, and inefficiencies associated with the inadequate input of data.

The Algerian planners were to recognize some of the dangers of insufficient accountability to the population at large to which they responded through the medium of the publication of Charters. It was the Charters which acted as the means by which the Algerian state discourse on socialism was articulated and they tended to appear at politically strategic moments. For example, the publication of the Plate-forme de la Soumam in 1956 was intended as much as a strategic declaration about the future of the Algerian liberation struggle and the political directions it would take as it was partly intended to establish the leadership of Abane Ramdane and Belkacem Krim (Harbi, 1975). Similarly, the Tripoli Programme was intended both to provide some framework for decision-making within the post-independence civilian government and to counter General de Gaulle's 1958 Plan de Constantine reforms which had aimed to seize the initiative from the FLN.

The third Charter – the Algiers Charter (*Charte d'Alger*) – was issued in 1964, when the Ben Bella Presidency thought that it had contained the various post-independence factions within the FLN and was trying to integrate the strategies of the planners with the autogestion movement. The next Charter came in the early 1970s, and was called the Charter for the Socialist Organization of the Firm (*Charte de l'organisation socialiste des entreprises*).[27] It was launched by Boumediene as the industrial equivalent of the Agrarian Revolution (*Révolution agraire*). Then in 1976, the Charter of the Boumediene Presidency was published – the National Charter of the Algerian People *(Charte nationale du peuple algérien)* – as perhaps Boumediene's last real attempt to confront the conflicts of interest which were emerging from the focus of planning on questions of industrial production alone.

While these Charters acted as official indicators of either changes in the direction of Algerian policy or as reminders to both people and policy-makers of what the Algerian liberation struggle was about, they were also to a large extent polemical in character, and therefore more closely related to the ideals of post-independence Algerian policy than to its practical expression. Of course, as has been indicated already, the main practical expression of post-independence Algerian policy was via the plans. However, while the plans themselves were the expression of Algeria's development policy intentions, even those intentions have always been further amplified by a certain amount of semi-official commentary from within the administration – most notably from Kaid Ahmed, who was both Boumediene's FLN spokesman and an important ideologue during the period of the liberation struggle. In an article in *Révolution Africaine* (**451**, 1972), Kaid Ahmed argued that 'the plan is above all a rational method that results from the encompassing in homogeneous evolution, the different sectors of a nation's activity and the way by which a nation's "spirit" could be translated into policy'.

The importance of Kaid Ahmed lies in the closeness of his relationship to Boumediene, which was established during the liberation struggle.[28]

Consequently, his discourse on the roots of the Algerian planning process that they lay with the October Revolution in the Soviet Union helped to construct the image of the Algerian state as a Soviet satellite. However, Kaid Ahmed's role within the FLN was ideological. Moreover, the FLN did not represent a single political tendency, so that Kaid Ahmed's discourse can also be seen as an attempt to indicate a particular ideological position on the nature of state power. In Kaid Ahmed's discourse, planning was an essential adjunct of the political goal of 'democratic centralism' and he illustrates his view of the role of planning in the economy by arguing that the development plan embodies two key ideas, *l'usager* ('the nation') and *l'architecte* ('the political power')(1972). He is here both explicitly indicating the space for the delegation of power and at the same time legitimizing the exercise of that power by those who already control it. The duality which (it has already been suggested) existed within the Algerian planning process is further illustrated by a second quotation from Kaid Ahmed: 'In political and economic terms, the plan is nothing other than a strategic order of combat by a society against the accumulated backwardness of an historic process.'

However, Abdallah Khodja (*La République*, 19.6.74),[29] the actual State Planning Secretary of the Boumediene period, argued that while in general the aims of the First Four-Year Plan and its predecessor the Three-Year Plan had been achieved, the whole system which they had set in motion was in danger of failing because the Plans had not taken into account the strains they would impose on Algeria's social fabric. This concern with the development of a gap between the perceived economic achievements of the early years of the Boumediene Presidency and the level of popular participation generated by it was, as later events were to illustrate, a legitimate concern. It did result in some conscious attempts to bridge the developing gap, an example of which is the attempt to introduce some form of popular consultation during the drafting stage of the Second Four-Year Plan. The introduction of the Communal and Wilayate Popular Assemblies (*Assemblées populaires du Commune et de Wilayate*) in 1974 and the publication in 1976 of the National Charter of the Algerian People can also be seen as attempts to lessen the distance between the state, the planning apparatus and the people.

In his Introductory message to the the First Four-Year Plan, Boumediene declared that 'the Nation was engaged in a new phase of its construction which would be marked by spectacular progress in the areas of education, industrialization and the transformation of the living conditions of the lives of the rural masses' (1970: 7). The Second Four-Year Plan was presented as 'a decisive stage towards "Horizon 80"' (*El Moudjahid*,

16.5.74) where 1980 was seen as 'the crowning of a long stage which over 15 years, will have permitted the radical transformation of our economy and have put in place the base of a sustained development which reflects the measure of the ambitions for the country's progress' (*Algérie-Actualité*, **449**, 1974). The idea of 'Horizon 80' was partly symbolic because 1980 was the year in which anyone born in 1962, the year independence was achieved, would be 18; thus in a sense it was also intended to convey the idea that the economy too had grown up. However, the proposals involved ambitious plans particularly in terms of employment, where it was anticipated that some 450,000 non-agricultural jobs would be created (*El Moudjahid*, 15.5.74): a figure which, as Table 4.2 illustrates, was in practice never achieved. Furthermore, the actual goal of the employment-creation programme was 'the guarantee of a lasting job to every member of the active male population' by 1980 (*Algérie-Actualité*, **449**, 1974). The limited nature of this guarantee and its restriction to the active male population help to illustrate the ways in which women were progressively excluded from direct benefit even from the proposed benefits of the revolution.

The lack of sufficient growth of the industrial labour force became one of the major long-term problems of the Algerian economy. The absence of growth can be attributed to the fact that while the Plans envisaged a number of more or less equal investment areas, in practice investment was concentrated on the petroleum industry. The First Four-Year Plan had designated five main areas for employment growth: mechanical and electrical engineering, construction materials, consumption goods industries, petrochemicals, and public building and works. It is certainly true that by the end of the period under examination here, Public Building and Works had indeed become the largest employer, but more than half of the employment it provided was being provided by the private sector. It had also identified a number of growth points in the Algerian economy. First among them was gas liquefaction where expected growth was to be around 45.5 per cent. The other industries which followed in decreasing emphasis were mechanical and electrical engineering, and public building and works. A rather general emphasis was laid upon the development of production facilities in the following industrial sectors: complex fertilizers (leading from the emphasis on the development of a petrochemical sector), iron and steel (particularly structural steels), and tractors. The consumption of output from the iron and steel industry was to be primarily by the petroleum industry, after which the emphasis would shift in favour of public building and works, and particularly of house building. The Second Four-Year Plan did not substantially change this orientation although it did promise a programme of medium and small firm creation at the local level (*El Moudjahid*, 15.5.74).

This emphasis on the local is what forms the key difference between the first two plans and the Second Four-Year Plan. It was translated into measures designed to encourage local initiative and, in a sense, in the preparation of the Second Four-Year Plan there was a conscious seeking after popular legitimation through methods of popular involvement which included a degree of decentralization and the adoption of local plans (*El Moudjahid*, 17.5.74). The problem was that the discourse underpinning these was calling for the continued 'pursuit of the politics of austerity' and a 'continuing priority for productive investment' – that is, the petroleum sector and heavy industry generally (*El Moudjahid,* 20.9.72). The next two chapters will explore in more detail the contradictions which these presented.

Notes

1. There is a growing literature on the Algerian War now available. For an indication of material, reference can be made to the bibliography in Benjamin Stora (1993) *Histoire de la guerre d'Algérie (1954–1962)*, Paris, Éditions La Découverte. The war also had a profound effect on French society and politics, most graphically illustrated by its role in the ending of the Fourth Republic, the accession to power by General De Gaulle and the creation of the Fifth Republic. However, for many of those who took part in the war, it has been in the words of Bernard Tavernier's film (1992), *La Guerre sans nom* (The War without a Name).

2. This is one of the most striking impressions given by the women talking in the documentary film *Algerian Women at War* made by Djamila Amrane and shown on the UK's Channel 4 in 1992.

3. The OAS was a body set up by dissident army officers and a section of the colon population once it became clear that despite his promise of 'a French Algeria', De Gaulle intended to grant Algeria independence. It was responsible in the final stages of the war for a campaign of bombings which was aimed both at the Algerian civilian population and at economic installations. It is reputed to have also intended to assassinate De Gaulle himself.

4. Messali Hadj had been responsible for the founding of the *Étoile Nord Africaine* (ENA) among migrant Algerian workers in France around 1926 (the date varies between 1923 and 1926) as well as its successor organization, the PPA (*Parti du Peuple Algérien*) in 1936. After the end of World War II, the PPA became a clandestine organization whose public face was the MTLD (*Mouvement pour le Triomphe des Libertés Démocratiques*). He remained a major influence in the nationalist movement but it was his opposition to the launching of armed struggle in 1954 that led to one of the splits in the nationalist movement. Both the founders of the FLN and their opponents claimed

descent from the PPA and the MTLD; and many had also been members of an earlier armed resistance group – the OS (*Organisation Secrète*), which had been broken up by the French police in 1950 and 1951. As a result, many of the founding members of the FLN had already undergone prison terms or exile. In response to the creation of the FLN, Messali founded the *Mouvement National Algérien* (MNA) in December 1954.

5. Harbi gives no information on Rabah Bitat's background (and neither does Stora), although Bitat was one of the few actually to survive the war, after which he married the woman militant Zohra Driff and served as a Minister throughout the Boumediene Presidency.

6. These were administrative areas of shared responsibility between the civil commissioners and the *bureaux arabes* (the military). The civil commissioners administered the affairs of the European population, and the bureaux arabes those of the Muslim population. A fuller account of their activities is given in Chapter 2.

7. The image of the FLN as the sole head of the independence struggle was achieved partly through its real dominance of the post-independence state, and partly through the impact of its own and others' myth-making. An example of this myth-making process at work is Gillo Pontecorvo's 1966 film, *The Battle of Algiers*. For an understanding of the conflicts which underpin the liberation struggle, a major source is Mohammed Harbi. Harbi was a young militant within that struggle who was subsequently regarded as both a leftist and a Marxist. He was imprisoned by both Ben Bella and Boumediene and was forced to leave Algeria in 1973. He was one of the authors of the Tripoli Programme

(see pp. 81–7) and editor of *Révolution africaine* (the mouthpiece of the new government) in the first days of independence. He has become a chronicler of the FLN and the liberation struggle with such books as *Le FLN mirage et réalité: des origines à la prise du pouvoir (1945–1962)*, Paris, Éditions JA 1980, and *Aux origines du FLN. Le Populisme révolutionnaire en Algérie*, Paris, Christian Bourgois 1975. The autobiography *Mémoires d'un combattant: l'esprit d'indépendance 1942–1952* (Paris, Sylvie Messinger, 1983) of Hocine Aït Ahmed – a politician still active in 1990s Algeria – also provides a context to the events leading up to 1954.

8. Lebjaoui is an Algerian exile in France who founded an organization called OCRA (*Organisation clandestine de la révolution algérienne*) which Ahmed Mahsas would join briefly after he left Algeria for France in 1966.

9. Of the five, other than Harbi, Ben Yahyia was a major figure during the Boumediene period and held several ministerial posts; Temman became Director of the National Bank of Algeria; and both Yazid and Reda Malek were Algerian ambassadors under Boumediene. Lacheraf was the author of *L'Algérie: nation et société*, Paris, François Maspero 1965.

10. Ramdane was assassinated in 1957, and Krim was to be accused of plotting against Boumediene in 1965 and condemned to death in his absence; he was assassinated in Frankfurt in 1970 (Harbi).

11. However, Stora (1993: 37) suggests that the published document is also clearly marked by the influence of Ramdane.

12. In other words, they perceived the FLN as forming the basis of an alternative government. However, the

formation of that alternative government did not necessarily mean that the FLN was committed to changing the bases on which society was organized, and very little had been attempted during the independence struggle to create alternative structures.

13. It forms part of a much wider debate at the time centred around the issue of whether or not Algeria had been a nation before the French conquest, whether it had become one as a result of colonization, and consequently whether the achievement of independence would result in the realization of the nation (Lacoste *et al.*, 1966). While the particular character of the Algerian debate crystallized (as discussed in Chapter 3: pp. 65–9) in the 1930s in the discourse of the Association of Reformist Ulama, it was also the discourse of the movements for national independence. It is representative of the view that state-building and nation-building were one and the same thing and that colonial independence would necessarily create the nation. The theoretical limitations of this view of the nation have been the subject of critical enquiry since the early 1980s; see also references in note 14.

14. Benedict Anderson (1991) *Imagined Communities*, London, Verso. This is the Revised edition, the first edition being published in 1983 in the same year as Ernest Gellner published *Nations and Nationalism*, Oxford, Basil Blackwell. These two works are the starting point for the development of what is now a large body of work in English on nationalism. Anderson's book became available in a French translation in 1996 under the title *L'Imaginaire national*, Paris, La Découverte.

15. Boumediene was to use this slogan for his Agrarian Revolution programme.

16. Autogestion is discussed more fully in the next chapter. It was, however, seen as the distinguishing feature of post-independence Algeria, with the result that many of the early studies of the outcomes of independence focused on it (Clegg, 1971; Chaliand, 1964; Chaliand and Minces, 1972). However, it was essentially the seizure of colonial land-holdings by those workers who were employed on these farms. Thus it was a redistribution of land from the colon to his Algerian agricultural workers but it was not a redistribution within the wider population dependent on land.

17. The word is derived from the Arabic word for 'school' and in this context means schools which were founded with the specific intention of preserving what were considered to be Muslim and Arab values against a background of French colonial education policies. Such schools were among the creations of the Reform movement of the 1930s and had provided an alternative education option to that of the *écoles françaises* (French schools).

18. See note 13.

19. Appiah's quote is from Chazan, Naomi, Robert Mortimer, John Ravenhill and Donald Rothschild (1988) *Politics and Society in Contemporary Africa*, Boulder, Colorado, Lynne Rienner Publishers, Inc.: 41.

20. These are 1965–78: Colonel Houari Boumediene, who had been the first head of the post-independence *Armée Nationale Populaire* (ANP); 1979–92: Colonel Chadli Benjedid, who was military commander of the eastern military region from 1964 to 1979. Following the forced

resignation of Benjedid in January 1992, the Higher Executive Council recalled Mohammed Boudiaf, one of the original founders of the FLN, from exile in Morocco to be Head of State from January until his assassination in June 1992. His immediate successor was Ali Kafi, Head of the War Veterans' Association, who had served for a period towards the end of the war as commander of Wilaya II. Kafi was replaced at the end of January 1994 by General Liamine Zeroual, who had held the Defence portfolio, and who became the first Algerian President to be elected, in November 1995. The Ottaways (1970: 305) calculate the size of the armed forces in 1967 as at least 75,000, with a Defence Budget of around $100 million (approximately 15 per cent of the total administrative budget).

21. Data for this has been extracted from RADP (1970), *Liste des sociétés nationales à activité industrielle en 1970*, Algiers; and RADP (1970), *Données 1969 sur le commerce de Gros Privé*, Algiers.

22. Immediately after independence the Algerian dinar was pegged to the French franc and at this point was technically equivalent.

23. Perroux's economic model is discussed in chapters 5 and 6.

24. Nove (1986: 11) discusses a similar elaborate construction of ministries and the problems of duplication of function which can result.

25. For information on the French planning process, see P. Bauchet (1964), *Economic Planning, the French Experience*, London, Heinemann; and J. Sheahan (1969), *An Introduction to the French Economy*, Charles E. Merrill Publishing Co.

26. For an account of the planning process in the Soviet Union, see Michael Ellman (1972), *Soviet Planning Today*, Cambridge, Cambridge University Press.

27. This is discussed in more detail in Chapter 6.

28. Kaid Ahmed's relationship to Boumediene was discussed on page 79.

29. The discussion of the Second Four-Year Plan uses newspaper sources because these illustrate the political discourse which the Boumediene government was using to gain popular support for its policies. Furthermore, *El Moudjahid* is the newspaper of the government and what it publishes represents current government discourse.

5

The Economic Origins of Crisis I:
Agriculture and the Boumediene Reforms

La terre à ceux qui la travaillent
(slogan of the Agrarian Revolution)

In pre-independence Algerian political discourse, agriculture represented as much a symbolic reclamation of the years of colonial domination as it did an economic resource. The importance attached to agriculture in a future independent Algeria was central to the vision of the post-independence Algerian economy held by the authors of the 1962 Tripoli Programme as they attempted to give some kind of form to the colonial successor state. In addressing the future organization of agriculture, they were also responding to two different realities. On the one hand, despite the discovery of oil in the Sahara and the beginnings of its exploitation, the colonial economy was still largely dependent on agriculture, but an agriculture controlled and managed by and for the benefit of the minority colon population. On the other, it was land and the struggle over its ownership which had lain at the heart of the resistance to the colonial project, and its loss signified the subordination that colonization had brought. Consequently, it had been ideologically impossible for the authors of the Tripoli Programme not to have a project which involved the reclaiming of land. To have not done so would have been to have recognized the validity of the colonial project itself and undermined the nationalist project for which Algerians had engaged in such a vicious eight-year struggle. However, it was not only the authors of the Tripoli Programme who recognized the ideological importance of land both as an issue of the struggle for independence and the issue which, for the general population, lay at the heart of the legitimacy of both the nationalist and the socialist projects which the post-independence governments sought to realize. Throughout the Boumediene period, agriculture and the improvement of rural living conditions dominated the political discourse. This ideological preoccupation with agriculture is graphically illustrated by the discourse which surrounded the presentation of the Second Four-Year Plan where the importance of land reform is always stressed but responsibility for its implementation is at the same time ceded to the Agrarian Revolution programme. It can be seen as Boumediene's key project as he sought throughout his Presidency to find a means to reconcile the industrialization programme with the needs of agriculture and to resolve the contradictions which agriculture presented for both the nationalist and the socialist project. Consequently, the Programme's use of the slogan 'the land to those who work it', which originates from the Tripoli Programme, illustrates both Boumediene's search for legitimacy and the problems which the dual character of land reform posed.

In the first place, while the struggle over land had lain at the heart of both the colonial and the nationalist projects, the impact of colonization on agriculture was more than the issue of ownership. Indeed, to some extent the mass departure of the colons resolved the issue of ownership by doing away with the need for expropriation. However, if the issue of the expropriation of colon land was solved, independence did not resolve the issue of the ownership of land acquired by Muslims during the colonial period. It also has to be remembered that, formally within Islam, the various systems of land-management give individuals access to the use of land which can be owned but they do not generally have the right to own the land itself. Colonization created an unambiguous system of landownership and, while clearly the principal beneficiary of this system was the European colon, it did not mean that some Muslims did not also become owners of land. Consequently, despite the fact that the agricultural sector had been dominated in resource terms by European farmers, it was also where vested interests of Muslims were significant. Mostefa Lacheraf writing in *La République* (19 June 1974) argues that the dislocation of rural life during the colonial period was caused by a pincer movement comprising European and local elites who had profited from colonization. Furthermore, because agriculture and commerce had been important activities during the pre-colonial period, some of the patterns of landholding from that period had also survived. This meant not only that there was the structural cleavage between European and Muslim landholders but also that there were internal structural cleavages between different classes of Muslim landholdings (Barbé, 1962). These can be summarized under the headings of *propriétaire* (landowner), farmer, métayers, and khammès, in conjunction with the difference in status between the permanent and seasonally-paid agricultural workers who were employed on colon farms. The effect of these divisions was accentuated by the fact that agriculture had remained the major actual employing sector.

As a result, the future of agriculture had been one of the principal concerns of pre-independence policy-making as is illustrated by the discussion in the Tripoli Programme. However, whatever would have been the result of implementing these initial plans for the restructuring of agriculture was overturned by the occurrence in the immediate aftermath of independence of the spontaneous occupation of many of the larger agricultural holdings by the permanent agricultural workforce. This action by these workers effectively pre-empted these early plans for the restructuring of land tenure. Consequently, the first post-independence governments were faced with the problem of rationalizing and incorporating an accomplished fact into policy-making. The manner in which this was accomplished can be illustrated by the comments made by Amar Ouzegane in his capacity as Minister of Agriculture and Agrarian Reform in March 1963 in an interview with François Perroux[1] (Perroux, 1963: 9–14); he had also been, in the main part, responsible for the published report of the 1956 Congress of Soummam.

Ouzegane's first point was that the principal heritage from the war for the rural population was that of displacement, with something like two and a half million people out of a population of seven million having been forced in one way or another to abandon their homes and livelihood; the result was that independent Algeria had only one option – to move directly to the stage of 'collective farms'. He argued that it was possible to skip the intermediate stages because any 'sentiments of attachment to private property' had been destroyed by the war and, furthermore, that famine had only been avoided by 'communal self-help' (*l'entraide communautaire*). He further argued that because landownership had been communal, it was accompanied by a tradition of collective work (*travail collectif*); and that both permanent and temporary workers on the colon and therefore capitalist farms also worked together. These meant that the essential base for a system of collective farming was already in place. Furthermore, it would prejudice the future development of agriculture to break up what he called 'modern production units'. It was instead necessary to reorientate actual production so that it could provide for the essential needs of the population. He also expressed the ideological importance attached to agricultural policy with the words 'At the moment the *fellahs* (agricultural workers) **believe** that their lot will improve and that the Government of independent Algeria is working for them' (Perroux, 1963: 11). How the practical realities of the time impinged and forced changes in direction is, however, illustrated in Ouzegane's argument that the farms which were under the control of the 'Autogestion Committees' were and could become the *pôles* ('centres of attraction') for the small peasant farmer. These remarks express how one of the more important pre-independence ideologues within the party and the government thought about agricultural policy. However, Ouzegane was a former General Secretary of the Algerian Communist Party and was consequently one of the few members of the Government to have had any systematic training in classical Marxist thinking. These origins are clearly present in his discussion of collectivization, which is seen as a logical consequence of the events which have taken place. However, the principal agricultural reforms of the period 1962–78 were introduced under Boumediene's Agrarian Revolution programme which was not nor was intended to be a programme of collectivization. Moreover Ouzegane, although he was using the language of Marxist-Leninist discourse which is reinforced by the language of collectivization and mode of production, signified by his argument that conditions in Algeria, that is, 'Algerian patterns of thinking, outdated and pre-capitalist, emerging from semi-feudal structures' (1963: 12), meant that it was possible for Algerian agriculture to go directly to a collectivist system and bypass the capitalist production stage. Nevertheless he made no concrete proposals for changing the status quo. Furthermore, although there would be an academic debate, it was a debate which *would* take place rather than one which *had* taken place.[2] Thus Ouzegane's essential concern here was with a theoretical discourse rather than a practical strategy for agriculture. His practical reference was in fact the Yugoslavian *autogestion* model and practice (1963: 11).

Ouzegane used two separate discourses to locate post-independence Algerian agricultural policy within a wider context. His first discourse employed the language of classical Marxism but turned to the former Yugoslavia for its practice. His second discourse foreshadowed the central discourse of the post-1965 Plans in which agricultural policy was both subordinated to industrial policy and conceived as an essential part of a development in which industry and agriculture were symbiotically linked. This second discourse can be traced to the French economist François Perroux, with whom this interview was conducted.[3] In fact, it is only possible to make sense of Algerian industrial policy planning, and consequently its view of agriculture, if one refers back to the writings of Perroux. In Perroux's model, 'a generalized theory of equilibrium and its application to contemporary realities' (1991: 51), linkages between different sectors are envisaged in two possible ways. In the first set of linkages, the central focus is linked between different classes of industry which are then sub-divided into entirely new industries, modern industries and traditional industries. In this version of the model, agriculture falls within the category of traditional industries. This model is represented in Figure 5.1.

Figure 5.1 Sectoral linkages in the Perroux model – version A

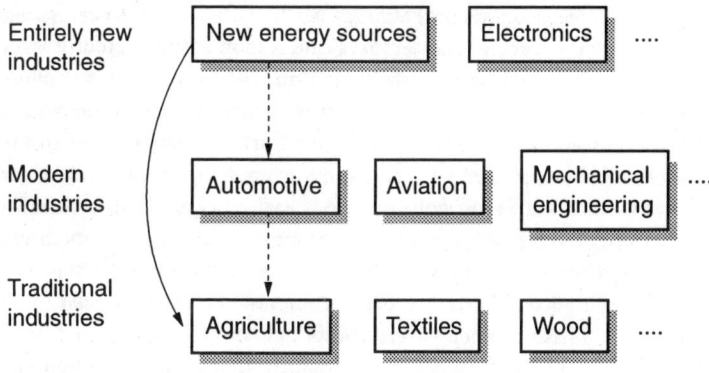

Source: François Perroux (1991) *L'Économie du XXe siècle*, 51.

In the second version of the model, agriculture is at the centre and inputs are made from two industrial groupings: 'upstream' industries and 'downstream' industries. This version is represented in Figure 5.2.

Figure 5.2 Sectoral linkages in the Perroux model – version B

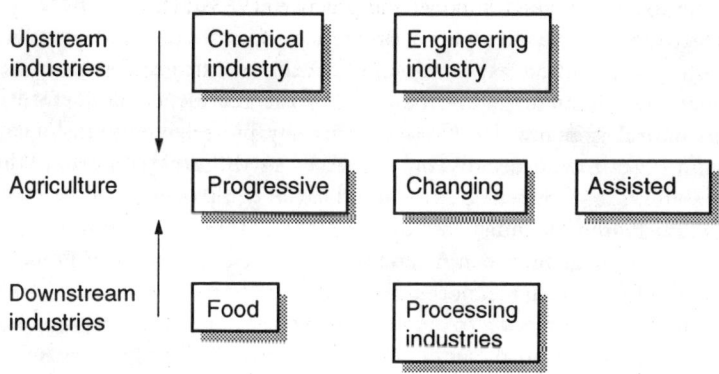

Source: François Perroux (1991) *L'Économie du XXe siècle*, 51.

The Algerian version is closest to the second version of the model as it argued that it was necessary to raise agricultural productivity in order that the increased capacity would then be able to absorb a higher industrial production and thus promote the development of the industrial sector.[4]

However, in practice, in the case of those sectors which were selected for industrial development – although in theory their development was linked to agriculture – the link was potential rather than real. Their actual lack of dependence on the agricultural sector is one reason for the rather limited release of budgetary resources to the agricultural sector in these first plans. It was also accompanied by a lack of development in the two sectors of industry with some direct relevance to agriculture, namely petrochemicals and mechanical engineering. Furthermore, even if these two sectors had been able to respond to agricultural needs earlier, agriculture lacked the means to utilize the products that were being generated. For example, fertilizers were not extensively used because of the absence of plant able to employ them and a labour force insufficiently qualified to use them appropriately. These problems were compounded by irregular supplies of fertilizer products and machinery. Agricultural machinery which was acquired was of poor quality and badly maintained once acquired. It is true to say, therefore, that by 1970 agriculture had accumulated a wide variety of problems and the various attempts which were made during the 1970s to resolve these problems were unable to achieve the improvements desired. At the same time, the decision to focus on an oil-based economy in practice switched the emphasis in policy-making from agriculture to industry.

In assessing the problems and difficulties which Algerian agriculture had in the 1960s and 1970s, it is also necessary to consider the nature of the problems which it had inherited. René Dumont, later Research Director at the National Agronomic Institute in Paris, had described North Africa as 'the last of the underdeveloped extra-European areas' which are 'characterized in the main by the prevalence of a retarded agricultural economy of very low productivity, by the undernourishment, qualitative if not actually quantitative, of the greater part of the inhabitants, and by the absence of industrial equipment, which even at best exists only in embryonic form' (1957: 207). In his view, modern techniques of agriculture in Algeria were confined to the European sector of agriculture which meant that in practice, most of agriculture was not 'modernized'. Dumont also argued that because the colons monopolized the best land, it had the effect of both an increased fragmentation of Muslim property and its confinement to less productive agricultural areas and to more ecologically vulnerable ones, such as hills and mountains. Thus, when such areas were ploughed for grain, erosion generally followed. In fact, Dumont calculated that erosion was proceeding at the rate of 85,000 acres per annum (Dumont, 1957: 168). Ouzegane also made a reference to the issue of erosion but in the context of conflicts within the colonial polity in which hostility between Public Works engineers (the constructors of large dams) and the Forestry department had resulted in erosion of the lakesides and reductions in water-use capacity (Perroux, 1963: 10). Dumont's final point concerns the predominance of the vine in colon agriculture and its occupation of the the more fertile lowlands. Such an occupation forced cereal production away from the fertile lowlands and into less fertile areas, with the result that a drop in production during the colonial period had made it necessary to import bread cereals. Furthermore, the level of importation was so high that in practice, vine produce sales were not sufficient to offset them (Dumont, 1957: 169). The result was that the agricultural economy was undermined at two levels: through the patterns of ownership and through the balance between different crops.

A later study of the future potential of Algerian agriculture by Dominique Badillo (1980) paints a similar picture. On the basis that the principal areas of colon agriculture in 1962 were the Chelif Plain, the Mitidja, Oranais and the Annaba plain, and that it was these areas which were both the most highly mechanized and specialized in the production of export-oriented crops such as the vine and citrus fruits, Badillo estimates that the vine accounted for 50 per cent of actual plant production and over 50 per cent of exports from the agricultural sector. However, another writer, André Tiano, argues that, while the vine was the major export earner in the agricultural sector and as late as 1960 still represented Algeria's principal export earner, bringing in 38 per cent of export earnings, oil was rapidly catching up and in the same year accounted for 29 per cent of export earnings. He goes on to argue that by 1963 the positions had in fact been reversed, with oil accounting for 63 per cent of export earnings and wine 17 per cent (1967: 566).

The final issue concerns the level of investment in agriculture. Dumont (1957) argues that under colonial rule, there was a general lack of investment in agriculture but that this overall lack of investment was particularly marked in respect of the Muslim sector of agriculture. Djilali Benamrane (1980) shows that in 1954 the total credits given to the European sector of agriculture were about 34,000 million francs; whereas that provided for the traditional (that is Muslim) sector was only 2.6 million francs. Benamrane (1980) also points out that despite agriculture's importance as a source of employment with some 350,000 permanent and seasonal workers employed in the sector, its overall role in the economy was less significant. For example, in his figures for Algeria's GDP in 1958, he shows that agriculture's share was 26 per cent, that of services 47 per cent, and that of industry 26 per cent. In his view the bias in the economy at this time was in favour of the services sector.

However, land and relations of the individual and the collectivity to it are able to provoke powerful images and this had certainly been true of colonial Algeria. Land and who owned it had also played a key part in the discourses of France and the nationalists during the independence struggle. Indeed it occupied an important part of the proposed reconstruction of the economy outlined in the Tripoli Programme. However, while agriculture held this prominent place in the nationalist discourse of the pre-independence period, in practice it would occupy a more minor role in the post-independence policy-making. The contradictions contained within policy-making are epitomized by the ambivalence towards autogestion and form the backdrop to the character of the attempted reforms of Boumediene.

Autogestion in agriculture

The spontaneous occupation of land by the permanent workforce (autogestion) was contingent on the fact that as independence approached it became increasingly obvious that the European population would quit an independent Algeria; thus a space was created for their Algerian agricultural labourers to seize control of the properties they deserted. The amount of land potentially available can be gauged from the fact that the European population which had numbered around one million in 1960 had declined to 150,000 in 1966. If this is taken into account alongside the fact that this population includes Barbé's 'gros colons' (Barbé, 1959: 12) who alone controlled 87 per cent of landholdings, it is possible to appreciate the amount of land that was involved. However, it needs also to be remembered that departure did not necessarily mean that colons abandoned their property and, in the case of some of the very large colon landholders, arrangements were made for the continued exploitation of their properties by the appointment of managers (Benissad, 1979). Estimates of the amount of land vacated vary. For example, Chaliand and Minces (1972) calculated that around 1.5 million hectares of land was initially affected by autogestion and that it represented around 13 per cent of cultivable land. However, this land area accounted for approximately one-third of cereal production, a quarter of wine production and about 45 per cent of citrus production, and had also employed approximately 80,000 agricultural workers. Benissad (1979: 76–84) argues that the autogestion sector accounted for some 1,994 *domaines* (farms) or 2.3 million hectares which represented about 35.5 per cent of cultivable land concentrated mainly in the fertile plain of the Mitidja, the Chelif plain and the Annaba plain, and employed about 255,000 workers of whom

135,000 were permanent. There is considerable discrepancy between these two sets of figures, which helps to illustrate some of the problems which were experienced by the planners and the statistical services in establishing an accurate picture of the agricultural economy.

Autogestion as it took place in Algeria was not pre-planned and, as has been suggested, formed no part of the various nationalist proposals for the management of agriculture. Attempts such as those by Ouzegane cited above were made to give it authenticity within the policy framework, but it was essentially something of a problem for post-independence government discourse. That this was so is illustrated by the variety of measures and institutions which were set up to regulate autogestion and to locate it within an overall strategy for the socialist economic development of Algeria (Marill, 1965). Other contemporary writers focused on the contradictions which this strategy produced (Minces and Chaliand, 1972; Clegg, 1971). They argued that the measures which were taken in the post-independence period to incorporate autogestion into broader Algerian economic policy-making were, on the one hand, no more than attempts to muzzle the development of forms of self-management in the post-independence Algerian economy and, on the other, conscious attempts to undermine its very existence. There were undoubtedly elements within the Algerian polity who did not favour autogestion as a means of managing either agriculture or industry; such opposition came from a number of different sources, as for example, those who favoured a Soviet-style collectivization of agriculture or who had vested interests in agriculture. However, such a view both underestimates the actual problems autogestion created for the post-independent Algerian governments and ignores the capacity of individuals like Ouzegane to employ both discourses at the same time. There is also a very real sense in which autogestion can be described as a counter-strategy to that which had been tentatively mapped out during the years of the independence struggle. In a sense, therefore, no one quite knew how to incorporate autogestion within an overall economic strategy, as a result of which agriculture was in practice neglected for the first ten years after independence was achieved.

It has already been suggested that figures from different sources give different estimates of the area of cultivable land within the autogestion sector and the amount of agricultural production it accounted for. For example, Chaliand and Minces (1972) estimates are lower than those of Benissad (1979). However, the Table they use was also reproduced by another author, Jean Teillac (1965),[5] and Krieger (d'Arcy et al., 1965) has similar figures derived from a different source.[6] The Table is included here in order to give a picture of the scope of the autogestion sector.

Table 5.1 Crop distribution and land area within the autogestion sector

Crop[1]	Hectares[1]	% of total[1]	Hectares[2]
Cereals	774,000	24.5	768,940[3]
Pulses	26,000	35.0	23,240
Artificial feedstuffs	46,600	57.5	11,010[4]
Industrial crops	11,800	46.0	44,380[4]
Market garden	29,700	48.0	28,730
Vine	333,000	89.5	64,800
Fruit trees	70,000	35.0	94,800
Natural grasslands	14,000	42.0	15,560
Total cultivated land	1,302,000[5]	32.5	
Fallow	748,000	25.5	856,640
Total cultivable land	2,050,600[5]	29.5	
Pasture and hunting	518,400	5.6	413,160
Total productive land	2,569,000[5]	15.8	
Unproductive land	76,700	14.5	325,460
Total land area	2,645,700[5]	15.7	2,648,890

Notes: [1]Figures from Chaliand and Minces (1972: 40); [2]figures from Krieger (d'Arcy *et al.*, 1965: 162, Table VI); [3]Krieger divides cereals into Summer and Winter, and these have been combined here; [4]these figures appear to have been reversed; [5]total figures are as reproduced in Chaliand and Minces (1972: 40) but actual totals are slightly greater.

Table 5.1 illustrates the problems in obtaining accurate statistical data on agricultural production and consequently why agricultural development was in practice so difficult to implement. Furthermore, the figures here represent the maximum area under autogestion and are a reflection of the series of land nationalizations which occurred after the promulgation of the March 1963 Decrees and which concluded in October 1963 with the nationalization without indemnity of all European land. While the land areas which came under autogestion represented the major part of agricultural production in Algeria – simply because they had been the former European landholdings – Teillac (1965) notes that the structure of production on them in 1963 did not differ greatly from that which had been in place in 1954. It can therefore be argued that this reflected the effects of the independence struggle in the rural areas and the accompanying underinvestment in agriculture. Another major problem was that sources of credit were also relatively underdeveloped. Certainly in the first stages of autogestion, the major source for credit remained the old Sociétés Agricoles de Prévoyance (SAP).[7] These were initially superseded by the Banque Centrale d'Algérie (BCA) and then in 1966 the BCA's role was delegated to the newly created Banque Nationale d'Algérie (BNA) in association with a central savings bank and regional agricultural credit savings institutions.

While the provision of credit to the autogestion sector was certainly a problem, what most concerned the early writers on autogestion were the institutional arrangements that the March 1963 Decrees on autogestion established. Essentially the decrees were composed of three elements: the Decree of 18 March 1963 which established what were vacant properties; the Decree of 22 March 1963 which was concerned with the managerial structure of the autogestion units; and the Decree of 28 March 1963 which dealt with the income and revenue distribution aspects of the autogestion enterprise.

The March 18 Decree basically legalized the status quo of property left vacant at independence and then taken over by the permanent workers; the second and third decrees, therefore, are of greater significance. The 22 March Decree established an essentially bicephalous managerial structure which juxtaposed on the one hand various interested parties of the state and, on the other, a structure of bottom-up control by the workforce. The state established a local watchdog body called the Communal Council for the Co-ordination of Self-management (*Conseil Communal d'Animation de l'Autogestion*) and appointed a Director as their representative to each individual autogestion unit. The aim of the Council was to ensure some form of local cooperation between the different units and the Director, to ensure that the wider aims of government policy were considered when drawing up plans for the individual unit. There were a number of reasons why these perfectly laudable intentions did not succeed, not least because in 1963 there was no established structure within which they could be situated. In addition, the Decrees created a potential for conflict between the Director and the President which in practice would be compounded by the Director being chosen from among workers of the old SAPs.

The other side of the managerial structure was based on the autogestion unit itself. This was composed of four elements. At the base was the General Assembly of Workers which included all workers over 18 and of Algerian nationality. However, there was one important caveat to membership and that was that the worker had to be a permanent employee. Moreover, a special clause was written in excluding seasonal workers both from being made members of the General Assembly and from enjoying any rights or privileges associated with such membership. The second organ of the structure was the Workers' Council, whose members were chosen from among the members of the General Assembly. It was the Workers' Council that had to decide on the purchase and sale of equipment for the unit and see to its maintenance. They also had the power within the constraints established by the General Assembly to make decisions on long- and medium-term loans, and decide who could or could not be a member of the General Assembly. Finally, it was the Workers' Council which elected the Management Committee.

The Management Committee comprised anything from three to eleven members and had to select one of its number as President of the unit. The Management Committee was primarily responsible for drawing up the unit's development plan, deciding on work schedules, instituting accounts procedures, producing marketing strategies, arranging short-term loans and attempting to diffuse problems which arose from the hire of seasonal workers. The President therefore was the spokesperson for the Committee and the workers; consequently, the post embodied a potential source of conflict with the Government-appointed Director.

While there were inbuilt institutional problems in the autogestion unit stemming from the attempt to represent both the views of the workforce and the views of the state, a further source of institutional problems was created by the establishment of a state regulatory body: the National Bureau of Agrarian Reform (ONRA). The idea behind ONRA was that there should be an overall supervisory body which would be able to co-ordinate agricultural policy at a national level. However, in practice, ONRA was to prove the principal focus of discontentment for the workers in the autogestion sector, and it was abolished in the 1968 agricultural reforms. In the late 1960s, some attempt was made to tackle systematically the problems which had arisen in the autogestion agricultural sector and in particular to attempt to reinforce the democratic aspects of autogestion. However, the methods chosen – a transferral of ONRA's functions to the BNA (National Bank of Algeria) and to the new Ministry of Agricultural Reform (MARA); and the reinforcement of the powers of the government-appointed Director rather than those of the elected President – did not improve the democratic functioning of the autogestion farms.

Autogestion represents an experiment in democratic methods of managing organizations in the context of newly achieved national independence. The other major example of a parallel experiment is in the former Yugoslavia, and Ouzegane in his interview with Perroux made explicit reference to the former Yugoslavia as a model of practice (Perroux, 1963: 11). However, the former Yugoslavia was not only a model for the Algerian government, it was also a model to which western socialists responded, perceiving in it an experiment which they believed pointed a way towards a more democratic form of socialism. The context within which the Yugoslav experiment took place was slightly different in that it was a conscious response to difficulties which had been experienced in the operation of a soviet-style centrally-planned economy within a multi-ethnic state. The interpretation of the reasons and the consequences of the Yugoslav experiment have been radically revised in the context of the implosion of the federal state in the 1990s (Ramet, 1992: 215). However, at the time it was seen as an innovative response to the central-planning model. It faced two specific problems, which to some extent the Algerian autogestion units also faced. The first of these was the problem of ownership – that is, within an economy where there was state ownership of the means of production/collective ownership by the community, how could you have individual ownership by a particular group of workers? The issue of ownership was also an issue for the Algerian farms because, in theory, all land was considered part of the national patrimony, while Islam also does not permit, except in certain specific circumstances, private or individual ownership of land.[8] The second problem, also a problem for the Algerian units, was an appropriate system of financing and distribution of revenue within the unit. Problems associated with the distribution of earnings meant that up to 1968, the autogestion workers received little direct return on profits. This absence of a means for ensuring a return meant that organizational learning was slow to take place. Coupled to this in the Algerian context was the absence of a skilled manpower reserve, which was as much a problem for agriculture as were the manpower problems experienced by industry. These were problems which had accumulated during the colonial period when it was not solely a question of the underfunding of agriculture itself but a question of the underfunding of rural communities and more particularly the underfunding of educational provision.

However, the central problem of the autogestion experiment lay in the fact that it was the large colonial farms which had been subsumed within this sector. Consequently, autogestion agriculture was organized on a division of landholding which had been established by colonial patterns of land distribution. It could not therefore tackle the question of the large disparities in land-owning capacity which existed in Algeria or relate to the dispossessed Algerian fellah. In many ways, therefore, autogestion farms perpetuated colonial patterns of landholding. Perennes (1979) illustrates how, in respect of date production near Touggourt, autogestion helped to maintain landholding patterns which suited the market in which the dates were sold and whose origins were colonial. He also illustrates that it did not change patterns of worker relationships as it was the permanent workers who were the beneficiaries and whose numbers were always less than those of the seasonal workers; for example, on one date farm the number of permanent workers was 140, whereas the numbers of seasonal workers was as high as 300.

However, the emotional pull of the autogestion idea was such that it effectively prevented any overview of agricultural policy being made and the much wider question of landownership in general being tackled at the level of state policy. In the meantime, however, industrial development had not only continued but had been gathering momentum, with the result that agriculture was not in a position to meet the new challenges that industrial development was creating. Pre-independence nationalist movement discourses had not envisaged that agricultural reform would occur through the medium of autogestion; consequently, the domination of autogestion as a method of agricultural ownership and production in the first eight years of post-independence policy-making in agriculture posed considerable practical and ideological problems for government policy-makers and, in 1970, they attempted to seize the initiative in agriculture by means of a reform programme called the Agrarian Revolution (*Révolution Agraire*).

The *Révolution Agraire* and agricultural policy in the 1970s

In the late 1960s, it had become increasingly clear that agricultural development had not been proceeding at the same pace as industrial development. In the first place, the development of the central-planning system with an industrial policy based on the *société nationale* (SN – 'state enterprise') had not had the impact on agriculture which the integrative basis of the planning model used suggested would happen. In theory, on the basis of the model, agriculture should have benefited from the development of industries like paper where the raw materials were derived from the agricultural sector. However, the proposed mutual dependence between agriculture and industry was a development which was still very much in its infancy. The second series of problems arose from the contradictions between the planning process and the effects of its implementation, and the parallel existence of the autogestion sector in agriculture, which affected the development of agricultural production. Finally, and in a sense this relates back to the original model, the dialectical relationship between agriculture and industry that was required had failed to take into account the extremes of the processes of dislocation which the creation of the European *colon*-centred agricultural system had caused and which the subsequent armed struggle had only served to exacerbate. It was the development of a landless army of former peasants without a corresponding development of industry that had created the impasse, and even emigration to France had never been sufficient to absorb this surplus population.

However, finding solutions was hampered by the ideological import-ance of land in the discourse of the nationalist struggle, by the fact that the choice of the motor for industrialization was oil, and that the pace of industrialization was not as fast as had been envisaged. It was also hampered by the lack of availability of data from the agricultural sector caused by the diffuse nature of the sector itself and from problems which had arisen from the mechanics of the operation of a planned economy. The development and use of plans were the key element of economic policy in the Boumediene era. However, the elaboration of the first plan was not completed until 1967 and it was marked by a lack of coherence in the programmes for the different sectors. This was the result of a planning process in which each sector Ministry elaborated its own plan, resulting in relatively little linkage between them. A co-ordinating national body, the Ministry for Planning (*Secrétariat d'État au Plan*) was not created until 1970. Even with the creation of the Ministry for Planning and the accompanying launch of the agrarian reform programme, the objectives set up for the agricultural sector were not achieved. The failure to achieve the objectives set out for agriculture were in part a reflection of the fact that by comparison with the oil sector, agriculture did not receive the same level of investment. For example, in the period 1970–73, actual investment in agriculture (Bedrani, 1982: Table 3, 10) was 10 per cent compared to 23 per cent for the oil sector and 31 per cent for industry and mining. Furthermore, in the period 1974–76, this share of investment dropped to 6 per cent while those for oil, and industry and mining, rose respectively to 24 per cent and 32 per cent. There were also other areas of failure; for example, in the First Four-Year Plan, there was a planned purchase of 30,000 cows but in practice only 16,000 were bought. Similarly in the Second Four-Year Plan, there was a planned purchase of 61,000 cows but only 24,358 were purchased (Bedrani, 1982: 31). However, the question of the effectiveness of local-level administration was also a problem; as a correspondent of the pro-government newspaper *El Moudjahid* (20.9.72) noted, even where funds for agricultural development had been made available, they had often got no further than the local *wilaya* (regional) treasury, something which he suggests was attributable to the shortcomings of local-level cadres. Indeed, the correspondent also argued that not only had the objectives of the First Four-Year Plan not been achieved, they had never in fact got off the ground.

As a result, and as part of a two-pronged campaign aimed at bringing about reform in both agriculture and industry, the Boumediene government drew up and launched in 1971 a campaign known as the Agrarian Revolution (*Révolution Agraire*). The seriousness of the problems in agriculture can be gauged by the fact that the Agrarian Revolution programme was established in parallel to the planning system, and in many senses remained outside that system. Consequently, when the Planning Minister Abdallah Khodja discussed employment creation in the context of the Second Four-Year Plan, he was exclusively concerned with non-agricultural employment (*El Moudjahid*, 26.6.74). The Agrarian Revolution programme was in the first place an attempt to tackle the question of landlessness. However, solving the problem of people without land meant that it was necessary to create land to be owned. The second major aspect of the programme was the reorganization of patterns of agricultural production. The question of landlessness was to be tackled in two stages, the first of which involved the assignment of publicly owned land to private ownership; and the second the expropriation of so-called surplus land of large landholders within the private sector. It was also seen as providing an opportunity to attempt to integrate autogestion within a wider programme of agricultural restructuring. This meant employing measures that would eliminate the distinctions between state-owned farms and the autogestion sector by incorporating the latter into a wider system of state-directed agriculture. The main mechanisms it chose in order to achieve these goals were, on the one hand, the creation of new forms of landholding which involved direct distribution of publicly owned land on the basis of screened applications; and secondly, the establishment of what were called 'agrarian reform villages' (*villages de la réforme agraire*) with their accompanying *attributaire* system, which was an allocative or grant-based system aimed at redistribution of land among the non-owning agricultural workers; and thirdly, the development of agricultural cooperatives.

The launching of this agricultural reform programme took some time and it was not really until 1973–74 that some progress could be said to have taken place. In fact, somewhat as with the socialist management programme (which will be discussed in Chapter 6), there was a time delay between the publication of the proposals and the beginnings of actual reform. Both the distribution of public land to private applicants and the reform of private sector agriculture were seen as a means to demonstrate the regime's credentials in respect of both the colonial past – where private-sector agricultural holdings often continued to reflect the pattern of landholding of the colonial era – and its own commitments from the independence struggle towards the poor and dispossessed. Furthermore, the statutes which had been drawn up in the early years of independence for the autogestion sector had made no attempt to touch the private sector. Within the private sector, the continuation of pre-colonial systems of labour such as the *métayer* and the *khammessat* was of concern to the regime. These were systems whereby an individual who worked a piece of land did not own it and instead paid a tithe in the form of four-fifths of the produce of that land as rent to a third party. Furthermore, the private sector still controlled approximately two-thirds of cultivable land and employed around one million people (Benissad, 1979). Badillo (1980) identified four main types of property ownership in the private sector of agriculture that survived independence. These were landowners who were rentiers only; agricultural landlords who owned land and farmed either through the use of wage-labour or through the use of family labour; tenant farmers, responsible for the organization of production but not themselves owners of the land; and agricultural wage-labour who neither owned land nor organized production but sold their labour power. Table 5.2 – reproduced from Bedrani (1982) – provides yet another illustration of the problems involved in acquiring accurate statistical data on the agricultural sector. This Table of changes in landownership in agriculture between 1966 and 1977 was compiled from the general population censuses for 1966 and 1977, the 1972–73 Agricultural census and a 1968 survey of workers in private-sector agriculture. In theory, the 1977 RGPH figures ought to record the effects of the implementation, however partial they may be of the Agrarian Revolution reforms; what they appear to record is a general decline in agricultural employment.

A central feature of the Agrarian Revolution, therefore, was land nationalization. Land nationalization was carried out by a new central body established for this purpose: the *Fonds National de la Révolution Agraire* (FNRA – Agrarian Revolution National Fund) illustrating once again the tendency of the regime to utilize bureaucratic solutions to solve political and economic problems. This was further illustrated by the manner in which the nationalizations took place. The first stage of redistribution involved public land owned by local and regional government authorities. Processes by which such land was redistributed and some of the attendant problems can be illustrated by the example of the Oran area (*El Moudjahid*, 31.8.72). First of all, the actual amount of land for redistribution could be quite small. In the Oran area, it was only 27 hectares, whereas in the neighbouring Arzew area there were

Table 5.2 The division of the agricultural labour force at the time of the Agrarian Revolution (after Bedrani, 1982)

	Private sector survey 1968	RGPH 1966	RGPH 1977	RGA 1972–73
Employing farmers		4,981	1,594	
Independent farmers		362,384	255,252	
Employing and Independent farmers	661,674			875,660
Cooperative workers			74,524	—
Permanent agricultural workers	35,061	212,824	192,604	7,070
Seasonal agricultural workers	493,467	571,475	114,000	177,662
Family help[1]	613,158	145,732	52,768	1,080,535
Apprentices	—	40	742	—
Not declared	—	1,627	678	—
Unemployed[2]			728,174	
Total active population	1,803,360	1,299,063	1,020,336	2,140,929
Occupied population	—	879,675	692,162	

RGPH, Recensement Général de la Population et de l'Habitat; RGA, Recensement Général de l'Agriculture.

Notes: [1] In the RGA, a very wide definition of *aide familiale* (family help) is used which may have had the effect of reducing the numbers of Permanent Agricultural Workers; [2] applies only to 1977 and to those who have already worked.

145 hectares available and only 40 applicants. However, the number of applicants for the land in question might be proportionately high. In the Oran area, there were 110 eligible requests and it is the eligibility criteria and the distribution of applicants between these criteria which perhaps illustrates the more serious problems which the programme faced. There were four criteria of eligibility which in descending order of priority were as follows: the first priority group were peasants already working on public land (in this instance, no applicants); the second priority group were *anciens moudjahidines* (veterans) and the *chouhada* (children of people killed during the war) of which there were 29 applicants; the third group were former agricultural workers without land and who were no

longer working in agriculture, and there were 42 applicants in this category; and the fourth category was 'others' in which there were 33 applicants made up chiefly from the unemployed, porters and dockers. In other words, these are applicants who are essentially desperate for work, whose knowledge of agricultural practices may be quite limited and who have no personal access to capital resources. In a sense, therefore, agricultural reform was also a means of finding employment for categories of workers either displaced by the colonial process or by the post-independence industrialization programme. They were not the basis on which an agricultural modernization programme could be built unless it was accompanied by large injections of both capital and educational programmes.

The second stage of land redistribution focused on the private landlord and involved both the nationalization of land belonging to absentee landlords, and the nationalization of what was considered to be excess land held by private landlords, but accompanied by the nationalization of various forms of pre-colonial landownership. These nationalizations involved 'arch' property – that is, the collective property of the 'tribes' – and 'habous' or endowed property. Both types of property were transferred into the ownership of FNRA. The measures failed to achieve their objectives on two separate counts. In the first place, they failed actually to transfer the amount of land which was marked out because, on the one hand, the definition of absentee landlord was sufficiently restrictive to exclude many properties which could reasonably be said to be the property of an absentee landlord; and, on the other, the definition of large landlord also served to exclude many properties. In the second place, what was in fact being achieved was the transfer from private landlords to a single state landlord. Furthermore, the process was faced with the same technical problem of the paucity of actual statistics available on agricultural property ownership as the first census of private land was carried out between September 1972 and March 1973. In addition, this was not a complete census as it covered 1.3 million landowners only. Consequently, it still meant that there was very little real data on which to base the decision-making processes within a planning-directed economy.

The Agrarian Revolution not only sought to bring more property under state control, it also attempted to introduce new forms of organizational structures. The form of organizational structure which it favoured was agricultural cooperatives. However, it was agricultural cooperatives under the direction of the state through a body called the *Coopérative Agricole Polyvalente Communale de Services* (CAPCS – Agricultural Cooperative Council for Multi-purpose Services). Legislation to establish cooperatives was introduced in June 1972 and it provided for two basic legal forms of cooperation: cooperatives and pre-cooperatives.[9] Cooperatives were then broken down into three sub-types: joint agricultural cooperative enterprises (*coopérative agricole d'exploitation en commun*); agricultural production cooperatives (*coopérative agricole de production*) and agricultural service cooperatives (*coopérative agricole de service*); and they were given the legal form of limited private companies with a variable capital (*sociétés civiles particulières de personnes à personne et capital variable*). However, the process of bureaucratization which these complex differentiations entail was compounded by the fact that the cooperatives were subject to two forms of tutelary authority: a cooperative higher council and the Ministry of Agriculture. In theory, the cooperative system was intended to benefit the smallest farmers by providing opportunities for democratic management and access to material resources. However, in practice – because the cooperative higher council was composed of representatives from the administration, the Party and agricultural cooperatives on an equal basis – it was the bureaucratic state which was enhanced. This is further illustrated by the fact that before a cooperative could be established, permission had to be sought from the Ministry of Agriculture; and MARA continued to control cooperative activity even after it had been set up, in the areas of planning, accounts and legal affairs, leaving the cooperative free of state control only with regard to marketing, the supply of farm implements and the upkeep and repair of all machinery and equipment. Access to credit also continued to be a problem and it was necessary for a further programme to be launched in 1974–75 to provide greater access to credit facilities.

The 1974–75 agricultural campaign through the medium of the National Bank of Algeria (BNA) aimed to provide new sources of short-term credit for both the autogestion sector and the Agrarian Revolution cooperatives. It also incorporated measures to devolve power to the local level by providing for direct negotiations between farm directors and BNA officials. However, Bedrani (1982) reports that the campaign had difficulty in achieving its objectives because of two main problems: first of all, a lack of cooperation at the centre between the Planning Secretariat and the Ministry of Finance over what monies should be made available for the purchase of equipment and machinery; and secondly, a continued preference towards irrigated agriculture as opposed to dry agriculture which had the effect of excluding the majority of poorer farmers. As a result, much of the loans and investment which were made reinforced colonial bias towards irrigated farming and, consequently, towards pre-existing social divisions. If agriculture was to become an active player in the economic development of post-independence Algeria, agricultural incomes had to be sufficient for the farmer to make the purchases of industrial products and the investments necessary for future development. Agricultural incomes are notoriously difficult to assess because of factors such as the element of family and therefore non-remunerated labour which they incorporate. However, Bedrani (1982) estimates agricultural-sector monthly incomes as 506 DA (Algerian Dinar) per head in 1969, and 613 DA in 1973 when the mean monthly national income was 2,214 DA per head. As these are average incomes, they ignore divisions within groupings and therefore do not record that, for some, agricultural income was even lower. Bedrani (1982) distinguishes between incomes in the autogestion sector which on average were higher and those in the Agrarian Revolution sector, suggesting that in 1975–76, mean monthly incomes in the autogestion sector ranged between 514 DA and 1,127 DA against a range of 300 to 600 DA in the Agrarian Revolution sector. The other side of agricultural income is prices; Bedrani (1982) suggests an initial period from 1966 to 1972 when there were regular rises in consumer prices, and the period after 1972 which coincides with the oil crisis and the resultant oil-price increases which, while they raised the price at which Algeria was able to sell its oil, also raised the level of consumer prices. As a result Algeria was also paying more for the import of goods, including agricultural products, as economic self-sufficiency was far from being achieved; and there was heavy dependence on imports. Bedrani also suggests that there were other problems which arose from the parallel existence of a state marketing system and private commercial networks, when the state marketing and supply bodies were experiencing problems in relations between them.

Conclusion

To conclude this discussion of the role of agricultural reform and the contradictions which it embodied, it is useful to turn to another of the theoreticians of the period of the independence struggle and one of the signed authors of the Tripoli Programme, Mostefa Lacheraf, who in a series of three long articles in Algeria's other major daily newspaper *La République* (19, 20 and 21 June 1974) entitled *Le Village algérien dans l'univers insaisissable du no-man's land* ('The Algerian village in the elusive/imperceptible universe of no-man's land') explored the problems which were faced by agriculture in Algeria. In Lacheraf's view, and his is a pessimistic analysis, colonization and the independence struggle had had the effect of breaking the links between the peasant and the land thoroughly enough to make it impossible to recreate the former agricultural community. He paints a picture of an agricultural landscape of abandoned villages, of depopulation, of an indigent population which is capable of doing no more than scratching a bare subsistence from the soil. As a result, the reforms which were being attempted under the heading of the Agrarian Revolution had no substantive basis on which to build, and the agrarian reform villages had no organic base. Consequently, the programme of the Agrarian Revolution had enormous obstacles to overcome. In other words, Lacheraf was essentially highlighting that the economic basis of agricultural reform was weak.

This perception of the weaknesses not only of the Agrarian Revolution programmes but also of the limited nature of an economic project concentrated solely on industrial development is to be found in Boumediene's own speeches. For example, at a seminar held in May 1970 on the Agrarian Revolution, he argued that 'our revolution itself will remain imperfect if it stays limited to the urban areas and the establishment of large industrial complexes. If such was her direction, it would inevitably be condemned to suffocation'.[10] However, it is also clear from other speeches that for Boumediene, the Agrarian Revolution was more than an issue of economics. He argued in a speech on the fifth anniversary of his Presidency that the industrial revolution would not be complete if there were not also a revolution in the countryside and 'the peasant masses continued to languish in poverty and underdevelopment'.[11] Similarly, when four years later the process of inauguration of those agrarian revolution villages was begun, the speeches he would make would consistently focus on the ideological nature of the project which was being undertaken. For example, at the inauguration of one of the pilot villages, Belahcel Bouzegza in the Mostaganem wilaya, Boumediene's focus was on the Agrarian Revolution programme and the villages built under its auspices as 'a work of social justice', which would provide 'a prosperous life for each citizen', and as an opportunity for the disinherited to have a new life (*El Moudjahid*, 24.5.74). What the Agrarian Revolution programme serves to highlight is the fundamental contradiction which lay at the heart of the Boumediene project of how to combine rapid industrial development with a redistribution of its benefits, and at the same time increase agricultural production. It was an ambitious and also a doomed project.

Notes

1. The other two interviewers of Ouzegane were Gérard Destanne de Bernis, the other principal French economist who influenced Algerian planners, and J. Guillot. The influence of de Bernis was probably more important in the industrial field and can be illustrated by his co-authorship with the Head of Sonatrach, Sidahmed Ghozali of, for example, 'Les Hydrocarbures et l'industrialisation de l'Algérie' in *Revue Algérienne*, 1, 1969: 253–94.

2. Valensi–Gallissot debate discussed in Chapter 2: (8).

3. Perroux, although barely known in Britain, can be seen as a major French economist. He is described in the 1988 *Petit Larousse* as having 'profoundly changed the analysis of economic facts, by the incorporation of factors of domination and power and the advocacy of a revised theory of development'. He died in 1987 and the François Perroux Foundation are engaged in the republication of his work.

4. For an example, the public discussion which surrounded the presentation of the Second Four-Year Plan (1974–77) is illustrative, and it is apparent in the press conference which the State Planning Minister Abdallah Khodja gave in June 1974 (*El Moudjahid*, 26.6.74).

5. Teillac says that the source of this Table was an insert into the March 1964 *Economic Bulletin*, 15 published by Algérie-Presse-Service Agency.

6. Krieger gives the source of her Table as *Jeune Afrique*, 141, 7 July 1963.

7. These had originally been called the Sociétés Indigènes de Prévoyance which were established in 1893 and renamed Sociétés Agricoles de Prévoyance in 1936.

8. For a discussion of Muslim systems of land tenure, refer to Chapter 2: (18, 24–5).

9. RADP, MARA: Commission Nationale de la Réforme Agraire (no date), *Coopération et Révolution Agraire – receuil des textes relatifs à la coopération agricole*, Algiers: Imp. El Baath.

10. Seminar held 25 May 1970 on the Agrarian Revolution, quoted in Part IV of Khalfa Mameri (1975), *Citations du Président Boumediene*, Algiers, SNED.

11. Speech at the Fifth Anniversary of the 19 June 1965 *coup d'état*, quoted in Part IV of Khalfa Mameri (1975), *Citations du Président Boumediene*, Algiers, SNED.

6

The Economic Origins of Crisis II:
Industry and Labour under Boumediene

The aim of this chapter is to explore the relationship between the industrial development strategy which the post-independence Algerian state adopted and the effects of this strategy on industry and labour. To some extent, understanding the nature of the choices which were made in respect of industrial development also depends on an understanding of what choices were available. As the focus is the Boumediene era, what we are concerned with is the period between 1965 and 1978, and more particularly the period which is covered by the First and Second Four-Year Plans (1970–77). The interest and importance of this period is that during this period one begins to see the difficulties which the government had as a result of its use of two different discourses. On the one hand, there was the discourse of the Algerian Revolution and its linked discourse of the construction of a socialist economy, and on the other, the discourse which was required in order to implement the industrial development policy. To situate these two discourses and to understand why they diverged requires a critical re-examination of the industrial-development theses which were available. When Algeria gained its independence in 1962, there were in fact two major types of industrial-development thesis which were current. The first of these had their starting point in the classical texts of Marxist economic thinking, in other words those of Marx himself, Engels, Bukharin, Preobrazhensky, Stalin, and more particularly in Lenin's *The Development of Capitalism in Russia* first published in 1899.[1] The second category of writing focused on a relationship between industrialization and processes of technical change.[2] Both of these industrial development theses were predicated on the basis of a progressive development of economic structures and on the historical experience of western Europe. Marxist economic thinking about industrial development in the Third World was based on the notion of 'transition' from one dominant form of the economic ordering of society or mode of production to another. The industrialization and technical-change models tended to identify a specific characteristic, such as Weber's 'Protestant ethic' (Weber, 1976) or

McClelland's 'achievement motive' (McClelland, 1970), as the reason why Western Europe had been the first to industrialize. It is within this context that the Algerian experiment has to be seen.

The phrase 'Algerian experiment' has been used because it helps to illustrate the gap between the economic models available and the political discourse used. Decolonization in practice raised real theoretical issues for both models of economic development. If the 1960s and 1970s were spent in a critique of the industrialization and technical-change models, the 1980s and 1990s have witnessed a parallel critique of the Marxist models. Furthermore, although the 1990s have seen the emergence of new economic powers in the so-called 'Asian tigers' of the Pacific Rim, and although in the preceding period after the ending of World War II Japan became one of the world's major economic powers, there is no real parallel between their histories and experiences and those of the ex-colonial world. This means that it is not a rhetorical question to ask exactly what prospects did the Algerian economy have in 1962 and what choices did the post-independence governments in fact have. Subsumed within this question is the issue already posed that the political discourses of the Algerian Revolution and the socialist economy were not necessarily a reflection of, or reflected in, the economic strategy that the Boumediene government was to adopt in the late 1960s and 1970s.

An examination of the Ordonnance (No 70–10, 20 January 1970) which legalized the First Four-Year Plan of 1970–73 provides an introduction to the political and economic discourses of the economic development process. In the first place, the Plan is seen as part of a long-term strategy to achieve economic and social development (Article 4). Secondly, it is seen as a means both to construct and consolidate the socialist economy and to achieve economic independence (Article 5). These would be achieved by a strategy which developed agricultural and mineral resources within the context of a modern process of industrialization (Article 5). The results of the anticipated expansion would be used to maintain the momentum of economic development and to satisfy the material and cultural needs of the population as a whole but in particular used to improve the standard of living of the poorest sections of the population (Article 6). In order to obtain these goals, the Government would promote organizational methods and interventionist structures in keeping with a state which ran a planned economy (Article 9); and those would be accompanied by an austerity policy which would particularly affect consumption and savings (Article 9).

A further examination of the text of the Plan reveals two further ambivalences in the discourses of this period. The first of these is contained in the opening sentence of the Introduction where it is argued that 'Seven years after independence, the Algerian Revolution was entering with confidence the decisive stage of the economic construction of the country.' The clear implication of this statement is that industrialization and economic development were short-term projects whereas more generally the discussion of economic policy emphasized the long-term character of that project. It illustrates the tension which was present between the view of economic strategy as essentially long-term, and the recognition that politically the State needed to show that there were going to be immediate and individual gains for most members of the population. The second of these ambivalences concerns women. This is because, while the Introduction gives a commitment to the provision of educational opportunities for women and men, it makes no equivalent commitment to the provision of equal employment opportunities for women and men. Indeed the inverse is true, as the commitment on employment restricts itself to providing by the end of the decade 'a stable job to every active male member of the population'. Thus the ambivalent nature of the discourse on women's role in post-independence Algeria which emerged immediately after independence and which can be observed in the absence of women from the post-independence political scene is also apparent here in the second of the dual discourses in which the State was engaged.

The Boumediene government chose to focus on industrial development because it wished to create the basis for an independent industrial base and provide Algeria with the capacity to control its own economic affairs. It was seen as the means by which dependence on the already industrialized countries in general and on its former colonial power France in particular would be weakened. Although this was a laudable intention, it could not hide the pervasiveness of French influence in Algeria. Tackling that influence at an ideological level to a considerable extent ignored the realities of economic structures and institutions which had been fashioned after their French counterparts. The banks, the insurance companies and the majority of the actual businesses in operation at independence were all French-owned, French-based or otherwise influenced by France. French influence was further emphasized by the fact that Algeria's currency had been the French franc which meant that Algeria enjoyed a much closer relation to France than did France's other colonies. Thus, unlike France's other colonies, Algeria had not needed to be a member of the 'franc zone',[3] because it already enjoyed an even closer monetary relationship with France. If commercial relations are then considered, then the major market for Algerian products and the major supplier to the Algerian market was France; thence French imports from Algeria in 1970 were 42.4 per cent,

Table 6.1 Algerian foreign trade in 1970 and 1971 (figures shown in Algerian Dinars)

Country	Imports from Algeria		Exports to Algeria	
	1970	1971	1970	1971
Western Europe	4,726,890	4,470,101	4,127,970	3,237,670
EEC:	4,059,104	3,687,948	3,662,412	2,719,393
France	2,631,278	2,273,449	2,667,180	991,119
FRG	619,807	567,910	640,296	1,013,863
Italy	451,509	515,285	209,737	317,293
Holland	140,880	163,616	43,735	191,188
BLEU	215,630	167,687	101,464	205,930
Socialist Countries	349,971	397,216	397,674	505,296
North America	576,803	669,276	41,023	77,833

Source: Chambre de Commerce et d'industrie d'Alger (1974), *Algérie, situation économique 1972–73.*

and French exports to Algeria in the same year accounted for 53.5 per cent of the total amount of foreign trade. Table 6.1 illustrates the importance of the European market in general in Algerian foreign trade, and that of France in particular.

If France was an important partner in Algeria's foreign trade, she was an equally important partner in industrial cooperation contracts. For example, in the month of July 1974, of nine contracts signed with foreign companies, five were with French firms, and three with West German firms.[4] France also continued to be a major influence in education and training systems with significant if declining numbers of French teachers and technical assistants in Algeria. Méducin (1974) records that in 1969, there were 6,350 teachers with French nationality in Algeria and 2,130 Technical Assistants. By 1972, the number of teachers had dropped to 3,750 but the number of Technical Assistants had remained stable and moreover the proportion of these who were National Service Volunteers (VSNA) had doubled. Furthermore, in certain subjects such as maths and the sciences, teachers of foreign origin were in the majority. The significance of the rise in the National Service Volunteers is that many of these were graduates of the Grandes Écoles, such as the École Nationale d'Administration, the École des Mines and the École Polytechnique.[5] At the same time, Algerians continued to travel to France to obtain further and higher education and thus imbue the *esprit du corps* of these same institutions. French influence was therefore as much indirect as direct.

The lack of independent access to markets for Algerian goods was apparent in a number of different ways. It was apparent in the first place through Algeria's dependence on the French market and the manner in which its economy was tied with the French economy. That can be illustrated by the fact that there was no initial need for Algeria to renegotiate terms with the European Economic Community because it possessed a privileged access to the Community via its special relationship with France. However, such a close relation of dependence had its own problems in that it also made the Algerian economy extremely vulnerable to any changes which might occur in that market. The evidence of that vulnerability was apparent in 1971 when Algeria nationalized all French oil interests in Algeria. Although the Algerian discourse emphasized the development of alternative markets for its products, in practice the policy was far less successful.

Algeria was not alone in choosing a strategy for economic development based on national plans and a system of state-controlled enterprise nor was it alone in the confusion of motives which prompted this choice. Whichever model is used as the reference for a system of national planning, whether it is Soviet or European (and in Algeria's case much inspired by the post-war French system of national planning),[6] planning and state-controlled enterprise models have a number of technical problems, some of which affect all systems and others particularly affect systems where infrastructure is weak. Algeria was an example of a system with a weak infrastructure and consequently was particularly affected by shortages of skilled manpower, the lack of independent access to markets for products, and the absence of the basic institutions for the process to take place. The actual structure of the labour market will be discussed in more detail later in this chapter, but what I want to focus on now are the consequences for industrial policy of this shortage of skilled manpower. The shortage of skilled manpower became a major issue because of the type of industries in which Algeria chose to concentrate development – the capital intensive, high skill-demand industries such as petrochemicals. That choice imposed a considerable strain on Algeria's labour market and led to a dependency, certainly in the early years of independence, on foreign nationals to supply the necessary technical labour for its industries. That technical labour was predominantly French but it also came from Eastern Europe, North America, the UK and the Middle East. A second point is that focusing on low-employment industries such as petrochemicals had the effect of creating a gulf between those who were able to obtain the necessary qualifications for employment in this labour market and the majority who could not gain these qualifications.

The absence of the basic institutions and infrastructure for industrialization to take place, and therefore of an adequate industrial base, led to the decision at the beginning of the Boumediene period to concentrate industrial development in particular geographic areas called 'industrial centres of attraction'. These were principally Algiers; Oran, Arzew and Mostaganem in the west; and Annaba and Skikda in the east. The other problems were the lack of skilled manpower, an insufficiently capitalized agriculture, and an industrial structure inappropriate to an industrial economy. One of the key issues for industrialization is timing, and the later a country's attempted insertion into world capitalist markets, the higher the ratio of capital to labour needs to be. It is possible that the exigencies of the world market can to some extent be deflected by concentrating on autonomous development after the pattern of the Chinese economy. However, in order to take that road, it is essential that the balance of forces internally are sufficient to be able to achieve that aim. In practice, Algeria's internal market was fragmented and, because of the effects of the colonial period on agriculture, unable of itself to generate the required resources for internal development. Furthermore, this would have held true even if Algeria had not had available a readily and comparatively easy to exploit raw material – oil – at a time when that raw material was in escalating demand by the actual industrialized countries and therefore capable, at least in the short term, of generating a high return.

Oil and gas: the petroleum sector in Algerian economic policy

While in reality it was the oil and gas sector which dictated post-independence Algerian economic policy, this is referred to only by allusion in the Introduction to the 1970–73 Four-Year Plan where the discourse focuses on agriculture and agricultural reform. The linked nature of the development envisaged in the Perroux model illustrated in Figure 5.1 on page 111 is explicitly stated in the Introduction in these terms: 'Industrialization works in tandem with the agricultural revolution whose success it will ensure.' Otherwise, all that is said is that there will be a 'systematic transformation of our natural resources'. However, the ambiguity of this statement is clear from a table in the Plan summarizing planned levels of investment. These allocate 49 per cent of total investment to directly productive investments split between agriculture and industry. What is significant is that the split is highly unequal, with industry receiving 76 per cent of the total. This inequality in actual investment is also illustrated by investment allocated to research of which, although it accounts for only 6.4 per cent of the total, 74 per cent is allocated to research in the petroleum field with the remaining 26 per cent divided almost equally between mining and hydraulic research. The importance of the oil and gas sector in practical terms is also summed up in the title of its *société nationale*: Sonatrach, the *Société Nationale pour la Recherche, la Production, le Transport, la Transformation et la Commercialisation des Hydrocarbures* (the state enterprise for research, production, transport, transformation and commercialization of petroleum and petroleum products), a name which graphically indicates the potential which it had to be – and in fact became – an unwieldy conglomerate but one which dominated the Algerian industrialization project both during and after the Boumediene years.

The importance of the petroleum sector in the Algerian economic policy can be seen as a reflection of developments within the world economy in the 1950s and 1960s. These developments placed a premium on cheap access to supplies of oil. As a result, research for new sources of supply were intensified and existing sources more fully exploited. It should be remembered that De Gaulle did not concede independence to the Algerian liberation movement until he had assured French interests in Saharan oil. However, the oil industry had developed particular patterns of exploit-ation as a result of the dominance of a restricted group of seven inter-national companies or oil majors who were able to control production and distribution (Odell, 1975). The effects of these were to survive the nationalizations of the 1970s with the result that those economies which are dependent on oil revenues have what Halliday (1995: 39) refers to as 'anomalous economic and social consequences of production'. This is most graphically illustrated by Saudi Arabia and the Gulf states; however, in spite of Algeria's political commitment to the integration of oil into a wider economic and social policy, nevertheless it was unable to escape the contradictions of this pattern of exploitation.

The Algerian economic planners argued that it was the petroleum sector which would act as the medium for capital accumulation within the Algerian state and provide the means to acquire foreign exchange which could then be used to develop other sectors of the economy. This argument was based on the 'industrializing industries' economic model illustrated in Figure 5.1 on page 111. A leading advocate of this model, the French economist G. de Bernis (1970, 1971a, 1971b), argued that the importance of such industries was that they encouraged three necessary developments to take place within newly industrializing economies, of which the Algerian economy was a prime example. He argued that these economies needed an industrial structure which would allow capital accumulation and foreign exchange acquisition to take place, but which would also, and most importantly of all, provide the basis for the establishment of the essential 'means of production' industries within the economy. The attractiveness of this model was that the 'industrializing industries' were variable and dependent upon the actual raw materials the economy possessed. Consequently, in the case of Algeria, it was the oil and gas sector which was the potential 'industrializing industry'. Its potential rested on the capacity of the industry to command relatively high prices on the international market and therefore provide the Algerian state with the capital and foreign exchange which could then be used to develop other industries. At the same time, oil itself forms the principal base material of one of the major modern industrial sectors, petrochemicals. Thus in theory oil should have provided the means for Algeria to develop the broad economic base which had been identified in the Plans.

The emphasis of the Algerian state upon this technologically complex and highly capital-intensive industrial sector of the oil and gas industry raised both practical and theoretical policy problems for the planners, not least because the oil and gas industry operates on the basis of a highly skilled labour force which is relatively small in number but which requires specialist educational facilities. In 1969, Algeria's technical educational programme had barely begun and, in fact, there were only 533 students undergoing a technical education in the higher education field. A further 246 students were attached to engineering schools in France and elsewhere (ASA, 1970). The absence of a sufficient number of highly trained workers for the industrial sectors forced Algeria to negotiate contracts with foreign firms which required that the foreign company undertook to train a certain number of Algerian cadres. For example, the contract with Parson and Whittemore Lyddon to build the Saida-Rebahia plant for SONIC required them to train a certain number of Algerian operatives in their own factories while the plant was being constructed. These were seen as essentially short-term measures while the infrastructure for training cadres internally was established. As a result, by 1977, there were approximately 8,000 students enrolled in technological studies at Algeria's two science and technology universities and at various other institutions (ASA, 1977–78). The increase in the number of students in higher education is a testament to the investment which was made in education and training, for example 12.5 per cent of the planned investment in the First Four-Year Plan. However, although investment in education and training was necessary, the size of the budget commitment which it entailed can be gauged by the fact that planned investment in agriculture was only 13 per cent. The result was to lay the basis for the development of a gap between the level of education of the future labour force and the technical development of industry and agriculture.

Algerian economic policy in the oil and gas sector was intended to transform the sector from a mere extractor and supplier of a strategic raw material – oil – into one which would be a producer of petrochemicals. In practice, it proved more difficult to achieve and the Algerian oil and gas sector remained predominantly an extractor and supplier of this strategic raw material, particularly to the industrialized nations of western Europe and the United States. Some changes did occur in the structure of the oil industry in the Middle East and North Africa during the 1970s but these were in the main limited to questions of the ownership of the crude oil. In other words, in 1970 the seven major oil companies owned 61 per cent of crude oil production, and other private oil companies 33 per cent. By 1979, following the 1971 nationalizations, the principal owners were now the governments of producing countries with some 55 per cent. However, it was not quite the same story on the marketing side where state marketing companies had 9 per cent in 1970 and 18 per cent in 1979 leaving the remainder divided almost equally between the seven majors and other private companies (*Financial Times*, 6.9.1980).[7]

The development of the oil industry structure in Algeria shows a similar pattern of movement away from dominance by the oil majors and other private companies to an increasing dominance of the state and state-run companies. The Algerian national oil company, Sonatrach, was founded in 1963 and was intended to take control of all aspects of the oil industry. It was formed as a giant conglomerate and from this initial starting point, it continued to expand its sphere of influence. For example, as early as 1966, a fertilizer and pesticide department was grafted onto it. Its expansion was also affected through the means of joint ventures, an example of which is ASCOOP (*Association Coopérative*) which resulted from the Franco-Algerian Agreement of July 1965 and which aimed to create an Algerian presence in the exploration field. However, the costs of oil exploration are such that such a venture was only feasible as a joint venture, and it is significant that the partner chosen for this joint venture was the French company SOPEFAL,[8] illustrating once again how close were the ties with the former colonial power – a pattern repeated in other joint ventures of the period. Consequently, despite the encompassing nature of the intent encapsulated by Sonatrach, in practice in the immediate post-independence period, the Algerian petroleum industry remained until the 1971 nationalizations largely in the control of foreign oil companies. The major foreign oil companies operating in Algeria were CFP and SN Repal (both French), and CREPS and CPA (both joint French/Shell operations). As a result Sonatrach, which had been formed to give an Algerian presence within the oil industry in Algeria, did little more than that during the first seven years of its existence.

With the choice of French partners somewhat compromised by the colonial past, Sonatrach was forced to look elsewhere for partners. This was only of limited success and, by February 1971, Sonatrach still only produced 30 per cent of crude oil and 25 per cent of natural gas production, and held just over 50 per cent of oil transport rights (Ghozali, 1972). As a result, an increasingly acrimonious debate developed between Algeria and France which led finally in February 1971 to the unilateral nationalization of French petroleum interests in Algeria. Although these nationalizations strained Algeria's diplomatic relations with France, in practice they amounted only to Sonatrach acquiring the majority shareholding in the various ventures it had undertaken with the French oil companies. However, although in many ways these nationalizations were no more than a symbolic act, they did result, during the initial period of estrangement, in the signature of a series of partnership contracts between Sonatrach and a variety of non-French partners, such as Sun Oil, Getty Oil and Amoco of the US, Hispanoil (Spain), Copex (Poland), Petrobras (Brazil), and Deminex (West Germany) (Mahiout, 1974; Mazri,[9] 1975).

After the 1971 nationalizations, Sonatrach grew enormously. For example, in 1972 it employed approximately 15,000 people but by 1978, its labour force had grown to 86,759 people (*Liste des Sns*, 1980) which made it the second largest employer after the Public Building and Works sector. It thus accounted for around 12 per cent of Algeria's industrial labour force and, while providing the bulk of Algeria's exports, also absorbed a considerable proportion of budget resources (36 per cent of industrial investment in the First Four-Year Plan). Furthermore, Sonatrach was a very active player in the international money markets, borrowing in the year 1979: $535m, DM 20m, Y 780bn – a total of some $447m. At the same time, Sonatrach made frequent calls in the international press for tenders to supply it with equipment and services; for example, of a random number of eleven tenders noted in the British press during 1980, five were for Sonatrach or her subsidiaries.[10] As a result of these actions, it was calculated that Sonatrach's share of Algeria's hard currency debt of $19bn in 1978 was $9bn or 47 per cent (*Financial Times*, 14.1.80).

These figures serve to illustrate that oil revenues were in practice insufficient both to cover new investment and fund the development of other industrial sectors.

This continual growth of Sonatrach and the expansion of her activities resulted in the creation of twelve subsidiary companies,[11] enlarging even further an already over-large industrial state enterprise.[12] A recognition of the potential dangers of this continuous expansion forced the Boumediene-successor government of President Chadli Benjadid to undertake a review of Sonatrach's economic performance, as a result of which there was a reorganization of both Sonatrach and her subsidiary companies. However, this reorganization created instead three large constituent companies: the Entreprise Nationale de Raffinage et de Distribution de Produits Pétroliers, the Entreprise Nationale de Grands Travaux Pétroliers, and the Entreprise Nationale de Plastique et Caoutchouc; this did not of itself solve the problems which had been accumulating as a result of the motor role which industrial development strategy had assigned to the oil and gas sector. Furthermore, even though Sonatrach itself had been broken up, its monopoly power remained as the whole enterprise was brought under direct ministerial control with the Minister of Energy combining his ministerial post with that of Head of Sonatrach. Indeed, in some ways the shift of power from Sonatrach itself to a Government Ministry only served to reaffirm the processes of bureaucratization. This reorganization also resulted in the departure of all three architects of Sonatrach's growth in the 1970s: Sidahmed Ghozali (President), Sidahmed Boukadji (Director of Finance) and Nordine Ait Laouissine (Director of Exports and Executive Vice-President).[13]

Algeria was similar to the other oil-producing countries of the Middle East in that oil exports made up the major part of its foreign commerce. This was a marked change from the colonial period in Algeria and even from the first years of independence. For example, in 1966 energy raw material represented 54–59 per cent of exports, the remaining 40 per cent being agricultural exports in which the most important individual commodity was wine (20 per cent). By 1973, the share of agricultural products in exports had declined to 7 per cent and continued to decline afterwards, while energy exports continued to acquire a more and more dominant position, so that by 1977 they accounted for 85 per cent of total exports (ASA 1977–78). Although the shift away from agricultural exports meant that Algeria's foreign trade was less dependent upon the vagaries of natural phenomena, petroleum-exporting is nevertheless subject to the vagaries of changing political and economic climates. This had already been shown by the effects of the 1967 Arab/Israeli war when it was the combined weakness of the Arab states that was most in evidence. As a result of a more successful intervention in the 1973 Yom Kippur war and the development of some solidarity between them, there was a translation of this solidarity into a more agresssive stance on the world oil scene. However, although during the 1970s oil prices grew steadily (for example, Algerian government oil revenues were $145m in 1966 but had risen to $280m in 1970), production did not grow as rapidly. In 1966, production stood at $33,868 \times 10^3$ tonnes; in 1969, $44,784 \times 10^3$ tonnes; and in 1977, $52,001 \times 10^3$ tonnes (ASA, 1970, 1970–78; CCIA, 1974). Moreover, by 1970 around 95 per cent of oil produced was being exported. Furthermore, production itself did not grow as steadily as the figures themselves suggest, with the years 1974 and 1975 showing a decline in overall production.

Oil is of course an exhaustible commodity, and Algerian oil reserves were not considered to be as large as those of the other main producers – Saudi Arabia, Iran and Libya. One result of this was to make Algerian Saharan oil the most expensive on the market in 1980 because of the fears that the earnings from it were only temporary. Certainly, the Algerian planners saw the future in terms of their country's natural gas reserves, even though exploitation of these was largely beyond Algeria's technical capacity in the 1970s and 1980s. Instead, Algeria exported the crude natural gas on similar terms to those for the export of oil. Among its major customers were the US El Paso company, Britain's National Gas corporation and Gaz de France. However, natural gas is highly volatile, and the form in which it was being exported from Algeria was that of LNG (Liquified Natural Gas). As a result, as its exports expanded, it was necessary for Algeria to invest continually in the extension of its storage facilities for LNG as well as in tanker bulk carriers for transport. Thus in order to export this commodity, extensive investment was necessary. However, this kind of investment is high-risk, for two main reasons. In the first place, there is the physical vulnerability of plant and equipment, illustrated by a freak storm in the Mediterranean in December 1980 which forced aground a Uruguayan tanker. The tanker damaged breakwaters, two jetties and the supply pipelines at the main LNG port, Arzew. As a direct consequence, Arzew's three gas-liquefaction plants had to cease activity as did the oil refinery and an ammonia and fertilizer plant. That so much productive capacity was affected was the result of Algeria's political economy of concentrating industrial development around selected towns – the industrial 'centres of attraction' – of which Arzew was one. In order to overcome this dependence on surface plant and equipment, the Algerian policy-makers sought the construction of a natural gas pipeline to Europe via Sicily and Italy. However, the project was not to be finally realized until 1983 (*Financial Times*, 14.12.83). However, while such a pipeline may have facilitated LNG supply to Europe, it was not doing much for either employment or technical development at home.

The second area of vulnerability lay in the actual pricing policies of natural gas. In world market terms, natural gas commands a much lower price than oil; however, for the Algerians, who saw their long-term future in natural gas and not in oil, there appeared to be a need to price up the country's natural gas, and more particularly to renegotiate the long-term supply contracts which had been signed in the early 1970s. The policy led in the 1980s to the suspension of several of these older supply contracts, most notably with the US company El Paso and with Gaz de France. In the short term of course, this meant reduced revenues for the Algerian state, with the result that the state undermined its own policies by seeking ways in which it could continue to supply LNG to those customers to whom, theoretically, it had suspended supplies. This was primarily done by continuing to supply the contract, billing at the new desired price but accepting in practice the original negotiated price.[14]

These difficulties over the pricing of Algerian gas indicate the problems which were faced in the attempt to compete in the global market. As a result, attempts were made to find alternative strategies. Among these alternative strategies which were tried by the Algerian government in the post-Boumediene era was barter. It was a policy which chiefly involved the Japanese and resulted from a Japanese trade mission of April 1981.

In practice, although Algeria's oil and gas were the major suppliers of foreign capital resources to the economy, the nation's industrial planning policies were dependent on its becoming more than a mere extractor and supplier of crude raw materials. Although in strategic terms it made sense for the Algerian economy to move into the petrochemicals industry proper, nevertheless there were many problems which it had to face in order to enter what was and is a highly competitive and relatively tight market. One of the major problems was the protectionist measures which were being taken by the existing producer countries and their companies. For example, in 1980 the European Centre of Chemical Manufacturers' Federations (CEFIC) opposed plans by the EEC to ease restrictions on chemical imports from Third World countries. At the time, quota restrictions on chemical imports into the EEC covered about thirty products and the EEC Commission wished to reduce this list to eleven products. However, CEFIC argued that there was already a serious overcapacity in basic petrochemical production in Europe and blocked the proposed changes. This blocking did not prevent the oil producing states from moving into the manufacture of basic chemicals (*Financial Times*, 29.3.84) but it did act to restrict their potential markets. One of the reasons they continued to pursue such developments was that during the 1970s the price of naptha (the basic raw material of the petrochemical industry) had risen sharply, from $125 a tonne in 1974 to between $323 and $335 in 1980. However, even an entry into the production of basic chemicals does not solve the underlying inequalities because all that the majors have to do is to shift their production into higher-value speciality chemicals and, as they have technical superiority, they can go on doing this for ever.

The Algerian planners tried to pre-empt this problem by seeking to develop their home market. However, that primarily meant a more technologically-orientated and capital-intensive agriculture. Unfortunately, as discussion in the previous chapter has already indicated, agriculture was seen primarily in political and ideological terms and its development was subject to the need to respond to the effects of rural dispossession. Consequently, agriculture was severely undercapitalized, which meant that it could not provide the necessary market for the products of the chemical industry. As a result, Algeria had to continue to rely on its export capacity, which was increased by extending the number of trading partners and replacing crude oil with natural gas, refined products, condensate and liquified petroleum gas (LPG) (*Financial Times,* 1.9.83, 17.10.83, 18.1.84) but this still did not achieve the planned development of the economy.

Algerian state enterprises – the *société nationale*

The utilization of the *société nationale* (SN – state enterprise) as the principal motor of industrial activity in the Algerian economy did not take place until after the accession to power of President Houari Boumediene in June 1965. Prior to 1965, only five SNs had been created. However, by 1970, the number of SNs in the industrial sector of the economy had risen to twenty-six. As industrialization continued, smaller SNs were absorbed within larger SNs as, for example, in the sugar industry, shoe industry, chemicals, wood and cork, textiles and mechanical engineering as well as the petroleum industry. At the same time as the number of SNs grew, so did the ministerial infrastructure which was required to maintain the SN system. The SN became the primary basis of Algerian industrial production as well as the means by which it was envisaged that a planned development of the Algerian economy would be implemented. The rationale behind this decision to adopt a system of state-controlled and -managed industrial enterprises was described in these terms as 'the recovery[15] and streamlining of the essential sectors of national industry' but where also 'this control by the state of the means of production is dependent on the support of the workers who will be associated with every aspect of the life of the enterprise.' (First Four-Year Plan, 1970)

The SN was therefore a state-owned enterprise regulated by Government statute, the complexity of whose structure varied according to the size of the industry it represented. However, the overall basic structure consisted of a national headquarters, usually in Algiers, which was responsible for the determination of general policy and the coordination of the activities of the various production units within it. In practice of course, some of the provincial production units enjoyed a considerable amount of local autonomy as, for example, the El-Hadjar plant of SNS at Annaba which as Algeria's largest iron and steel plant operated as a largely self-contained unit. Each SN was supervised by a minimum of three Government ministries, usually the Ministry of Finance, the Planning Ministry and one of the sector Ministries such as the Ministry of Energy and Petrochemical Industries, the Ministry of Heavy Industry or the Ministry of Light Industry. This expansion of sector Ministries was a product of the Boumediene period and reflects two simultaneous processes which were both the cause and the result of the decision to attempt the industrialization of Algeria through a system of state-controlled and managed industries. As Nove (1986: 20) points out, the share size of planning requirements in a state-controlled enterprise system means that the sytem is forced to expand its planning apparatus because as the number of industries under its control increases so does the complexity of the decisions which have to be made about the interrelationships between each component of the system.[16] However, the technical problems which were associated with an integrated state enterprise and planning system had not been subject to much serious analysis and the contemporary critiques of the Algerian system did not focus on these internal structural issues but were concerned with it at an ideological level, as a model of an ideal socialist economy.[17]

The ideological role of the SN in Algeria's industrial development and planning structure as well as the practical problems of the system can be illustrated by an examination of one such SN: SONIC (Société Nationale des Industries de la Cellulose), which had responsibility for the development of the paper industry. SONIC was in fact one of the smaller SNs but it embodied the central principles of Algerian planning. Essentially, this meant both the designation of the SN as representative of a particular sector of economic activity and its use as the means of mutual dependence between sectors. SONIC illustrates this principle in that it derived its raw materials from Algerian agriculture but was also dependent for certain processing techniques upon the production of chemicals from the chemical industry and, finally, was a sector whose finished products feed simultaneously into both industrial and consumer markets. The Algerian national daily, *El Moudjahid* (24.8.72)argued that as 'a big consumer of chemical products, the cellulose [i.e. paper] industry will encourage the development of other chemical industries', while 'the modern role played by this base industry will have the effect equally of giving a major boost to the level of agricultural production' and as a result the paper industry 'will contribute to the economic take-off of our country and towards her independence'. However, the paper industry is also internationally a highly competitive industrial sector which in the early 1970s was severely hit by recession in the western economies; consequently it also provides an example of the tensions within a system designed to encourage the internal development of industrial production but also required to compete within a global market.

SONIC was created by a Government Ordinance in January 1968, in other words after the inauguration of the first planning exercise of the Boumediene era – the 1967–70 Three-Year Plan. It is therefore a product of the shift in economic policy towards planning and the creation of state enterprises. The paper industry itself was not envisaged as being at the cutting edge of economic policy during the period of the First Four-Year Plan. However in certain wilaya, for example the Mostaganem wilaya, paper might in practice be more important locally. For example, the SONIC plant at Mostaganem was described as 'one of the largest industrial plants in the Mostaganem wilaya' (*El Moudjahid*, 24.5.74) because although its permanent industrial staff was only 650, it made use of some 20–30,000 seasonal workers in the cultivation of esparto grass (*alfa*).

On establishment in 1968, SONIC was little more than a 'paper' creation, as the first of the two initial plants under its control, El Harrach, was not nationalized until the end of 1968; and the second, Ain El Hadjar, was nationalized in October 1969. Furthermore, even together these two plants accounted for only 6 per cent of Algeria's paper and board production.[18] It was not therefore until the nationalization of two further plants – the Cellunaf plant at Baba Ali in May 1971, and Sonic Chlore (a subsidiary of the Belgian firm of Solvay) in January 1972 – that SONIC could be said to have had any real impact on production within the Algerian paper industry. The nationalization of these two plants increased its share of paper industry production to 46 per cent. The ex-Cellunaf plant was an integrated esparto pulp and paper mill which produced around 22,000 tonnes of paper per annum, of which about one-half was then exported. It employed six hundred people. The Sonic Chlore plant (also at Baba Ali) employed fewer than one hundred people, but its production process – the manufacture of sodium chloride – was the only one of its kind in Algeria. It was with the nationalization of these two plants that it is possible to say that the basis of an Algerian paper industry was laid. However, this also serves to illustrate just how cautious in practice the nationalization policy was.

The subsequent expansion of Algeria's paper industry was mainly concentrated at El Harrach (near Algiers), where what began as a plan merely to modernize existing facilities became one where an entirely new plant would be built to be able to produce annually 25,000 tonnes of folding box card and 21,500 tonnes of kraft paper (compared to the Saida plant which aimed to produce 33,000 tonnes of printing paper, and 66,000 tonnes of bleached *alfa*). The El Harrach production was to be used in the manufacture of cement sacks and wrapping paper and the expansion was intended to create 250 new jobs; and indeed by 1978, El Harrach was employing 722 people in its folding box card section and 130 in the paper sacks section. However, the market for the output of paper sacks was dependent upon the development of the cement industry; consequently, its continued expansion was heavily dependent on industrial development in other sectors of the economy.

Unfortunately, the cement industry upon which El Harrach's production capacity of paper sacks relied consisted of two automated cement plants at Hadjar Soud (which was severely affected by floods in 1973) and Meftah (Algiers); and three medium-capacity plants at Sétif, Saida and El Asnam (which suffered a severe earthquake in 1980); plus three former plants from the colonial era at Rais Hamidou (ex-Ponte Pescade, Algiers), Zahana (Oran), and Meftah (Algiers). Besides its dependence upon the cement industry, the El Harrach plant was also dependent upon the supply of straw pulp, manufactured at the SONIC plant at Saida, as well as imported unbleached and bleached kraft and waste paper. However, the reconstruction of the Saida plant was not begun until December 1973, and can be seen as part of the project to ensure that materially poorer and more marginal areas were not neglected. The Saida wilaya is a relatively large wilaya which covers the western part of the Saharan Atlas mountains and was consequently not particularly prosperous and had suffered from rural depopulation stemmed only by the imposition of restrictions on emigration. The reconstruction of the

Saida complex was thus intended to provide industrial employment and prevent further emigration, thereby illustrating another of the tensions within the Algerian project of simultaneously attempting to compensate the poor while building an industrial base. The aim of the reconstruction of the Saida plant was to increase employment within a plant which had employed fewer than 60 people to one which was capable of employing more than 1,000.

The third of SONIC's major new plants – the Mostaganem complex – despite construction having begun in 1970, was not completed until 1974. While the El Harrach plant was linked to the projected development needs of the cement industry, the plant at Mostaganem was projected to use the increased acreage given over to growing esparto grass, hence its design as an integrated esparto pulp and paper mill. Moreover, Mostaganem is situated in Algeria's major esparto-growing area. The esparto plantations of southern Oran in fact supplied around 60 per cent of Algeria's esparto.[19] Consequently at the same time as the paper industry grew so did the area which was under esparto cultivation. Although Mostaganem illustrates the potential for the integration of agriculture and industry, it also illustrates the gap which existed between the creation of modern industrial plants with relatively a small labour force and the technological level of agriculture where it was labour that was most abundant. This is also another illustration of the delays which often took place in the actual building of key industrial plants.

The use of esparto grass in the Algerian paper industry and its importance to it stem from esparto's unique fibre character which makes it one of the finest pulps for high-grade printing papers. Apart from esparto, the other major raw material in the Algerian paper industry was wood pulp, of which the greater part was imported. However, in an attempt to fill this gap, eucalyptus trees were planted. Although these grow fast, they are not particularly good environmentally as they prevent natural regeneration of the soil. Furthermore, the demand for wood pulp exceeded Algeria's capacity to produce it, and its importing continued. However, in other respects, the paper industry did go some way towards the fulfilment of the planners' ideal of one industrial sector feeding off another, in that SONIC could be supplied with soda and liquid chlorine from the chemical complexes at Skikda; nitric acid and ammonia from Arzew; sulphuric acid from Ghazaouet; and sulphur, kaolin, lime and glue from local sources; which left only sulphate and sodium chlorate to be imported.

Although the paper industry was an example of internal linkages at work, it is also an international industry just as were many of the other industries which Algeria was seeking to develop – an international industry dominated by North America and to some extent Japan which in the early 1970s was contracting with a number of large European paper companies already experiencing difficulties. Examples of such companies were Bowater (UK), Groupement Européen de la Cellulose (France), and Norrlands Skogsågares Cellulose (Sweden). Algeria was therefore attempting to develop a paper industry at a time when internationally the industry was in difficulty and when internally her own consumption of paper and board was low; for example, in 1969 it was around 14.5 kilos per head (ASA, 1970), whereas in the US at the same time it was 250.7 kilos per head and in Japan, 108.8 kilos per head (OECD, 1972). Since 1969, Algeria's paper industry has grown rapidly at a time when the overall production of paper packaging and wrapping products has been declining.

Thus SONIC founded in 1968 to create a state presence in the paper industry, with four plants at the beginning of 1972, had increased the number of plants under her control to eleven and its workforce to more than five thousand in 1978. As with the majority of SNs, its headquarters were in Algiers and it was administered through a formalized pattern decreed by the Government Ordinance which created it. The Director-General was appointed separately by means of a Government decree and on the advice of the tutelage ministry, in this case the Ministry of Light Industry. The amount of basic or social capital allocated was a decision of the Light Industry Ministry and the Ministry of Finance. This was a fixed amount which the Director-General could not increase independently but only following advice from an 'orientation committee' which was comprised of thirteen members: six Ministry representatives (Light Industry, Agriculture and Agrarian Reform, the Interior, Commerce, Finance and the Plan), a representative from the ruling party (the FLN), a representative from the main trade union organization (the UGTA), plus two employee representatives, two advisors (both chosen by the Ministry of Light Industry), and the Director-General. This 'orientation committee' had to meet a minimum of three times a year, at meetings called not by the Director-General but by the non-executive President who was also a Government nominee. Committee members held office for a period of three years. Although it was a system designed in principle to ensure the accountability of all parties at all levels, in practice it displays once again many of the self-generating features required to operate a planned economy which results in the control of industry being seen as an administrative process rather than a market-dependent process (Nove, 1986). The result was a system which could not avoid bottlenecks, and which was frequently characterized by a lack of decision-making and individual enterprise.

The failure of the SN to generate the industrial development envisaged by the planners was not unique to Algeria. Furthermore, the scale of the Algerian project was in practice quite small; mass movements of population such as those which fed the Soviet industrialization project of the 1920s and 1930s were not part of the vision of the Algerian planners. Their goal was industrial development in tandem with a reconstruction of agriculture which would both enable the mass of the population to stay on the land and also reward it for the losses it had suffered as a result of colonization and the liberation struggle. It was not a project of dislocation, which is why it should be seen as being in the tradition of the French economic planners of post-1945. The problems which arose can be seen as a consequence not only of the limitations of a centrally-planned economy but also of the nature of the project undertaken, built as it was upon the foundations of a disequilibrated colonial economy. However, the project raised high expectations among a rural and industrial labour force excluded from the benefits which had accrued within the colonial economy. Furthermore, the project's failure to provide the employment promised helped feed the disillusionment of the new labour force, created by the educational reforms of the planning system, who were to reject the basis of the project itself and turn to other ideologies for answers. The next section of this chapter will therefore focus on the impact which these developments had on the formation of the labour force in post-independence Algeria.

Labour in the post-independence economy

This section turns its attention to the labour market and its interaction with the planning project. If the industrial structure reflected Algeria's colonial past, so did the labour market, with particular consequences for the skilled sector of the labour market which had previously been dominated by foreign or colon labour, leaving the unskilled-labour market more or less exclusively to the Algerian Muslim. The post-independence governments were very conscious of the distortions within the labour market both from the ideological stance of justice and from the practical stance that the mass departure of the colon population had also effectively taken with it the bulk of the skilled industrial labour force. Consequently, there was yet a further tension as demands for justice and positive action by the victims of this distorted and unequal labour-market structure met the effects of its unequalness in terms of the constraints which they imposed on its restructuring. For example, the massive shifts in the structure of the labour market which needed to take place in order for there to be equal representation for the new Algeria could not be achieved instantaneously as neither was there a nationwide system of industrial education nor had even basic education been widely available. The goal of the planners to revalorize the labour market could not be met in the short term. In effect not only was the discourse of industrialization dependent on establishing the required industrial base, it also had to create the conditions for the expansion and development of a qualified industrial labour force.

In considering the labour market of the Boumediene era, the following general points need to be made. One of the most significant aspects of the labour market was that, while the population always showed a steady increase, the actual officially registered working population remained largely static at around the two and a half million mark. Secondly, while there was an overall increase in the industrial working population, the distribution between the sexes also remained largely static. Thirdly, and perhaps not surprisingly, the structure of male employment was different from that of women's employment and did not change dramatically in spite of the industrialization project. The main areas of male employment were in Public Building and Works, the Iron and Steel Industry, the Petroleum sector, Transport and the Food Industries; and the main employment area for women was Textiles.

In the 1966 Census, Algeria's total population was calculated to be just over 12 million and was divided almost equally between men and women. In the 1977 Census, the total population was now almost 17 million with a slight balance in favour of women (8.6 million women to 8.4 million men). During this same period the industrial labour force doubled but from a very low base, i.e. from 310,106 in 1970 to 632,510 in 1977. Tables 6.2 and 6.3 help to illustrate the main lines of development which were occurring in the labour market in this early period. These were a slight shift in employment from the private sector which accounted for 34 per cent of employment in 1970 and 30 per cent in 1977 to the public sector (66 per cent in 1970 and 70 per cent in 1977). This shift was partly accounted for by the fact that three sectors – namely, petroleum; finance and banking; and gas, water and electricity – were by 1977 exclusively in public ownership. Although overall there was a move away from the private sector to the public sector, in three sectors the shift was in the opposite direction. These sectors were public building and works (47 per cent in 1970 to 53 per cent in 1977), the food industries (26 per cent in 1970 to 29 per cent in 1977), and more particularly textiles, where private-sector employment accounted for 25 per cent of the total in 1970 but in 1977 accounted for 45 per cent of employment in this sector. In addition, in three other industrial sectors, while private-sector employment had declined overall, it still accounted for a substantial proportion of employment in the sector as a whole. These three sectors were wood and timber products (63 per cent in 1970, 46 per cent in 1977), chemicals and rubber (55 per cent in 1970, 45 per cent in 1977), and leather and leather goods (35 per cent in 1970, 29 per cent in 1977). The third factor to emerge from these employment figures is that they mirrored the image of Algerian industrial policy during the Boumediene period, that is a concentration upon the heavy goods sector of the economy and in particular the petroleum sector. This meant that there was a neglect of the consumer industries sector, which had two main consequences. In the first place, it created the classic problem of state-controlled economies, the inability to meet expanding consumer demand; and secondly, it left the consumer sector largely in the private sector and orientated towards the import of consumer goods.

Tables 6.2 and 6.3 show that the industries which experienced the greatest growth in employment had very different skill requirements, even though they were all primarily sectors where a high skill content was required: petroleum, iron and steel, gas, water and electricity; as well as, but for different reasons, finance and banking. However, while it was these sectors along with the construction materials sector which grew the most rapidly, the major employing sector remained public building works which demands a large but relatively unskilled labour force. Tables 6.4 and 6.5 show in greater detail how the labour force was divided within each industrial sector between the different skill categories. In a sense, what one observes is a parallel process of the bureaucratization of the labour market in which there is an increasing differentiation between different categories of workers. For example, the former category of 'qualified and highly qualified personnel' (*personnel qualifié et hautement qualifié*) is now two separate categories of 'qualified personnel and qualified workers' (*personnel qualifié et ouvriers qualifiés*) and 'technical staff and higher qualified personnel' (*agents techniques et personnel hautement qualifié*). This process of sub-division and differentiation can be attributed to the growth of industry and to the elaboration of educational facilities; and more particularly, to the development of technical education in Algeria after 1970. This was characterized by the creation of Science and Technology universities at both Algiers and Oran, as well as the development of professional training courses at a variety of Institutes and Colleges directly associated with the relevant industry sector. Examples of these are the 'Post and Telecommunications Central Schools' which were responsible for training technicians for the postal and telecommunications industry, and the 'Training Centres' of the SNs which provided training for technicians and unskilled workers. Perhaps, from the point of view of the ideological links with France which have underpinned most of post-independence Algerian policy-making, the most significant of these new forms of professional training came from the creation of the *École Nationale d'Administration* for the purpose of forming the upper administrative cadres.[20]

Table 6.2 Main sectors of employment in the Algerian economy in 1970

Industry sector	Total employed	Public sector		Private sector	Total men	Total women
		State	Self-managed			
Public building and works	106,925	54,354	2,087	50,484	106,069	855
Iron and steel	9,024	8,426	—	598	8,474	550
Engineering	22,595	9,915	3,028	9,652	21,804	791
Petroleum	16,240	10,155	—	6,085	15,477	763
Transport	32,743	19,137	6,646	6,960	32,088	655
Food and tobacco	28,032	19,140	1,653	7,239	26,574	1,458
Textiles	26,245	16,553	3,032	6,660	18,293	7,952
Paper	5,535	2,516	1,531	1,488	5,225	310
Timber	8,876	2,631	606	5,639	8,769	107
Construction materials	8,404	2,614	4,902	888	8,354	50
Mines and quarries	14,760	13,355	752	653	14,730	30
Finance and banking	9,031	8,242	—	789	7,414	1,617
Gas, water, electricity	6,344	5,972	—	372	6,109	235
Chemicals and rubber	7,411	3,110	212	4,089	7,011	400
Leather and leather goods	5,828	3,577	121	2,130	5,391	437
Other	2,113	166	90	1,857	2,029	85
Total	310,106	179,867	24,660	105,583	293,811	16,295

Source: RADP, Direction des Statistiques (1970) *La Situation de l'emploi et des salaires 1970.*

Table 6.3   Main sectors of employment in the Algerian economy in 1977

Industry sector	Total employed	Public sector[1]	Private sector	Total men	Total women
Public building and works	200,468	94,956	105,512	197,740	2,728
Iron and steel	28,486	27,680	806 }	78,052	4,662
Engineering	54,228	38,464	15,764 }		
Petroleum	73,870	73,870	—	69,397	4,473
Transport	63,875	54,654	9,221	60,839	3,036
Food and tobacco	43,804	31,255	12,549	41,151	2,653
Textiles	33,699	18,470	15,229	23,646	10,053
Paper	10,889	8,860	2,029 }	22,416	1,215
Timber	12,742	6,844	5,898 }		
Construction materials	22,780	20,628	2,152	21,328	1,451
Mines and quarries	19,746	16,524	3,222	19,258	488
Finance and banking	22,266	22,266	—	18,378	3,888
Gas, water, electricity	16,593	16,593	—	15,794	799
Chemicals and rubber	14,704	8,041	6,663	14,031	673
Leather and leather goods	7,366	5,203	2,163	7,068	298
Other	6,994	614	6,380	6,657	37
Total	632,510	444,922	187,588	595,755	36,755

Note: [1] After 1973, there is no separate accounting in the Public Sector between the *sociétés nationales* or state enterprises and the *autogestion* or self-managed sector.

Source: RADP, Direction des Statistiques et de la Comptabilité Nationale (1978) *Les Résultats de l'enquête emploi et salaires de 1977*.

The development of educational opportunities formed a central part of the rhetoric of the post-independence Algerian government, and education was projected as a means by which inherited inequalities of the colonial period could be eliminated in the post-colonial era. Education and culture may have been seen at an ideological level to form part of a triad comprised of industry, agriculture and culture (as, for example, in a speech by Boumediene on 4 July 1971, when he declared: 'The cultural revolution is the culmination of our all-embracing revolution built upon the three pillars of the industrial, agrarian and cultural revolutions' (quoted in Baghli 1978)); in practice, however, the Algerian regime neglected the cultural aspects of the revolution. Furthermore, the focus

Table 6.4 Skill categories of Algeria's industrial labour force in 1970

Industry sector	Unskilled workers / unqualified personnel			Skilled workers / personal assistants			Higher qualified and qualified personnel			Foremen and middle management			Management and senior management		
	Public state	Public S-M	Private	Public state	Public S-M	Private	Public state	Public S-M	Private	Public state	Public S-M	Private	Public state	Public S-M	Private
Public building and works	20,763	1,128	25,394	7,066	409	8,380	22,557	789	15,398	3,153	27	858	815	27	454
Engineering	1,894	939	1,351	2,875	757	1,757	4,144	1,138	5,550	535	103	492	367	91	502
Iron and steel	2,292	—	219	2,460	—	228	2,932	—	128	489	—	5	253	—	18
Petroleum	1,584	—	955	2,051	—	1,667	5,135	—	2,860	676	—	384	709	—	219
Transport	4,574	917	1,406	3,311	798	1,323	9,970	4,838	3,306	938	33	466	344	60	459
Food and tobacco	8,479	714	2,765	5,129	474	2,143	4,728	321	1,853	498	88	232	306	56	246
Textiles	4,966	1,128	2,597	3,774	540	1,978	7,168	1,101	1,845	513	215	140	132	48	100
Paper	541	404	661	448	484	262	1,282	563	466	148	31	44	93	49	58
Timber	835	202	2,024	700	—	1,393	1,002	337	1,940	51	45	175	43	22	107
Construction materials	1,059	3,044	516	551	921	257	891	804	82	76	64	15	37	69	18
Mines and quarries	7,826	467	197	67	132	147	3,432	132	204	1,563	7	79	467	14	26
Finance and banking	676	—	234	1,343	—	21	5,349	—	354	470	—	121	404	—	59
Gas, water, electricity	478	—	143	615	—	76	4,324	—	106	310	—	31	245	—	16
Chemicals and rubber	1,067	41	973	967	64	1,145	833	94	1,460	162	6	356	81	7	155
Leather and leather goods	622	45	584	175	38	628	2,601	19	816	104	6	62	75	13	40
Other	3	45	962	63	—	416	83	—	371	9	34	65	8	11	43
Total	57,659	8,781	40,981	31,595	4,617	21,821	76,432	10,136	36,739	9,795	659	3,525	4,378	467	2,517
% in each category	32.1	35.6	38.9	17.6	18.7	20.7	42.5	41.1	34.8	5.4	2.7	3.3	2.4	1.9	2.4

S-M, self-managed sector.

Source: RADP, Direction des Statistiques (1970) La Situation de l'emploi et des salaires 1970.

Table 6.5 Skill categories of Algeria's industrial labour force in 1977

Industry Sector	Unskilled workers State[2]	Unskilled workers Private	Skilled workers/personal assistants State	Skilled workers/personal assistants Private	Qualified workers/personnel[1] State	Qualified workers/personnel[1] Private	Technicians and higher qualified personnel State	Technicians and higher qualified personnel Private	Senior technical staff State	Senior technical staff Private	Management and senior management State	Management and senior management Private
Public building and works	33,425	49,591	14,623	13,717	30,481	27,433	10,540	11,606	3,608	2,110	2,279	1,055
Iron and steel[3]	9,128	3,870	16,230	2,895	22,703	6,223	10,972	2,240	4,096	845	3,015	497
Petroleum	25,336	—	10,333	—	23,734	—	—	—	8,533	—	5,934	—
Transport	16,888	1,936	8,635	1,752	15,139	3,781	8,471	1,199	3,553	461	1,968	92
Food and tobacco	11,033	5,271	6,282	2,133	6,282	3,137	4,407	1,255	2,407	502	844	261
Textiles	3,140	4,112	3,602	2,894	7,296	6,701	2,383	914	1,477	303	572	305
Paper and timber[4]	2,361	1,770	2,890	3,010	5,427	2,372	2,808	358	1,542	238	676	179
Construction materials	6,786	1,097	6,003	732	4,146	258	1,444	65	1,341	—	908	—
Mines and quarries	7,056	1,547	330	354	4,313	644	2,231	451	1,768	65	826	161
Finance and banking	2,672	—	3,496	—	7,437	—	5,165	—	1,581	—	1,915	—
Gas, water, electricity	4,621	—	615	—	4,825	—	2,874	—	2,764	—	894	—
Chemicals and rubber	1,222	666	1,198	3,798	3,257	999	1,053	933	700	200	611	67
Leather and leather goods	385	411	1,072	779	2,201	325	1,056	497	359	108	130	43
Other	73	2,360	50	1,276	407	1,978	61	—	13	447	10	319
Total	124,126	72,631	75,359	33,340	137,648	53,851	53,465	19,518	33,742	5,279	20,582	2,969
% in each category	27.9	38.7	16.9	17.8	30.9	28.7	12.0	10.4	7.6	2.8	4.6	1.6

Notes: [1] This represents the former 'Higher qualified/qualified personnel' category. [2] The self-managed sector is included within the state sector. [3] Includes engineering. [4] Paper and timber are one category.

Source: RADP, Direction des Statistiques et de la Comptabilité Nationale (1978) *Les Résultats de l'enquête emploi et salaires de 1977.*

on industrial education ignored the fact that over 20 per cent of the labour force was still directly involved in agriculture and a further 7 per cent was in different forms of non-permanent employment.

Furthermore, even though general education expanded[21] – for example in 1965–66, just after independence, the ratio of primary to secondary pupils was 11:1; by 1977–78, this was 4:1; and the number of pupils in each sector had risen from 1.3 million primary students in 1965–66 to 2.9 million in 1977–78 and secondary pupils from 0.1 million in 1965–66 to 0.7 million in 1977–78 – it should be remembered that this expansion was accompanied by an increase in both population (which meant more young people) and numbers of young people whose education had been interrupted by the independence struggle. Such students were still entering mainstream education in the 1970s. The other major factor concerns the ratio of girls to boys at the different levels of the education system. These changed much more slowly than the overall increase in the numbers of young people entering the system. At the primary level, girls were 38 per cent of the school population in 1965–66 and 41 per cent in 1977–78. At the secondary level, they were 29 per cent in 1965–66 and 36 per cent in 1977–78. In higher education, where the numbers of students in 1965–66 had been eight thousand, the ratio of girls to boys was 1:4; and although by 1977–78, there were then almost 50,000 students in higher education, girls were still only 1:3 of the student population; moreover they were heavily concentrated in certain subject areas. The two broad sectors which young women were choosing were those of Medicine, Dentistry and Pharmacy and the Arts, Human and Social Sciences. In the former they made up almost 40 per cent of the student population and in the latter just under a third; whereas in Science and Technology, and Law, they numbered less than one-fifth of the student population. The unevenness of the impact of post-independence education policies on girls and boys also reflects the ambivalent discourse in the Plans to equal opportunity for women and men in the post-independent state.[22]

The level of education and training of the workforce is one aspect of labour market policies; the other concerns the organization of labour and how it impacts on industrial structures. Post-independence Algeria had only one trade union, with the result that collective bargaining between labour and capital was not a feature of Algerian industrial relations. Instead wages and salaries were determined by the state as part of overall economic planning. This included a ceiling on earnings which in 1974 was 2,000 DA (or £200) per month. Table 6.6 gives an official view of the development of wages and salaries during the Boumediene period.

Table 6.6 Evolution of hourly wage rates by level of qualification, all sectors, 1969–77

Level of qualification	1969	1970	1971	1972	1973	1974	1975	1976	1977	1969–77 % increase
Higher qualified workers	3.51	4.10	3.95	3.86	4.39	4.43	4.71	4.93	5.55	+58
Qualified workers	2.06	3.20	3.25	3.58	3.49	3.88	4.30	4.41	4.71	+129
Skilled workers	2.33	2.55	2.64	3.18	2.87	3.35	3.45	3.77	4.23	+81
Unskilled workers	1.82	1.85	1.81	1.89	2.12	2.35	2.62	2.87	2.35	+29

Source: RADP (1978) *Annuaire statistique de l'Algérie 1977–8.*

Table 6.7 Evolution of monthly salaries by level of qualification, all sectors, 1969–77

Level of qualification	1969	1970	1971	1972	1973	1974	1975	1976	1977	1969–77 % increase
Management/senior management	1765	1871	1809	1887	1939	2120	2221	2413	2686	+52
Senior technical staff	1238	1171	1263	1356	1328	1480	1518	1608	1754	+41
Technicians/section heads	935	929	970	980	1009	1085	1301	1263	1376	+47
Qualified/higher qualified personnel	783	764	760	790	810	912	934	1055	1174	+50
Personal assistants/admin staff	614	526	639	610	675	734	776	817	880	+43
Unqualified admin staff/other	498	512	516	529	553	573	580	667	656	+32

Source: RADP (1978) *Annuaire statistique de l'Algérie 1977–8.*

The purpose of imposing a ceiling was to prevent the growth of disparities in income between wage-earners and salaried staffs that were such a feature of Third World countries. However, although the ceiling did prevent the development of substantive differences in salary levels, it did not prevent the development of differentials generally. This was because the different SNs were able to, and exercised their right to, provide different levels of 'perks'. For example, a wealthy SN like Sonatrach was able to supplement its employees' salaries by such things as the provision of special housing (important in an economy where housing was difficult to obtain), car allowances, etc. This gave the different SNs opportunities to attract better qualified staff and indirectly bring out the latent inequalities of opportunity between different sectors of the Algerian population.

While there were indirect income differentials between employees in different SNs, there were also continued income differentials between 'white collar' and 'blue collar' workers as Tables 6.6 and 6.7 indicate. These differences in earnings were an inheritance from the colonial period and, in spite of the apparent attempt to contain salary levels, an examination of patterns of salary increases at the time indicates that in practice, earnings at the lower levels were increasing more slowly than those at the higher levels. If earnings differences were the negative aspect of the inheritance from the colonial period, the commitment to the improvement of minimum wages represented the transformation of a policy whose purpose had been to 'assure the European population heavily concentrated in the coastal area and the urban centres of their better conditions than those of the "autochtones" pushed back into the interior'.[23] If wages and salaries were determined by the administrative structure, what role did the trade union organization play in labour relations? The next section examines the relationship between the trade union organization, the UGTA, labour and the Government.

The UGTA

The role of the trade unions in mediating the labour-capital relation in the Third World is complicated by several factors. These include the historically short period within which labour movements have developed, the ambiguity of the primary ownership of capital actually lying with the state, and the relatively small size of the industrial labour force. As a result, there is a pervading sense that the interests of labour and capital are not opposed and that the parameters of the relationship between labour and capital can be determined without recourse to oppositional institutions but through co-optive and cooperative organizations and institutions. Thus while a country like Algeria has continued to sustain a trade union movement in the post-independence period, the role of this movement has lacked clarity. It has been further hampered by the fact that the actual structure of its institutions reproduced the patterns of organization of the former colonial country.[24] Labour interests with respect to trade-union organization in post-independence Algeria have been represented by one trade union – the *Union Générale des Travailleurs Algériens* (UGTA). The UGTA was constructed along the lines of French trade unions like the CGT and the CFDT, with both of which it had historic links. This meant that its structure consisted of a national secretariat which aimed to coordinate the activities of industry federations and territorial unions.

However, although the formal structure of Algeria's trade union organization was a reflection of its colonial inheritance, the UGTA itself had been a direct creation of the nationalist movement and of the FLN which in the absence of an independent Algerian trade union movement in 1954 chose to establish a confederation which would be reflective of its own objectives. That there had been no independent trade union confederations in Algeria was partly due to the fact that during the colonial period Algerian territory had been subsumed as an integral part of France; thus trade union organization during the colonial period was carried out under the name of its French originator, the CGT.[25] The CGT only revendicated its Algerian organization in 1954 when it permitted the establishment of an autonomous Algerian central: the UGSA (*Union générale des syndicats algériens*). While the UGSA can be said to have had authentic trade union origins, this cannot be said of the UGTA. However, the colonial government was to treat them both as threats to its security and banned them in November 1956, just after the UGTA's founding. The creation of the UGSA also led to the founding of a second autonomous Algerian trade union central, the USTA (*Union des syndicats de travailleurs algériens*), by the Messaliste section of the nationalist movement (Weiss, 1970).

The sudden flowering of trade unionism in Algeria and its associated rivalries is illustrative of the problems which confounded the nationalist movement and which affected all the Algerian post-independence governments. It reflected the dual base of the nationalist movement and the intense ambiguity of the interactions of the Franco-Algerian relationship which on the one hand shaped an industrial working class but one whose entire experience was in France, and on the other excluded most Algerian Muslims from an industrial experience in their own country. Consequently, the trades-union movement in Algeria did not perform the same function within the nationalist movement as the trade unions were able to do in the development of the nationalist movements in Algeria's neighbours Tunisia and Morocco, which was to provide continuity and stability. The split within the Algerian trade-union movement at its birth was such that the major part of the USTA support came from Algerian workers in France; this acted to confirm the divisions within the nationalist movement itself. The antagonism between the two trade-union federations was not improved when the USTA's General Secretary, Ahmad Berhat, was assassinated in France in October 1957 and responsibility was attributed to the UGTA.

Meanwhile, in Algeria itself, the UGTA was forced underground virtually as soon as it was born. Furthermore, it was to be engaged from its foundations in demonstrations and strikes directed against the colonial government, reflecting its political role in the nationalist movement rather than its trade-union role. As a result, the majority of its officials were very soon arrested and imprisoned; this also contributed to the formation of an essentially unstable organization which by February 1957 was into its seventh secretariat. Finally in mid-1957, the UGTA went underground, moved its operational headquarters to Tunis and set about countering the influence of the Messalistes in France by founding the *Amicale Générale des Travailleurs Algériens*. The effects of exile, and the essentially political nature of its foundation, meant that the UGTA's links with its parent organization the FLN became even closer in terms of both the structure of its organization and the experiences of its members. It was, like the FLN, to see many of its officials disappear and some to die in French prisons, including one of its General Secretaries, Aissat Idir. Consequently, when independence came, only a rump of the original organization was left, with the result that the UGTA experienced the same difficulties as the FLN in the immediate post-independence period in establishing its legitimacy as the heir to the 1956 UGTA.

In the confusion which prevailed in Algeria after independence, sections of the UGTA would become involved in the autogestion movement. However, the limitations of the UGTA's base meant that it did not possess a coherent ideology from which it could either sustain ideologically the movement or provide a consistent political and economic opposition to the positions taken by the new government. Consequently while it would overstate the case to say that the rapprochement which characterized the relations between the UGTA and Government policy-making was one entirely without strains, nevertheless the very similarity of their histories helped to maintain a commonality of interest and purpose which was translated into an organizational structure which was virtually a mirror image of Government structures. Consequently, it would frequently act as the instrument for the enablement of Government policy decisions. Its role in the socialist management programme well illustrates this relationship.

Although the UGTA was the Government's arm within the working class and historically it was founded to represent nationalist interests to the Algerian working class, the relationship between the UGTA and the Algerian government has not always been as close as this might imply. For example, when the UGTA held its First National Congress in January 1963, its secretariat was unilaterally replaced by one nominated by Ben Bella's government. Moreover, at the time of the government power struggles which took place during the summer of 1962, the UGTA adopted a neutral stance. The leaders who took control of the UGTA in 1962 were some of those who had been involved in its foundation in 1956. Even so, they chose not to take an identifiably pro-Government and therefore pro-Ben Bella stance in the period immediately after independence. Furthermore, some sections of the leadership were opposed to the direction which his government was taking. It was to resolve these tensions that the Ben Bella government decided unilaterally to remove the UGTA's secretariat at its first congress and replace it with a government-nominated secretariat. Although the UGTA continued to function after this coup and Ben Bella was replaced by Boumediene in 1965, the UGTA was to hold only four national congresses between 1962 and 1974 and these were held at irregular intervals. Consequently, its functioning as a trade-union organization was severely compromised, reflecting its relatively weak power base with the result that it cannot be seen to have been an independent political force.

The close relationship which developed thereafter between the Algerian government, its policies and the UGTA is best illustrated by the fact that after its 1973 National Congress, a series of national conferences of the different industry federations was held throughout 1973 and 1974 at which UGTA national officials and Government ministers outlined what they considered to be the main tasks to be undertaken by the UGTA and its constituent federations, all of which were essentially tasks informed by Government needs. How these tasks were represented is illustrated by a speech given by the UGTA's National Secretary to the *Fédération Nationale des Travailleurs de la Métallurgie* in June 1974. The tasks were grouped around four principal themes:

1. To organize all workers in such a way that they take part through their organizations in national development. To defend them by contributing

as much as possible to their material well-being, by raising their purchasing power, and improving living and working conditions.

2. To defend the gains of the Revolution, to avoid every form of exploitation of man by man, and to reinforce workers' power at the level of the management of their factory.

3. To develop and raise the workers' political involvement; to sharpen their awareness of their responsibilities in order to produce men who are informed and able to develop efficiently the country's economic potential.

4. To work unceasingly to raise the level of workers' consciousness. (*El Moudjahid*, 5.6.74)

This aspect of the UGTA's role – that of reinforcing Government policy at the popular level – can be further underlined by its habit of making public proclamations in advance of key dates in the Algerian national calendar. One example of this is again in June 1974, when the UGTA made what it called the UGTA Appeal (*Appel de l'U.G.T.A.*) in the official daily newspaper, *El Moudjahid* on 15 June 1974, the purpose of which was to remind workers that 17 June was the National Day of the Agrarian Revolution. In this Appeal, the UGTA's National Secretary emphasized the role which the UGTA had to play in such commemorations and in particular its role as the agent for the elimination of the divide between the urban worker and the rural labourer. There is an interesting distinction which is made through the use of different words to describe 'industrial work' and 'rural work' which suggests that they were being conceptualized in a different way. He goes on to argue that the importance of seeking ways to eliminate that divide was based on the need to ensure a popular base for the Agrarian reform programme because without the success of that Programme, Algeria's socialist policies would fail to gain mass support. The Programme, he continued, was also important because it was a policy which met the objectives of the 1954 Revolution. How then to provide support – to organize a mass 'Volontariat'[26] on the day before (a Sunday) which then left the day itself free for the FLN to organize a mass demonstration in support of the Programme? The speech ended with the words: 'Vive le FLN, vive la UGTA, vive la révolution socialiste'.

The speech illustrates once again the difficulties which the post-independence Algerian policy-makers faced in transmitting to the grass roots their centrally arrived at policy decisions. While creating popular support for the government's economic policy was a major problem for the Boumediene regime, it would also have been a problem for any

Algerian regime which adopted a central-planning-based model. It reflected both the absence of democratic institutions and the original pattern of organization adopted by the FLN in the independence struggle. Both of which meant that after independence, political and civic institutions tended to merge. Furthermore, even if a central-planning model had not been adopted, the actual trade-union organizational model on which the UGTA structure was based (in the absence of other political parties or alternatively with only a single political party, the FLN) would have tended to push the UGTA towards a commonality of interests with the government.

The UGTA's role was not only to provide public support for Government policy, it was also to be an integral part of the process of government. In this capacity, it was an automatic member of Government committees and quangos. One such example is the National Commission established in February 1974 to study 'the harmonization of pay scales applicable to personnel in the public and para-public sectors' (*La République*, 13.2.74). As a trade union whose membership might be affected by decisions which were taken to harmonize pay scales, the UGTA would have had an interest in the outcome of the debate. However, its role was less to represent membership interests directly than to form part of the government decision-making processes. The other issue which arises from the establishment of this Commission is that it illustrates the problems which the planning system had in regulating wage levels which in the absence of a market tended to reflect the unequal distribution of resources between different state enterprises.

The involvement of the UGTA in government policy-making was well established by 1974. It was, as has been suggested, both a result of the dynamics of the post-independence Algerian political system and a reflection of Algeria's former status as a French colony. Thus it also reflected a more general pattern of development associated with trade unions in the Third World. These last were developed by the colonial powers either to protect the interests of the settler worker or to set up clearly defined channels among indigenous labour forces for labour-management relations. As a result of this usually top-down introduction, trade unions in Third World countries were set up as direct copies of the trade-union structure prevailing in the colonial *metropole*. Thus in the former British colonies in Africa, the trade-union organization was patterned on British trade unionism, while in the former French colonies, it was patterned after the French model. The next section looks at one government programme, the 'socialist organization of firms', in whose dissemination the UGTA was intimately involved.

Autogestion and the *organisation socialiste des entreprises*

The post-independence debate both in and outside Algeria on the best forms of managerial control to adopt in both industry and agriculture were, as has been argued already, dominated by the issue of autogestion. To some extent, the debate outside Algeria on the merits of autogestion was part of a wider search among western socialists for alternative models of economic organization. As knowledge about the Soviet economic system (Nove, 1977) and its political discourses became more widely available the problems with both the economy and the political system led socialists in the west not towards a questioning of the feasibility of a socialist economy in the manner of Barone (1908/1972) and Mises (1920/1972; Steele, 1992) but to a search for alternatives. It was in this context that the autogestion or self-management model which had also been taken up by the Yugoslav government appeared to offer a level of plant-level democracy which the economic planning model did not. However, the attachment of the name of 'autogestion' to the Algerian post-independence takeover of colon-vacated farms and enterprises was an attempt to legitimize both practically and theoretically a *de facto* situation. Further-more, its enacting took place before any system of economic organization had been adopted by the post-independence Algerian government. At least the Yugoslav system had developed as a response to the specific economic and political situation of the establishment of the new post-war Yugoslav state. Even so, general knowledge about the system and its operation did not begin to emerge until the 1970s (Vanek, 1972). Consequently, the basis on which the Algerians were working compounded lack of knowledge at the economic level of the model's viability with a political commitment to retain and validate the workers' seizures. Whatever may be the merits of autogestion at an ideal level, in the Algerian context it was an experiment which was taking place within an economy in which basic economic structures had still to be established. The struggle to establish autogestion and the struggle to construct a labour/trade union movement were illustrative of the problems which post-independence industrial strategy faced in reconciling the aims of economic growth with workers' interests. In an attempt to deal with these contradictions, the Boumediene government launched in 1971 a programme known as the 'socialist organization of firms' (*organisation socialiste des entreprises*). This programme was an attempt to answer both external and internal critics by offering a management reform programme.

The programme was launched with a 'Charter for the Socialist Organization of Firms' *(Charte de l'organisation socialiste des entreprises,*

RADP 1971; *Visages de l'Algérie*, 22, 1973) which set out specifically to expound some theory of what socialist development in the Algerian context meant. In order to convey a sense of motion, the Charter referred to itself as the second phase of socialist development in Algeria, a phase which would aim to marry the needs of increased production and economic efficiency with a substantive redefinition of the worker's social relationships within the firm. This process of redefinition would result in gains by means of increased production and economic efficiency. The introduction of what it termed this second phase had been made possible because its two principal preconditions – nationalization, and the establishment of a solid and stable state – had been met with the creation of the SNs and the Boumediene Presidency. It also argued that prior to the Boumediene Presidency, the material conditions for socialist development had not existed because in spite of a commitment to ideals of workers' self-management and other types of worker-centred management practices, the objective conditions for their realization had not been present. The significance of this programme is that it shows how important it was to the Boumediene regime to have popular political legitimacy.

The 'socialist organization of firms' programme can therefore be seen as an attempt by the Algerian state to counter the centralizing tendencies inherent in its industrial-development programme of large state corporations. The socialist organization of firms programme envisaged that it would be possible to decentralize power within the state corporations and create within them more democratic organizational structures. The aim was to create a process by which an individual worker would move progressively through the stages of producer and manager to become a *responsable* (someone who felt responsible for production). Throughout the process, the Algerian state acting in its capacity as the 'nation' would be the guarantor of the totality of the interests of Algeria's working people. The use of the abstract notion of 'nation' creates Benedict Anderson's 'imagined community' (Anderson, 1991) as it makes the attempt to bypass differences between groups through recourse to the notion of an abstract community or 'nation'. The underlying premiss that the state's interests and those of the worker were not the same is conveyed by the emphasis within the charter on worker duties, and more particularly statements such as there will be 'an adoption of more serious attitudes to work (which is taken to mean, spending the whole of paid working time on the job); a concrete interest in improving his technical competence; and a faithful observation of those rules and regulations which are laid out for the factory'. It is clear that the aim behind these exhortations is to bring about increased productivity and therefore to improve overall industrial efficiency. What they also reveal is the difficulties which were being faced in the attempt by Algeria to become an industrial economy in the twentieth century both at the level of production and at the level of the individual worker in the enterprise.

Socialist management was essentially a product of state policy. However, the nature of the role of the state in the process is a little more ambiguous. It can be seen either in classical Leninist terminology as a vanguard, or as the agent of the statist economic model (Perroux, 1991: 316). Either model envisages the state as simultaneously responsible for formulating, promoting and administrating the different measures. This self-appointed role posed considerable practical problems for a Government which not only lacked an administrative structure to carry out these functions but also popular channels through which its policies and ideas could be conveyed to the populace and legitimized. The party, the FLN, was not sufficient for the enormous task entailed; hence the reason for the Government's attempts to use the trade-union organization UGTA as an additional mediator. In the Charter, the role of the trade union is described as follows:

> . . . In the socialist economy, the trade union represents in effect, the effective mobilizing nucleus for the active involvement of the working masses in the realization of the objectives of socialist construction. It must organize the workers, sharpening their political consciousness and their sense of their responsibilities, and work towards the improvement of their technical competence. The trade union is the organization of the working class which contributes to the building of the new society. That is to say, that it takes upon itself heavy responsibilities with regards to the fulfilment of the task in hand.

The worker was seen as someone for whom everyday economic and social problems meant that on the one hand they did not always perceive the benefits of programmes like the socialist management programme, and on the other such problems affected their capacity to implement them. The Charter also reflected some of the concerns which were emerging as a result of its political and economic policies and in particular what was referred to as the emerging dangers of *l'ouvrierisme* (workerism or workerist trends), and tendencies towards bureaucratism and authoritarianism.

Although the Charter and the the Ordinance governing its application were first published in 1971, the socialist management programme did not become effective policy until 1973, and then actual elections for the workers' councils which it established did not take place until January 1974. The principal reason given for these delays was that the industrial workers were not yet prepared for radical change in the management of the firm. Consequently, prior to introduction of the programme, an extensive and intensive education programme was necessary. The means chosen to carry out this education programme were bureaucratic in that first of all, two national commissions were set up: the National Commission for the Socialist Management of the Firm (CNGSE, Ordonnance No 72–47) and the National Operational Commission (CNO, Ordonnance No 72–78). At the same time as this national structure was created, various local and regional committees were also set up to promote these same aims at the local and regional levels. Finally, it was decided to give the Programme a trial run in the Spring of 1972 at plants of SN Metal: a state enterprise which manufactured railway rolling stock as well as small metal items such as picks and shovels.

In spite of the SN Metal experiment and perhaps because of the setting up of the CNGSE and the CNO, the Programme itself made little progress until the initiative was taken by Boumediene himself with a speech on 19 June 1973 at which he called for further initiatives to implement the old 1971 Charter. Again the speech indicates the real problems which the Algerian regime was facing in its attempts to bring about industrial change as well as its failure to evolve effective means for either the enactment or the propagation of its policies. The speech argued that there was a need for a broad-based campaign led by the organizations involved in socialist management to explain as clearly as possible the meaning and purpose of the proposed new management system. An effective campaign, Boumediene argued, would require that all workers attend at least one explanatory session, presented in a language they would understand. It also meant encouraging debate among the workers on the various issues raised by the programme, even though such a debate was to take place strictly within the terms set by the Charter. In other words, it was not a free debate; and the emphasis here on the restricted nature of the debate which was to be allowed was repeated by other Government Ministers, for example by the Minister of Labour and Social Affairs, Mohamad Said Mazouzi in a speech to the CNO (*El Moudjahid*, 28.12.73; *RAT*, **13**, 1974), in which he argued that personal interpretations of the meaning of socialist management, however well-intentioned, would always incur the risk of leading 'in a higgledy-piggledy fashion to reformist systems of co-management, to libertarian self-management and even to authoritarian capitalist management'. Mazouzi's speech also displays a certain ambivalence towards self-management and its ideological interpretations. However, it also illustrates the way in which the State tried to take the lead in introducing new methods for the management of firms but in practice, beyond the level of discourse, lacked the means or the constituency with which they could be implemented.

The difficulties which had been experienced in getting the socialist management programme off the ground in the period prior to Boumediene's 19 June 1973 speech did not disappear. The elections which Boumediene had said were scheduled for November 1973 were first postponed to December 1973 and then to January 1974 and then to February 1974. The UGTA's National Secretary in charge of Socialist Management (*Révolution et Travail,* 235/12, 1973) accounted for these delays as resulting from difficulties experienced in dividing up the state corporations into electoral units, where a lack of coordination between the parties involved – that is the UGTA, the state corporation's management and the Government sponsoring ministries – had been the most significant. This lack of coordination was embodied in the process of setting up candidature committees, particularly as a decision had also been taken to enlarge them to include two representatives from the sponsoring Ministries. He also argued that the propaganda campaign had been less effective than had been anticipated. Each of these factors serves to illustrate that the regime's attempt to direct and consequently also control everything from the centre in practice had a negative effect on the implementation of its policies. Simply the fact that the number of institutions which had to be involved in the decision-making process shifted the emphasis from the policy to the achievement of consensus (or alternatively, to an emphasis on homogeneity and common organizational forms) meant that the process itself was stifled.[27]

When the CNO was finally able to agree on the conditions under which elections could be held, it had agreed conditions for only eleven of the state corporations and, of these eleven, only SNS – the iron and steel state corporation – had a central role in economic policy-making. The state corporations which were selected were not, with the exception of SNS, central to industrial strategy; however, they did include several who were major state employers of industrial labour – that is, SNS, Sonacome (mechanical engineering), SNMC (construction materials), Sonitex (textiles), and SN Sempac (foodstuffs). Elections for the socialist management committees in these corporations finally took place in 1974; an event which did appear to make at least some workers in these corporations more optimistic that the Programme would both improve their personal position and increase productivity within the enterprise as a whole. An example of this is given in an interview recorded in *El Moudjahid* (27.3.74), in which the workers being questioned gave this response:

> If we have the right to look over the financial side of management, it is a clearly defined task, that is to be aware of what is going on and to be able to check if production and financial results are in harmony. We do not want to imply that it is our desire to upset the power relations in the factory. On the contrary, we are working for a sensible management system, in which all human potential is recognized, from the workers to the management.

There are several interesting aspects to this interview, not least being a clear implication that workers felt undervalued within the state corporations and that they were not entirely convinced that there was proper financial management. However, even though they were drawing attention to internal organizational problems, they were also quite careful to define the limits of their own competence and consequently make a clear distinction between themselves and their function and the functions of management.

The elections of February 1974 were, however, concerned only with the workers' councils at the level of individual factory plants or 'units' within the state enterprises. The election of workers' councils for the state enterprise as a whole had not taken place at the same time because there had been no agreement on either the proper unit of representation or what level of representation each unit should have. The argument over the terms of representation also indicates how complicated the intended processes of management which the socialist management programme sought to implement. The chosen solution was to bring in the CNGSE in May and June 1974 as a mediator, which effectively meant that decision-making was once again ceded to the bureaucratic process and the legislature so that what should have been resolved by organic processes was dealt with by a mechanical process through the drafting of further legislation. The socialist management programme provides an example of the problems which the Boumediene regime found to be involved in reconciling economic objectives – that is, the desire to create an efficient industrially-based economy – with political objectives which sought to ensure that benefits were evenly distributed. It illustrates the complexity of the issues which the Boumediene regime was attempting to resolve, and why each attempt that was made resulted in the use of bureaucratic methods.

Conclusion

This chapter and chapter 5 have sought to show how the economics of the industrialization project was constantly checked by the political imperatives to respond to the expectations which Boumediene's discourse of revolution and change raised. However, they have also argued that what appeared to be a means to ensure a planned programme of growth, the centrally-planned economy, in effect constantly shifted economic decision-making towards bureaucratic and administrative solutions. The effects of these were to stifle individual enterprise and also economic growth. What is perhaps less clear is the extent to which the choice of a different economic model would have produced different results given the conditions under which Algerian independence was achieved. The next two chapters shift the emphasis away from internal conditions in Algeria to Algeria's relation to the wider world and focuses in particular on the Franco-Algerian relationship (chapter 7) and the role of the European Union (chapter 8).

Notes

1. For a selection of material on the form a socialist economy might take, see the readings in Nove, A. and Nuti, D.M. (1972) *Socialist Economics*, Harmondsworth, Penguin. It should be noted that there is a distinct gap between the material of the classical authors and the early years of the Soviet Union and the contemporary or near contemporary material. In other words there is an absence of material from the period between the mid-1930s and the early 1960s. However, as Nove himself notes in his 1977 Preface to the First Edition of *The Soviet Economic System*, there is a similar gap in work by Western economists who also showed very little interest in how the Soviet economy actually functioned until the late 1960s. Consequently the amount of information which was available on the actual functioning of communist economies was quite limited. Because of this paucity of analytical material, there are implications both for the way in which the Algerian view of a socialist economy (as it was articulated by Boumediene) was developed and for the basis of the contemporary critique of the Algerian model.

2. For a selection of some of the key themes of this class of writing, see the collection edited by Hoselitz, B.F. and Moore, W.E. (1970), *Industrialization and Society*, UNESCO, Mouton. This collection contains a summary – 'The Achievement Motive in Economic Growth' – by David C. McClelland of his controversial but much referred to study (1961) *The Achieving Society*, Princeton, N.J., Van Nostrand Co.

3. The 'franc zone' was established in 1939 as a form of monetary union between France and her colonies (Bloc-Laine, 1956).

4. *Bulletin Économique* (Algiers), 2–4, 1974.

5. The role of the Paris-based *École Nationale d'Administration* (ENA), founded in 1945, has received both fame and notoriety, in the sense that in the upper echelons of both French business and the French government, graduates of in particular, the ENA, but also the École Polytechnique are virtually ubiquitous.

6. As a result of the collapse of France in 1940, when liberation came in 1945, a joint socialist and communist government was elected which nationalized most of the key sectors of French industry including several banks, established a system of national planning and, among other innovations, inaugurated the *École Nationale d'Administration* (ENA). For a short introduction to these develoments, see Ardagh, J. (1977), *The New France*, Harmondsworth, Penguin.

7. The seven international oil majors were respectively Standard Oil of New Jersey (Esso), Standard Oil of New York (Mobiloil), Standard Oil of California (Chevron), Gulf Oil (Headquarters actually in Pittsburgh, USA), Texaco – all US-based; plus Royal Dutch/Shell group, and British Petroleum (Odell, 1975: 12–13).

8. SOPEFAL was part of the ELF-ERAP group. Information on Sonatrach is derived from its own publicity including a superb coffee-table-sized 100-page Introduction to its operations published in 1968, and from Rabah Mahiout (1974), *Le Pétrole algérien*, Algiers, Eds En AP.

9. Hamid Mazri was at one time Head of Operations for the Beni-Mansour-Algiers pipeline.

10. Compiled from press notifications of loans to Algeria during 1979. These including floating-rate loans, medium-term loans, buyers' credit, etc.

11. These were ALGEO, ALFOR, ALFLUID, ALTEST, ALTRA, ALEIP, ALCIP, ALDIM, ALDIA, ALRID, ALCOTRA, and ALGEC (*Liste des sociétés nationales* 1980).

12. There are interesting parallels here with the attempts at privatization by the Russian government and the resistance it has encountered from the Russian oil giant Lukoil to these attempts.

13. In spite of their departure from Sonatrach, Sidahmed Ghozali held the Chair of the High Executive Council and was Prime Minister from 1991 to July 1992; Ait Laoussine headed a consultancy in Geneva but was recalled by Ghozali in June 1991 and remained in his post until July 1992 when he was replaced by Hacen Mefti, another former Sonatrach cadre, in a reorganization resulting from the appointment of Belaid Abdessalam (also ex-Sonatrach) as Prime Minister. While this argues for the pervasiveness of the influence of Sonatrach in Algerian political affairs, it could equally well illustrate that as Sonatrach was the most sophisticated of the Algerian state companies, it attracted the most talented applicants. In some senses, the ambivalences which are expressed about the role of Sonatrach are not dissimilar to the arguments which are used about the *Enarque* (graduates of the Paris-based *École Nationale d'Administration*) who tend to go on to hold leading posts in politics, government and industry. This can be illustrated by the fact that the French President, Jacques Chirac, is a graduate as is former Prime Minister Alain Juppé. A result of this convergence of education and employment, it has been suggested, is a tendency towards conformity or what Dimaggio and Powell (1991)

refer to as 'institutional isomorphism'. See also note 6.

14. Various prices were being paid by different customers; for example, British Gas was paying, after July 1981, $4.80 per million BTU, while Gaz de France was paying $4.35 per million BTU; and Belgium's Distrigas was also paying $4.80 per million BTU following a contract concluded in April 1981, but also indexed to 50 per cent of the value of a basket of oils imported into Belgium (*Financial Times*, 13.4.81).

15. The French word is *la récupération* which can also be translated as 'appropriation'; however, in this context it would have been more usual to use the word *l'appropriation*; I have chosen to translate it as 'recovery'.

16. In his Introduction to the Soviet economic system, Nove (1986: 1) remarks that 'planning methods, or practical problems of operating a socialist economy were not seriously discussed by Marxists (or non-Marxists) before 1917'; one of the few exceptions being an essay by E Barone in 1908. This essay is republished in Nove, A. and Nuti, D.M. (1972). However, it tends to imply that the practice was studied after 1917; but Ellman (1972), *Soviet Planning Today* uses almost exclusively Russian-language sources, which suggests again that in practice not much more was known in the West about how the planning system functioned, which makes Nove's subsequent statement – that the general sentiment was that 'Full-fledged socialism, or communism, would be a state of affairs in which scarcity would have been overcome, and production would be for use and not for exchange, socially planned for the benefit for the educated and participating working masses'

(1986:1) – all the more revelant to the Algerian planning context.

17. Several of the principal critiques have already been referred to, for example, Chaliand and Minces (1972), and Maschino and M'Rabet (1972); others were Kader Ammour, Christian Leucate, Jean-Jacques Moulin (1970), *La Voie algérienne: les contradictions d'un développement national*, Paris, François Maspero; and Marc Raffinot, Pierre Jacquemot (1977) *Le Capitalisme d'état algérien*, Paris, François Maspero.

18. Information about SONIC has been put together from the following sources: RADP (1971) *Annuaire statistique de l'Algérie 1970*; RADP (1972) *Industrie 1969*; RADP (1970) *Liste de sociétés nationales à activité industrielle en 1970*; RADP (1980) *Liste des sociétés nationales ayant une activité industrielle et leurs unités de production*; daily newspapers and journals

19. During the colonial period, most of the Algerian (and North African) esparto crop was exported to Great Britain (particularly to Scotland) and to France as Algeria's own paper industry was negligible.

20. The creation of the Algerian *École Nationale d'Administration* (ENA), the purpose of which was to produce senior executive personnel, mirrors the foundation in 1945 of the institution of the same name in France. See also notes 5, 6, and 13.

21. Figures on education have been compiled from the following sources: Ministry of Primary and Secondary Education (no date) *Enseigner en Algérie*, Algiers; (1979) *Annuaire statistique de l'Algérie 1977–78*; (1973) *Visages de l'Algérie* 24.

22. For discussion of the First Four-Year Plan, see pages 101–2, 131–2.

23. RADP (1970) *La Situation de l'emploi et des salaires 1970*, Direction des statistiques, Sec. d'État au Plan.
24. The manner of the reproduction of metropolitan trade-union structures within the colony was the subject of a research project carried out by Ron Dore at the Institute of Development Studies, University of Sussex in the early 1970s, on which the author of this study worked as a Research Assistant.
25. For example, the CGT (*Confédération générale du travail*) is often seen as close to the French Communist Party although its origins were partly in the anarchist movement, while the CFDT (*Confédération française démocratique du travail*) is close to the Socialist Party; and there are other confederations such as the CFTC (*Confédération française des travailleurs chrétiens*).
26. The Volontariat was a day of action on which non-agricultural workers would give unpaid labour on some project which the State considered to be useful. It was particularly aimed at students and young people.
27. This is a reference to an article by Paul J. DiMaggio and Walter W. Powell (1991) 'The Iron Cage Revisited: Institutional Isomorphism and Collective Rationality in Organizational Fields', 63–82 in W.W. Powell and P.J. DiMaggio, *The New Institutionalism in Organizational Analysis*, Chicago and London, University of Chicago Press; they argue that with the achievement of the bureaucratization of the corporation and the state, there is a shift to the internal structure of organizations with the effect of reproducing conformity both within and between organizations.

7

Algeria and France

The focus of the discussion so far has concerned the impact of France on Algeria. In this chapter, the focus will switch to a consideration of the ways in which the modern French state has been shaped by events in Algeria before returning in the final chapter to a consideration of the impact of globalization on Algeria. In other words this chapter takes up the argument proposed by Homi Bhabha (1990a: 218) that there is a 'repressed history' in the West which is 'the history of the West as a despotic power' and that 'the material legacy of this history is inscribed in the return of post-colonial peoples to the metropolis. Their very presence there changes the politics of the metropolis, its cultural ideologies and its intellectual traditions, because they – as a people who have been recipients of a colonial cultural experience – displace some of the great metropolitan narratives of progress and law and order, and question the authority and authenticity of those narratives'. France provides an interesting example of the enacting of this process. It is only necessary to consider the responses of the French state to the bomb explosions of 1995 and again in December 1996, and to read the back page of the book written under the pseudonym of Lucile Provost (1996) *La Seconde Guerre d'Algérie: le quiproquo franco-algérien* to understand how this can be effected.[1] There is the obvious sense of ambiguity which the use of a pseudonym characterizes but it is the opening statement of the back page summary which encapsulates to perfection the point which Bhabha was making. This statement reads in translation 'Assassinations of French foreign nationals in Algeria, attacks perpetrated on the Paris Métro, the year 1995 will have marked the beginning of the Second Algerian War. In a conflict which opposes Algerian state power to the Islamists, France plays again a leading role. Because more than 30 years after independence, Algeria has not left France and France has not left Algeria. She remains present both as a political and cultural mirror and through the economic interests and the networks of influence she mobilizes.'

There are a number of crucial images which are conveyed by this short extract. The first of these is the acknowledgement in the book's title that there was a First Algerian War, as for many years this was – as it is captured in the title of the 1992 film of Bernard Tavernier *La Guerre sans nom* ('The War Without a Name') – an unacknowledged war. Unacknowledged because of the legal status of Algeria as a French *département* which meant that technically, the French state could not be at war. Nevertheless, for many of the conscripts and the *rappelés* ('recalled reservists')[2] it was difficult for them to understand how France was not at war with Algeria. The ambivalence of the French state to the Algerian war continues in the 1990s: on 11 November 1996, President Chirac inaugurated a monument on the Boulevard d'Algérie in Paris dedicated to 'victims and fighters killed in North Africa 1952–1962' (*victimes et combattants morts en Afrique du nord 1952–1962*) which, as the national President of Fnaca, Wladyslas Marek, wrote in *Le Monde* (18.12.96), means that an opportunity was lost finally to acknowledge that France fought a war in Algeria. Marek writes that this is to be even more regretted because in September, the President had in a reply to a request from Marek agreed to substitute the expression *guerre d'Algérie* ('Algerian War') for the expression, used until now in official texts, of 'operations and maintenance of order in Algeria'. The second of the impressions is conveyed by the use in the subtitle of the word *quiproquo* as this has the sense of a 'case of mistaken identity', a view which the book's reviewer in *Le Monde* (29.3.96) considered as reflecting on the one hand, the 'famous love-hate relationship' between the two countries which itself was a reflection of the failure of the two countries to surmount the old colonial relationship. This image is also conveyed by the metaphor of Algeria not having left France and France not having left Algeria. That these are not simply metaphorical images is clear from their juxtaposition with the political and economic realities of the relationship, and from Provost's view that these are responsible for the French state's support for the Algerian central government's repression of opposition whether or not that opposition is always, or necessarily, Islamist. The result of this policy is that in practice, the cause of democracy in Algeria is not assisted. The question for this chapter is the extent to which political discourses in France are influenced by the Algerian relationship.

The discussion of the creation of the modern Algerian state, and the impact upon it of France through the medium of colonization and post-colonial relationships, cannot be completed without a discussion of the role which Algerian emigration to the French mainland has played in shaping not only the image of Algeria and the Algerian immigrant but also the particular dualities of French state policy with regard to immigration and the immigrant. The importance of this emigration is that it needs to be seen as a dialectical relationship in which the experience of Algerian emigrants in France not only had and has an impact on the development of ideology in Algeria but also had and has an impact on the development of ideology in France. The dualistic nature of this relationship is well illustrated by the events that have taken place since the 1992 crisis in Algeria. On the one hand, the current crisis means that for some Algerians, France is a place of refuge. On the other, the struggle for hegemony between the different forces in Algeria has led, it would seem, to the importation of that conflict to France, which has had the effect of the enacting of a series of repressive counter-measures by the French state against the Algerian presence on mainland France. These actions are at the same time the essential ingredients for a right-wing trajectory which has enabled the French National Front to establish itself in both national and local politics. However, as Bhabha suggests, the debate is more than a debate about immigration and the immigrant; it is also a debate about the nature of French identity.

The problem of French identity

In the same way that Algerian emigration to France has a history which predates World War II, so also is it necessary to view the history of the rise of the National Front in the 1980s as part of a longer history of an 'idea of an exclusive identity of France' (Lebovics, 1992: xiii) which Lebovics goes on to argue 'was the chief strategy, the hegemonic project, of conservative cultural thought and practice from the time of the Dreyfus affair to the end of World War II'. However, if the articulation of this project has been the property of the right, the formulation of the ideas upon which they were able to base this project were not necessarily their exclusive property. In the wider construction of such ideas, Algeria, as Patricia M. E. Lorcin (1995) shows, played a key role in the sense that in order to realize its conquest, the French state found it necessary to carry out in parallel a series of scientific studies. The underlying aim of these studies was to make conquest easier to accomplish, and their importance can be underlined by the fact that a Scientific Commission was in place and engaged in collecting data by 1840–42 (1995: 35). The purpose of the Commission was to collect sufficient scientific information, in the sense of science as information and categories, which would enable the colonization process to take place. An aspect of this research was an assessment of the security risks posed by different population elements. In deciding who would be most likely to cooperate with the colonial authority, and where, and at some time also become its agents, the researchers of whom the majority were in one way or another in active military service used the construction of two opposing categories of Kabyle/Berber versus Arab. Lorcin argues that these categories were distinctions drawn initially to represent proximity and distance from the colonial authority and to distinguish those who it was thought could be most assimilated by the colonial project. However, the manner in which these categories were constructed also reflects currents in European scientific thinking at this time where issues of language and origins had become major subjects of enquiry (1995: 42). In the Algerian context, it had the effect of reinforcing the incipient categories of Kabyle/Berber and Arab by establishing a history of origins based on language (1995: 44). Later these categories would become divisions within the population which were exploited by the colonial authority in terms of, for example, the provision of schools (Colonna, 1995: 342). They would also affect the naming of the Algerian immigrant in France, where early immigrants were usually referred to as Kabyle. Thus as Lorcin argues what these studies served to achieve was the creation of a particular racial paradigm.[3]

According to Lorcin, the role of science and scientific ideas in French society had been given a considerable boost as a result of the 1789 Revolution. However, science had also become 'linked to the military and hence to colonial experimentation' (Lorcin, 1995: 10). The other defining element was the struggle by the Republican state to confirm the establishment of a secular state in France, and it is this struggle which influences both the understanding and the representation of Islam. Furthermore, it lays the foundations for the creation of the link which is then established between Islam and the issue of security (1995: 37). The obsession with security, Lorcin argues, was also a specific legacy of Algeria's Governor-General of 1840–47, General Bugeaud. However, if in origin security was the result of the confrontation between General Bugeaud and those resisting the imposition of French rule in Algeria itself, the issue of security is one which occupies the French state in France and dominates official discourse on the Franco-Algerian relationship. The result is the introduction of measures such as *vigipirate*[4] when the French state feels threatened.

In his monumental study (1988, 1990), *The Identity of France*, Fernand Braudel describes the identity of France as 'a residue, an amalgam, a thing of additions and mixtures. It is a process, a self-inflicted conflict, destined to go on indefinitely . . . A nation can have its *being* only at the price of being forever in search of itself, . . . ; a nation will recognize itself in certain stock images, in certain passwords known to the initiated' (1988: 23). However, in volume I which is entitled 'History and Environment', where is Algeria? For Braudel, Algeria is present in terms of the shortening of the time it takes to fly between Paris and Algiers, and in terms of it being fortunate to inherit the oil wealth of the Sahara, but in no direct sense has Algeria played a role in the history of France's identity. In volume II, 'People and Production', his references are to the alien nature of Islam and the fate of the *harki*; thus the interconnections which are discussed here between history and politics in France are in a sense mislaid exactly in the way of Bhabha's 'repressed history' (1990: 218). This absence is even more striking if one considers that in his other monumental work, Braudel's focus was the integrality of the Mediterranean in the sixteenth century as a historical, economic, political, geographic and cultural world (Braudel, 1972).

So what are the images of identity which France seeks to project of itself? There are some which are humorous, such as the notion of a France obsessed by issues of food and where images such as *Mon pote le bistrot* ('my best friend is the café') (*Le Monde*, 27.3.96) abound. Another instance of a humorous representation, but this time with a rather more serious edge to it, is the Astérix series in which in text by R. Goscinny and drawings by A. Uderzo an image of France through the notion of Gaul is created. Here history and myth unite in the image of the undefeated village filled by warring Gaulish (but also friendly) villagers possessed of a magic potion which means they are able to defend themselves against all comers (particularly the Romans). They also discover the new world but are of course unaware of their discovery; they enjoy enormous feasts (where they can be outdone by only the Belgians) and help the oppressed. It is easy to dismiss Astérix, but it should be remembered that the history of Algeria was rewritten to give precedence to the pre-Muslim or Visigoth period, and Hocine Aït Ahmed records how at school in the 1930s he was taught about his 'Gaulish ancestors' (1983: 14). Lebovics records that it was during the nineteenth century that French schoolbooks were written to give an idea of 'a virtual France existing before the historical France' (1992: 3). That these ideas continue to have a resonance today can be illustrated by the semi-legendary figure of Clovis.

On 22 September 1996, France celebrated the 1,500th anniversary of the baptism of Clovis, King of the Francs, which is reputed to have taken place in AD 496. The reason for these celebrations is that the baptism of Clovis is seen to mark the transformation of Gaul into France. Consequently, Clovis's baptism according to Alain Juppé, the French Prime Minister, signified Clovis as the 'founder of French identity' (*fondateur de l'identité française*) (*Le Figaro*, 3.4.96). The first reports that the French administration were intending to commemorate this event appeared in the press in April 1996 when it was announced that Alain Juppé had set up a Committee to oversee festivities which would mark this important event in the history of France. However, as the debate which ensued indicated, Clovis is an ambivalent hero for the cause of French identity. He is described in the *Petit Larousse illustré* as king of the Francs, 481–511. However, the Franks are recorded as a Germanic people concentrated in the lower Rhine area who gave their name to Roman Gaul after conquering it in the fifth and sixth centuries. As a result, Clovis would become the first 'barbarian Catholic king' (*roi barbare catholique*). In establishing his kingdom, Clovis also defeated Syagrius (described as a Gallo-Roman chief who governed what was left of Roman Gaul between the Somme and the Loire), the Alamans (a confederation of Germanic tribes who had settled on the Rhine in the second century), the Burgondes (described as a Germanic tribe which first settled on the Rhine and then in the Rhône basin giving their name to Burgundy), and the Visigoths (or western Goths), who originated from the Danube area in the fourth century where they converted to Arianism, a Christian heresy centred around a priest based in Alexandria called Arius (256–336), but which was rejected as a doctrine by the Orthodox church in 325 and 381; they took Rome in 410 and then settled in south-west Gaul from where after 476 they conquered a large part of Spain and North Africa until they were *submergés par les Arabes* ('swamped by the Arabs'). The complexities of the population movements involved provide rich material for both history and myth. They can as easily be translated into a storyline for the Astérix series – Book 5 is the story of *Astérix and the Goths* – as provide the basis for Ernest Renan's reflections on 'What is a nation?' (1990: 8–22). These ancient tribal groupings are used to provide evidence of ancestry in the same way that the 'saints' in Algeria sought evidence of Arab ancestry, even though in the above commentary the Arabs are established as the countervoice to the European experience.

The ambiguity comes about because the figure chosen, in this case Clovis, was a real figure whose achievements during his lifetime did include the creation of a united kingdom sufficient to provide the material evidence for the country and state which became France. However, as with all such figures, they are to some extent ambivalent. In Clovis's case, the kingdom he created did not survive his death, being divided up among his four sons. The other level of ambiguity contained in the Clovis story concerns the variable meanings which can be attached to the ethnic origins of peoples. The question can equally be posed: does the history of Clovis make the French French; or are the French German? It is, in the words of Benedict Anderson (1991: 6–7), an example of an 'imagined community', one in which a 'subjective antiquity' is employed to provide the French nation with a longer pedigree. Clovis has proved particularly useful in this respect and it is perhaps not surprising that he was employed in a similar fashion to unify the religious and the secular in the post-Revolutionary French state exactly one hundred years ago. On that occasion the Pope, Leo XIII, who was engaged in a project to reconcile anti-Republican Catholics with the republican state, wrote in a letter to the Archbishop of Reims, Cardinal Langénieux, that he saw France as 'the Church's eldest daughter' (*la fille aînée de l'Église*), a phrase which the Cardinal then popularized. It has been further argued that this was an attempt by the Church to turn round for the purpose of improving Church-State relations a much older designation applied to the French kings of 'the eldest son of the Church' (*le fils aîné de l'Église*).[5]

The other less benign significance of Clovis is that because he belongs to the tradition of Gaul – of blond hair and blue eyes – he can become, as Joan of Arc has also become, a symbol of the right, of the National Front of an exclusive France. The appeal of such historical/mythical figures and the ambiguous message they carry can also be illustrated by the use of another such eponymous hero by National Front members in Marseilles. Here the occasion was the stabbing of a Marseilles schoolboy by a young Moroccan, and the hero was Charles Martel (*Le Monde*, 17.9.96). Charles Martel was, like Clovis, a Frank and he was responsible in AD 732 for the defeat at the Battle of Tours and Poitiers of (depending on whose version) either a Muslim army or a Muslim raider group (Lewis, 1982: 18–20). Lewis uses Charles Martel to illustrate how the same events can have a different signification depending on whose text is read. In this instance, the texts are western European/Christian historical writing and Muslim historical writing. Lewis illustrates the different textual treatments by a quote from a passage in Gibbon's *Decline and Fall of the Roman Empire* which says 'From such calamities was Christendom delivered by the genius and fortune of one man' (Lewis, 1982: 18), compared to the Muslim historical tradition, in which 'the Battle' is perceived as a minor skirmish or the defeat of no more than a band of raiders (Lewis, 1982: 19) and historically of no significance, in strong contrast to the struggle which was going on at the same time to conquer Constantinople.

Lorcin (1995) in her discussion of French scientific study in Algeria drew attention to the way in which such studies used language as a means of signifying difference, and in particular to create the dichotomous categories of Kabyle/Berber and Arab. This concern with language reflects in the French what Lebovics (1992: 202) calls 'one of the most language-sensitive cultures in the world'. Consequently, in the debates over what constitutes French identity, language and the uses and abuses of the French language play a key role. It involves campaigns to remove foreign and in particular English/Anglo-Saxon words from the French language and the creation of specific bodies whose role it is to monitor the use of the language. Such organizations are both voluntary and state sponsored. Examples of such organizations are the *Délégation générale à la langue française* (DGLF) and the consultative *Conseil supérieur de la langue française*. It can also involve the use of the law; for example, the association *Avenir de la langue française* (ALF) used the 1994 Toubon Law to instigate proceedings against Body Shop for selling products without labelling in French.[6] Another example of the concern about the use of French can be illustrated by discussion of the use of both oral and written communication in French within the European Commission in Brussels where oral use of French in relation to that of English is 22 per cent:32 per cent, and written use is 6 per cent to English 59 per cent. ALF in association with a group of 1,000 intellectuals were the coordinators of a further 17 movements of protest against this. However, despite these activities on the language front, the body responsible for French cultural activity, the *Alliance française*, has like its British counterpart, the British Council, experienced a 15 per cent cut in its budget in recent years (*Le Monde*, 24–25.3.96). However, for the first time since Georges Pompidou was President (1969–74d), responsibility for *la politique linguistique*, which should be read both as linguistic/language policy and the politics of language, were taken up by the then Minister of Culture Philippe Douste-Blazy (*Le Monde*, 27.3.96). While an obsession with language is not of itself necessarily problematic, in a country where immigrants form some 10 per cent of the population, this preoccupation with language spoken and written within defined limits contains the potential for discriminatory practices, perhaps most apparent in the debate on integration where the use of language becomes a criterion of the capacity of the immigrant to become integrated into French society.

Increasingly, the issue of French identity has become a hostage of the French right, where the National Front sets out the terrain for the right in general. The National Front uses the issue of identity as a means to launch its attacks on immigrant communities. This is best illustrated by the National Front education trade union which is called the National Education Movement (*Mouvement pour l'éducation nationale* – MEN), the aim of which is to spread National Front ideas on 'identity and national preferences' (*Le Monde*, 24.10.96). What these are can be illustrated by the three founding aims of the National Front trade union formed in March 1996 within the RATP – the regional transport system.

The aims espoused by this new trade union were the protection of statutes (*défense des statuts*); preference for the recruitment of French nationals (*priorité aux Français*); preference to be given to the children of existing employees (*priorité familiale*) which effectively excludes the immigrant entrant; as well as improved working conditions such as the provision of late-night security, and quality of service. The context is unemployment, specifically youth unemployment, and continuing industrial unrest in cities like Marseilles where there are also significant populations of North African immigrants and former *pieds-noirs* ('black-feet', the *colons* who fled in 1962). The founding of trade unions in selected employment areas such as education, transport, the police and the prison service is strategic, not only in the sense that these are the key areas of contact between the state and the immigrant communities, but also in the context of a general political philosophy in which the National Front is hostile to trade-union objectives. For example, in the major public-service strikes which took place in November/December 1995 Le Pen, the National Front leader, was consistently hostile (*Le Monde*, 24.3.96).

However, there has been a spectacular growth in the vote of the National Front during the 1980s and the question of their future growth has been raised further by attempts to introduce a new electoral system which, while aimed at blocking the election of the Socialist Party, might well have the effect of providing new possibilities for growth by the National Front (*Le Monde*, 8–9.9.96). The key point in the National Front vote was the Presidential elections of 1988 when they gained 14.5 per cent of the vote, a share of the vote which was retained in the Presidential elections of 1995 when it rose to 15.5 per cent. They now have mayors in a number of municipalities in the south elected in June 1995, including Toulon and Orange; while the mayor of Nice, although now a member of the RPR (President Chirac's party), is an ex-member of the National Front. In the September 1996 local elections, although the RPR finally headed the list, in the first round a National Front candidate was at the top. The situation in Nice and the cities actually governed by the National Front brings into focus the uneasy relationship with the mainstream Right.

Immigration and identity criss-crossed one another in 1996 as the celebrations over Clovis were accompanied by the struggle by groups of Africans to retain the right to stay in France. In this struggle, they were given the title of 'people without papers' (*les sans-papiers*).[7] This struggle which began with the occupation of the Parisian church of St Ambroise (XIe arr) on 18 March 1996 culminated in hunger strikes in July–August 1996 involving 294 Africans, mainly Malians. Such hunger strikes and demonstrations are not new; they occurred in the early 1970s after the introduction of the Marcelin-Fontanet circulars which sought to 'regulate and control immigration' (Silverman, 1992: 85). However, the identity of the immigrant groups involved has changed because in 1972 it was mainly North Africans. As a result of this campaign for legal status, there has been a prolonged debate about the role of immigration in French society and the treatment of immigrants. This has led the government to propose a new anti-racist law and to a series of government ministers, including the President on 10 December 1996, condemning racism and xenophobia (*Le Monde*, 11.12.96). However, Chirac's condemnation has been very much in the context of these being outside the French republican tradition, and the essential ambivalence of his discourse is captured by the continued expulsion of the Africans involved in the protests and the continued construction of a linkage between immigration and illegal working. For example, President Chirac may have condemned xeno-phobia on page 7 of *Le Monde* (11.12.96), but on page 9 of the same issue, it is reported that the French Assembly is studying the issue of illegal working before it examines new controls on immigration; and the President's speech itself juxtaposed Muslim religious extremism with French xenophobia.

Some of the current problems arise from changes in French nationality law which have shifted its basis from the *jus solis* principle – that is, nationality granted as a result of where you are born – towards the *jus sanguinis* principle – which stresses who you are or who your ancestors were and conveys nationality by descent. They are consequently also concerned with the issue of identity as the *jus sanguinis* principle conceives the nation in its narrowest sense. New nationality laws came into force on 1 January 1994 and it is the effects of these, promoted by the then Interior Minister Charles Pasqua, which are now beginning to be felt (*Libération*, 25.3.96).

The role of Algeria in French identity

Algeria was not France's first colony, but the colonies which she possessed before Algeria were at the same time individually small and geographically remote. However, this did not mean that events in France did not have an impact on events in the colony or that events in the colonies did not have effects on events in France. The most well-known example of the impact of this dialectical relationship is the case of San Domingo which, in the wake of the Revolution in France, challenged the power of France using the rhetoric of that revolution to articulate demands for independence. It took a twelve-year struggle for this particular colony to achieve independence and create the black state of Haiti (James, 1989). In fact, San Domingo had been France's most profitable colony in the Caribbean as it was one of the most important markets of the European slave trade and it was the defeat of an expedition by Napoleon in 1803 which finally secured the colony's independence. At the same time as he was being defeated in one colonial arena, Napoleon was seeking to extend France's colonial rule into Africa, sending an expedition to Egypt as well as considering an invasion of the Ottoman Turkish Beylik of Algiers. Furthermore, it was under Napoleon's aegis that French interest in the Orient began to emerge. However, Napoleon himself did not succeed in building a colonial empire in Africa and it was left to his successors to begin the process of constructing France's new colonial empire. In this new empire, not only would Algeria be the first and the primary acquisition, it would also be France's closest geographical colonial possession. It is for these reasons that the relationship between Algeria and France would from the beginning have more than ordinary importance.

The importance of this relationship was illustrated by the close institutional arrangements for its governing. Algeria, as the discussion in chapter 2 indicates, was for much of the nineteenth century the subject of direct government by France. At various times, it was a part of France, a relationship of proximity which even the 1956–62 independence struggle made neither Algeria nor therefore Algerians any less a part of France (Provost, 1996: 7). This idea of Algeria as a part of France can also be illustrated by the legislation on nationality and citizenship in which immigrants of Algerian origin have a special position (Hargreaves, 1991). At the same time, Algeria has had and continues to have a decisive impact on internal French politics. The conquest of Algiers in 1830 took place as the French government of the Bourbon king Louis XVIII fell to his cousin Louis-Philippe, and such concurrences occur throughout the history of the two countries, culminating in the events of the independence struggle which not only led to independence for Algeria but were also responsible for the creation of France's Fifth Republic. The fall of the Fourth Republic in 1958 was as a direct result of its failure to end the war in Algeria with a French victory. General Charles de Gaulle became President on the promise of a 'French Algeria' (*l'Algérie française*) but was nevertheless responsible for conceding independence in 1962. As the cause of the creation of the Fifth Republic, the Algerian War can be seen as a defining moment in French politics and the origin of the creation of the contemporary French far right, in the form of the National Front, whose leader Jean-Marie Le Pen not only was a member of France's military forces in Algeria during the independence struggle but also was based at the Algiers headquarters where many of the recorded cases of torture occurred.

How can the contradictory nature of France's relationship with Algeria be explained? Bhabha (1991) offered one explanation; Edward Said (1993) suggests that the problem for France was that the existence of its colonial empire made necessary a number of philosophical compromises, in that it required, on the one hand, the union of the philosophical tradition of the Enlightenment with the intrinsically conflictual position of the ideals of the 1789 Revolution – liberty, equality, fraternity – and, on the other, their universalization expressed through the imperial project of *la francophonie*. Silverman (1992: 5) argues that the contradictions which are present in the French model result from the fact that 'there is a French national idea which could constitute the *optimal version* of the nation in the contemporary world' which he goes on to suggest is true as long as it is seen 'not as the universalist *as opposed to* the particularist model, but rather as one in which the tension between universalism and particularism is best exemplified. In other words, the French "version" of the nation is perhaps the clearest manifestation of the contradictions in the formation of all modern nation-states: contradictions which emerge within Enlightenment formulations of the individual and the collectivity.' (Silverman, 1992: 6) This is because in Silverman's view 'Questions of immigration and racism are not adjuncts to the development of the modern nations but a fundamental part of that development.' (1992: 6)

These ambivalences, Said would argue, are often most visible in literature and are to be found in Albert Camus' writings, particularly in his (1942) semi-autobiographical novel, *L'Étranger* (*The Outsider*) and the series of short stories (1957), *L'Exil et la royaume* (*Exile and the Kingdom*). Said (1993: 210–19) argues that despite being set in Algeria, where Camus was born of Breton and Spanish parentage, the events of the novel and these short stories take place essentially without reference to this environment and the political events which were taking place there. However, Cyril Connolly's Introduction to the First English Edition (1946/1961: 5) graphically illustrates the ideological environment which made this possible when he writes of Camus 'He is an Algerian. What is an Algerian? He is not a French colonial, but a citizen of France domiciled in North Africa, a man of the Mediterranean', but one for whom there is 'nothing but the Roman Empire, decaying dynasties of Turk and Moor, the French Conquest and the imposition of the laws and commerce of the Third Republic on the ruins of Islam'. Another example of the use of the territory of the colony as a backdrop is given by Ernest Gellner (1981: 150–4) in his discussion of André Gide's *L'Immoraliste* (*The Immoralist*) which Gellner uses to introduce a discussion of the life history of a 1930s member of the Association of Reformist Ulama, Tayyib Uqbi. Gide's concern is his discovery of homosexual love (Gellner, 1981: 151) whereas Gellner's interest is the clash between the 'saints' and the ulama epitomized by the career of Tayyib Uqbi. The two histories are juxtaposed in order that Gellner may draw a comparison between two philosophical stances, Gide's Nietzschean search for self-fulfilment and western Marxist search for socialism in Algeria (1981: 154). However, although Gellner and Said are in many ways providing illustrations of the same phenomena, their starting positions are very different (Gellner, 1994: 159–69). These examples help to illustrate that until the end of the Algerian War in 1962 the Algerian was a Frenchman. The importance of this discourse is that it affects the conceptualization of the immigrant from Algeria in France. In effect, this immigrant had no name, as the name had already been appropriated by the French immigrant in Algeria. This question of who the immigrant from Algeria is can be said to be a continuing theme of relations between immigrants from Algeria and a French population on the territory of mainland France. Its importance rests in the long duration of an emigration of Muslims from Algeria to France, which began as the twentieth century opened (Beauge, 1985; Wihtol de Wenden, 1988: 27).

There are a number of consequences which arise from the long period during which emigration from Algeria to France has taken place, not least of which is the development of several communities of Algerian origin in France. It would also not be the case that attitudes to immigrants from Algeria in France have remained the same throughout the whole period of migration. Just as Miles (1989) has argued, it is probably unhelpful to see a single racism as having defined relations of the immigrant from Algeria in France. The reasons for arguing that there have been a number of changes can be clearly linked to Algeria's changing legal position from that curious status of being at one and the same time a colony and a *département* of France to the impact of the creation of the post-independence state and the reclaiming of the name 'Algerian' for the Algerian and not the Frenchman in Algeria. These changes have also been accompanied by shifts in the political complexion of both states, which have had an impact on policies in Algeria on emigration and in France towards different immigrant groups. There are a number of ways in which these changes and the impact which they have had can be explored, for not only is there extensive literature in French,[8] but an increasing interest in Britain on questions of immigration and racism in France which has seen the publication of Maxim Silverman's (1992) *Deconstructing the Nation: Immigration, Racism and Citizenship in Modern France*, and John Hargreaves's (1995) *Immigration, Race and Ethnicity in Contemporary France*, as well as the translation into English of various articles by Colette Guillaumin (1995).[9]

Immigration from Algeria to France can be dated back to as early as 1905–06, with the result that by the mid-1920s numbers had increased to around 70,000 (Therborn, 1995). Immigration therefore provided for some of these immigrants an early experience of proletarianization, an experience which would have an impact on the development of the nationalist movement in Algeria. For many, it was also – given the structure of the labour market in Algeria itself and the relatively circumscribed development of industry within the colony – their primary experience of the industrial labour market. The experience of industrial labour conditions in France was to be important in a variety of ways. However, perhaps the two most significant were first the impact which it had on the development of the nationalist movement, and secondly, the creation inside French industry of important concentrations of Algerian-origin labour. Experience of industrial labour in France led to the creation among immigrant workers in France in the mid-1920s by Messali Hadj of a radical nationalist movement, the *Étoile Nord Africaine*. The creation of *Étoile Nord Africaine* led ultimately to the development of two separate strands within the nationalist movement which would split the movement at the very point of the launching of the armed struggle, even though in practice the immigrant workers in France would be a source of support for the struggle. The FLN would create a specific wing, *Fédération de France*, to organize on-the-ground support for the nationalist struggle in France, and it was the demonstration by these workers in France on 17 October 1991 and the subsequent repression carried out by Maurice Papon[10] which helped to show that the ideological battle for Algeria was lost.

This long history of immigration from Algeria to France and the special relationship which Algeria had in the configuration of French politics meant that in the post-World War II establishment of a system of regulation for immigration in 1945 when the ONI (*Organisation Nationale de l'Immigration*) was set up, immigrant workers from Algeria were to be exempted from its provisions by a special Ordonnance of 1947 which allowed virtual free movement of labour between Algeria and France (Hargreaves, 1995: 178). Such special status has also been translated into special arrangements over nationality and citizenship. Thus Algerian immigrants and children of Algerian immigrants have a wider access to French nationality than other immigrant groups. These arrangements reflect the special relationship which France has had with Algeria and have also played a role in directing most of the emigration which has originated from Algeria exclusively to France. This is illustrated by European Union data (RIMET, 1995) whose figures for Maghrebine immigration into the European Union provide only a single destination for Algerian immigration – France. The consequence of this particular directional flow are that it has had the effect of focusing the concept of immigrant in France on the Algerian in which Algerians are perceived as not only the pre-eminent migrant group but also the pre-eminent group of Muslims in France. In fact, other migrant groups in France, some of which are also Muslim, are almost as large. For example the RIMET (1995) figures suggest that Moroccan migrants now constitute almost as large a group as Algerian immigrants (Table 8.1); while the 1982 Census enumerated the size of the Algerian immigrant population as equal to that of the Portuguese (INSEE quoted in Lloyd, 1991).

At the same time, migration both internal and external has been a significant element in French demography since the nineteenth century. The reasons for this are complex; however, Ogden and White (1989) argue that there are four major reasons for the specific patterns of migration in France: a low overall population growth; the maintenance of a significant agricultural sector with its accompanying creation of a large class of small rural proprietors with both a relatively low birth rate and a low propensity to move; widespread rural industrialization; and the specific locations of urban and industrial growth in the North, Lorraine, Alsace, Lyons, and St Etienne as well as the port cities of Marseilles and Bordeaux. As a result, almost a third of France's population has foreign ancestry including major political figures such as Charles Pasqua himself. These factors have also meant that the number of foreign migrants in the French population has remained consistent over the last 100 years, as Table 7.1 illustrates.

Table 7.1 Percentage of foreigners in the French population

Year	Percentage
1881	2.7
1921	3.9
1936	6.5
1950	4.1
1990	6.4

Source: Göran Therborn (1995), *European Modernity and Beyond*.[11]

Table 7.1 shows that the numbers of foreign migrants in France's population today is only marginally higher than it was in 1936; and that it took until 1990 for the number of foreign migrants in the population to regain the pre-World War II high of 1936. Thus the conditions in which anti-immigrant measures have been taken cannot be said to have been influenced in the first instance by actual numbers. The political nature of the issue of immigrant status is clearly illustrated by current discourses on immigration and the discussions in the National Assembly during December 1996 over reform of the Pasqua laws. Moreover, any account of migration in France cannot ignore the issue of internal migration. The changes which have occurred in external immigration centre principally around its ethnic composition, and it is the impact of this changing ethnic composition which lies at the heart of the current debate. However, one particular effect of the changing pattern of immigration has been in the location of immigrants, in that in the 1990s a far greater proportion of immigrants are concentrated in urban areas; for example, immigrants now comprise 16 per cent of the population of Greater Paris whereas in 1890 the figure was 7 per cent (Hargreaves, 1995). These changes in location have had an impact on how immigrants are viewed by the wider population. However, as in Britain, hostility towards immigrant groups is not a new phenomenon; in the case of France, such early hostilities include the communal attacks on Italians in 1893 in the Aigues-Mortes region near Marseilles (Hargreaves, 1995: 7). That the principal discourses on immigration take as their text Algerian immigration is therefore not a function of the numbers of Algerians in France but of the position Algeria and therefore the Algerian and/or Algerians hold in France.

One effect of this tendency to view the Algerian immigrant as a representative type is, as has been indicated, that it ignores some of the complexities of Algerian immigration to France and in particular that, with a history of migration which goes back over 70 years in which the political status of the emigrating country has changed, it means that it is not really possible to speak of a single Algerian presence in France; what should be thought of instead are several different communities of Algerian origin. If communities of Algerian origin are approached in this way then it is possible to see that the experience of the conditions of migration may be different from group to group, with the effect that all the communities do not necessarily have the same interests. This is important to remember because of the history of the Algerian War which created two specific categories of migrants: the *Harki* and the *pieds noirs* (former colon population which left Algeria en masse at independence). Consequently in the conceptualization of Algeria in France, Algerian communities in France can be divided into six broad groupings:

(i) Migrants who settled after World War I and formed part of the early recruitment in the 1920s to the newly-established car factories of Renault and Citroën. They were also employed in substantial numbers in mining, construction, the iron and steel industry and mechanical engineering. However, on the whole, the working population has been unskilled or semi-skilled, as for example in the iron and steel industry in the Moselle area where some 43 per cent were unskilled and 54 per cent semi-skilled (Association-France Algérie, 1966). It is this group of migrants who became members of Messali Hadj's *Étoile Nord Africaine*.

(ii) Post-World War II immigration (until 1962): despite the independence struggle, immigration was to continue throughout the war. This reflects the intensification of industrialization in France and the fact that there was free movement between Algeria and France reflecting Algeria's status as a French department. However, with the creation of independent Algeria in 1962, such migrants had to choose whether to take up Algerian nationality or French nationality and because many chose Algerian nationality there can be some extremely complex family statutes.

(iii) *Harki*: soldiers, and members of the police during the independence war, who found themselves initially abandoned by France in 1962 but in the face of massacres and their potential execution, France was reluctantly forced to evacuate a substantial number of the remainder. Braudel (1990: 215) gives a figure of 400,000. Most obviously have French nationality as they have no possibility of return to Algeria. They are probably still the least integrated into French society, as many *harki* communities were located in isolated units on the edges of small towns in rural France.

(iv) Post-independence immigration: continuing migration by nationals and citizens of independent Algeria to France and subject to changes in regulation by both governments. For example, in 1973, following attacks on Algerians living in France, the Algerian Government suspended emigration.

(v) People of Algerian ethnic origin: born in France and therefore usually in possession of French citizenship and therefore, technically at least, French.

(vi) The *pieds-noirs*: settled mainly in the south of France. Their impact on one small community is recorded in André Téchiné's film *Les*

Roseaux sauvages (The Wild Reeds) (1994). More generally, they have been an influence on French politics in the south in the Provence-Alpes-Maritimes region, and in particular can be linked in some instances to the success of the National Front in some of the cities in this area.

The need to distinguish more precisely within immigrant communities is something to which Modood (1991) has drawn attention. Early immigrants from Algeria in France experienced a process of proletarianization and were politically radicalized. Post-1992 immigration is primarily of professionals, journalists and academics whose lives have been most threatened by contemporary political events in Algeria. At the same time, not all Algerian immigrants are radical; for example, President Chirac appointed as Public Prosecutor for the Court of Appeal a long-standing political associate of the Right (*Le Monde*, 26.7.96), the lawyer Alexandre Benmakhlouf who was born in Oran, Algeria in 1939. In spite of this diversity, the Algerian immigrant in France tends to be seen as a threat to the integrity of the French state, and nowhere is this imagery more apparent than in the responses which have been made by the French state to the bomb attacks which took place between July and October 1995, and recurred in December 1996. In this dialogue, the Algerian becomes at one and the same time a criminal and a terrorist.

Terrorism and crime

The representation of immigrant groups as criminals is not that unusual; there is plenty of evidence from the British context to illustrate the manner in which this linkage is made (Gilroy 1987). What is perhaps more unusual is the representation of Algerians as being simultaneously both criminals and terrorists.[12] However, the linkage with terrorism is less surprising if a European-wide perspective is taken, as this linkage was codified in Title VI of the Treaty of European Union of 1992 and in the Schengen Accords of March 1995; and it is a link which is fundamental to the construction of policing within the European Union. However, while this forms part of the explanation, there are also certain specificities in respect of Algerians which, as has already been suggested, arise from the particular character and history of the Franco-Algerian relationship.

Consequently, to explain the Algerian as terrorist, it is necessary not only to go back to the Algerian war of 1954–62 where bombing campaigns aimed at the colon population played a key role in FLN strategy, particularly in the struggle for control of Algiers, but also to recall the discussion earlier of Lorcin (1995) and the role which was played scientifically by Algeria in the construction of racial categories and co-related stereotypes. The bombing campaigns of the latter half of the liberation war had the effect of destabilizing the colon by depriving him of the certainty which he had felt about his position in Algeria prior to the war, and as a result helped to contribute to the mass exodus of this colon population at independence. The principal destination of this colon population was of course France. The violence associated with the Algerian War was not in any sense a prerogative of the Algerian; French violence towards the Algerian was recorded by Frantz Fanon in *Sociologie d'une révolution*, not published until 1968 after Fanon was already dead. It is recorded in Gillo Pontecorvo's film of 1966, *The Battle of Algiers*, whose fictional representation of the activities of the French paratroopers has always been acknowledged as an accurate representation.[13] The uncertainties which surrounded the end of the Algerian war were intensified by a particularly brutal campaign of violence unleashed against the Muslim community by an army group which took the name OAS (*Organisation Armée Secrète*). Furthermore, the personnel involved in the OAS were also linked to a group which planned to assassinate De Gaulle.[14] Consequently, there are two distinct strands to the construction of the Algerian as terrorist: on the one hand, the realities of the Algerian War; and on the other, the ideological impact of the construction of hierarchical racial categories which depicted the Muslim of Algeria as an inferior category. The double impact of these two strands enables the Algerian immigrant to be constructed as first of all criminal and, secondly, subversive – two constructions which the events which have taken place since 1992 have served only to reinforce.

By contextualizing the position of the Algerian immigrant in France in this way, state practices that serve to focus on the Algerian immigrant as a criminal and a terrorist are more clearly visible. In clarifying the processes involved and their effects, the Roubaix incident of 29 March 1996 is useful. Roubaix involved a gun battle, carried out by the Belgian police but in collaboration with a section of the French police in Lille called RAID, which left four men dead: two Moroccans both in their 30s including the tenant (*locataire*) of the flat against which the raid took place; a third Moroccan wounded; then one Algerian in his 50s killed; and the final man killed identified as French (but who had converted to Islam as a student) whose name was given as Christophe Caze, aged 27, and who was later identified as the leader of the group. In the initial stages of reporting, the French newspapers found it difficult to decide whether or not the group had been involved in crime (*banditisme*), or if there was an Islamist root (*dérive islamiste*) resulting from fundamentalist activities (*des activités intégristes*) (*Libération*, 1.4.96; *Le Monde*, 2.4.96; *Le Figaro*, 3.4.96). In constructing the events within the Islamist framework, Caze's history was used. Here was a young man from a working-class background who had attended private schools and gone to university to study medicine then abandoned his studies having been influenced by his Islamist neighbours. The Islamist motive was construed from the presence of material from the Islamic Salvation Front's official political journal, *Al-Ribat,* and its army-wing bulletin *Tabsira* in the house in Roubaix where the seige had taken place. A fifth man, also a Moroccan, was wounded at the same time in Courtrai after a shoot-out at a house where he had been holding two women hostage. The whole affair had begun with a mini-explosion of a booby-trapped car in Lille. What this illustrates is that even though only one of the people involved was of Algerian origin, the others being Moroccan and French, it was still possible to construct the affair as Algerian and to give it Muslim terrorist overtones which then allowed the discourse of a threat to the state to be triggered and the wider Algerian community to be targeted. Its location within this wider context can also be gauged by its globalization with the involvement of cross-border police cooperation. Final reports of the incident in *Le Monde* (12.4.96) then stated that the interrogation of the sole survivor pointed to the group as criminal, the words used to describe them being organized crime (*grand banditisme*), and they were not as had been intimated Islamist; but presumptions about the individuals concerned had already led to community targeting and the arrests of other Muslims on non-specified charges.

This is well illustrated by the fact that following the terrorist discourse, eight people had been arrested in Nice (*Le Monde*, 2.4.96) on 26 March (3 days before). Two of these were identified as belonging to the Islamist movement (*la mouvance islamiste*) and in the same manner, this group also then became 'presumed Islamist terrorists', and part of a new 'Islamist terrorist network'. This reduction of all encounters between Muslims and the police authorities as the consequence of the activities of Islamic terrorism allows other issues to be subsumed. In this case, the issue was immigration and the contradictions and difficulties which had arisen as a result of the current ambiguities in the law have made many formerly legal immigrants illegal. The Nice affair as it was reported in *Le Monde* began as an enquiry about immigration control and in particular, that of the struggle against the employment of illegal workers (*l'emploi des clandestins*) through the auspices of the organization responsible for combatting illegal immigration and employment, Diccilec (*Direction centrale pour la lutte contre l'immigration et l'emploi clandestins*). In spite of this, the direction and the focus of the reporting were to change over time so that in a report in *Le Monde* (6.4.96), one of the men released had been rearrested in Monaco on 4 April because his name appeared on the papers in the Roubaix house. To confirm this interpretation, it was added that this man was thought to be close to the Islamic Centre of the Alpes-Maritimes.

What this incident helps to illustrate is how policies which are already in place, in this case counter-terrorist and anti-immigrant, are upheld by a pattern of construction of events which implies that a crime or an act of terrorism has been committed to which the state is reluctantly forced to respond. However, even before the July 1995 Paris Métro bomb which inaugurated the present public campaign against terrorism, the French police had already carried out a police operation which had led to the arrest of some 66 'islamistes' throughout France (*Le Monde*, 27.6.95), and while some were reputed to belong to Algerian organizations, there were also among those arrested members of the Tunisian Islamist Front. However, it is the Algerian groups and in particular the GIA (*Groupe islamique armé*) which dominate public discourse (*Le Monde*, 26.12.96).

Islam in France

In the discussion about terrorism and crime in the previous section, for the discourse to be complete a third element was required, namely Islam or more particularly Islam presented in the form of 'Islamist' and/or 'fundamentalist' (*intégriste*). Indeed the discourse on terrorism in particular is dependent upon a construction in which the question of the presence of Muslim communities in France means that the integrity of the French state is threatened by Islam. Indeed the issue of the religious preferences of immigrant communities in France has played a much larger role in the debate on immigration than has been the case in Britain. In Britain, writers such as Tariq Modood (1991) have struggled to incorporate some consideration of the impact of religious belief on the development of relations between migrant communities and the British state. In France, there is an extensive literature which examines the impact of Muslim communities on politics and society.[15] The very different treatment and the much higher profile which are accorded to the discussion of the role which Islam and Muslims may have within the Fifth French Republic reflect the tension within the republican state between official secularity and a Catholic Church which is not only a social force but also, as the events surrounding the Clovis celebrations indicated, a continuing political force.

While the debate today is about the relationship between Muslims and the republican state, the background to that debate and the perceptions as to the content and meaning of Islam have been constructed out of the French colonization of Algeria. Indeed, most of the major spokespeople on Islam within France have behind them the experience of Algeria; these include Mohamed Arkoun, Jacques Berque, Bruno Étienne, and Ali Merad. However, although all of these can be seen as sympathetic to and supportive of the Muslim communities in France, nevertheless as Lorcin (1995) has shown the practices of colonization influenced the particular type of formation of the categories used to describe Islam. Furthermore, this encounter with Islam took place at a time when the French state was engaged in a long struggle over the secular nature of the republican state which would be resolved at the end of the nineteenth century in favour of secularism. Consequently, the manner of the viewing of Islam in France in part reflects this struggle but it also has the effect of the elision of the two words 'Muslim' and 'Algerian'. The impact of this fusion of categories can be seen in the presentation and interpretations of various incidents in schools over young women and their wearing of a headscarf for religious reasons. Interpretations of these incidents often do not provide any information on the ethnic origin of the wearer even though reporting in the French press of other events will generally provide this information. At one level, it might seem perfectly reasonable to ignore this information; however, because of the way in which the idea of Islam and Muslim and consequently Muslim terrorist and fundamentalist are constructed so that they become Algerian, the omission of ethnic origin tends to infer that the person is of Algerian ethnic origin, which then nourishes the prevailing discourse.

This has also been true of writing in Britain on France and occurs in the two important recent works by British writers on immigration and race in France, Hargreaves (1995) and Silverman (1992). Both of these authors explore the signification of what became the celebrated affair of the Headscarf in 1989 at a school in Creil (Hargreaves, 1995: 31, 125; Silverman, 1992: 1, 111). However, neither draws attention to the fact that the young women who were involved were not Algerian but Moroccan. Thus they too in effect become part of the process by which Islam and, in particular, Islamic Fundamentalism is perceived as an Algerian issue. Secondly, the issue is posed as a confrontation between Islam and Christianity and, while such a view is consistent with the idea of a growing antagonism to migrants as the result of an encounter between radically different cultures embodied in the opposition of Muslim and Christian, this subsumes the fact that because of the 1789 Revolution, at least at an official level, the state is aggressively secular. This means that the problem is not one of confrontation between two religions as such, but a reflection of two different confrontations. The first of these is between a secular state and a section of the population which, in spite of the final acceptance by the Catholic Church in 1905 of a secular French state, still seeks to depict the one through the other. The second confrontation is as much about the internal struggle (within Muslim communities living in non-Muslim countries) over the relationship between the secular and the religious as it is evidence of a confrontation between Islam and Christianity.

The Creil headscarf affair occurred in 1989; in 1996 a similar incident occurred at a school in Albertville (Savoy) and again the young women involved were of Moroccan origin although with French nationality (*Le Monde,* 8.11.96). In this case, an additional factor has been that the teaching trade union concerned here and at a *lycée* in Paris 8 (*Le Monde,* 18.12.96) is federated to *Force Ouvrière*. These incidents serve to illustrate that not only is Muslim practice in France not uniquely an affair of Algerians, but that confrontation between Muslims and the state involves other Muslim communities. That there are other Muslim communities living in France has already been indicated – Moroccan immigration is now almost as large as that from Algeria, and there is a sizable Tunisian community, while increasingly, new immigration in the 1990s is bringing African Muslims to France. One of the major effects of these new movements is to problematize the emergence of an institutional structure for Islam in France. The necessity for such a structure reflects the patterns of organization of the French bureaucratic state; however, the problems which have been encountered are a reflection of one of the central problems which face both Muslims living outside Muslim states and the non-Muslim states in which they live. In other words, processes of representation which are possible where the state is also Muslim do not exist where the state is non-Muslim. Thus both the state and Muslims are confronted with the need to create formal systems of representation in an essentially informal religious structure. Consequently, both individuals and organizations are invested with a formalization of power and authority which would otherwise be unnecessary. This evokes a struggle for power between those who have been included within the formal structures of representation and those who have been excluded.

Institutional representation of Islam in France has in the past been focused on the Paris mosque and its head: Dalil Boubakeur, of whom many Muslims in France are suspicious both because of his close links with the Algerian government and because of the fact that the Paris mosque has been promoted by the French Right, including Charles Pasqua. The attempt to develop other institutions may be illustrated by the meeting in Paris on 15 December 1995 of a newly constituted representative group calling itself the *Haut Conseil des Musulmans de France* (HCMF – High Council of Muslims in France) (*Le Monde*, 19.12.95). This group sought to inaugurate a constitutional assembly of some 120 delegates which would represent the 400-plus organizations to which Muslims in France belong. The principal leaders of this new initiative were: Khadidja Kali (President of the Union of Muslim Women), Abderrahmane Dahmane (Radio-France-Maghreb), Embarek Kari (regional councillor of the RPR), Khalil Merroun (founder of the Évry mosque), Ahmed Baba (former Mauritanian Ambassador in France), Rachid Kaci (President of Democratia), Mohamed Mebtoul (producer of Connaître Islam), Hassan Ben Ghabrit, and Didier Ali-Bourg (a convert). A number of originating nationalities are represented among the signatories which again reflects the fact that not all Muslims in France are from the Maghreb – immigrants from French-speaking Black Africa, for example, may also be Muslims. A second point to note is that, in fact, twelve members of this group were also dissident members of Mr Boubakeur's representative council/management committee. Although it was intended to hold elections in Spring 1996 throughout France's Muslim communities to elect representatives for a General Islamic Assembly, the group split in July 1996 following the election of two Presidents. In addition, one of the founders of HCMF, Khalil Merroun, is in dispute with other Muslims in Évry over the construction of the mosque. He is accused by them of *gabegie* (mismanagement) of the funds for the construction of the mosque which has been under way for some twelve years (*Le Monde*, 11/12.8.96)

The problems encountered by the HCMF are in some respects part of the struggle for a wider control of the Muslim community in France. It united some of the principal opponents of Dalil Boubakeur, whose family has controlled the principal mosque in Paris since 1957. One of the main leaders of this opposition is Abderrahmane Dahmane, who had been ousted from direction of Radio-France-Maghreb and is under investigation for fraud and deceit, but who regained control of the radio station at the beginning of August 1996. As a result of the split in the HCMF, six of its founder members had left including Embarek Kari, an RPR regional councillor for the Île-de-France and Hassan Ben Ghabrit. These had been replaced by Laredj Nizar, *aûmonier* (chaplain) at the Fleury-Mérogis prison but also leader of the group of Muslims opposed to Khalil

Merroun as Head of the mosque at Évry and who occupied the mosque in August 1996 (*Le Monde*, 11/12.8.96 and 6.9.96); Hocine Chabaga, assistant to the mayor of Villeurbanne; and Kamel Mansour, President of the Association of Young Lyonnais who is one of the principal opponents of those running the main Lyons mosque. In fact, this mosque is also facing legal challenge. Again, although the mosque was finally inaugurated in September 1994 by Charles Pasqua, it was only after fifteen years of political and judicial wrangles and a present from the Saudi King. All of these examples are illustrative of the considerable problems faced by Muslims in organizing not only within France but within non-Muslim countries in general.

Other players and organizations in the attempt to formalize the presence of Islam in France have been CORIF (*Conseil de réflexion pour l'avenir de l'Islam en France*) which was created in 1990 by Pierre Joxe, the then Integration Minister; and Mohamed Arkoun who along with Ali Merad and Étienne Trocmé is attempting to create a national centre for the study of Islam which would also provide training for imams and community workers. The original proposal was to locate the centre in Strasbourg but this proposal was rejected by Pierre Joxe. However, it has now been revived and presented to Eric Raoult, the minister currently responsible for integration (*Le Monde*, 11/12.8.96). This episode indicates other difficulties which are faced by the attempt to realize President Chirac's July 1995 statement that Islam should now be recognized as the second religion in France. It also illustrates the cross-linkages which exist between the different organizations and how difficult that makes it in practice to create unique forms of representation.

Conclusion

Although twentieth-century migration to France has brought migrants of many different nationalities, of which some of the most significant numbers have been those of the Italians, the Portuguese and the Poles, the Algerian – although only one out of many migrant nationalities who have come to France – is still in many ways seen to define the immigrant in France. It has been argued that this importance of the Algerian in French thinking has its roots in the peculiar symbiotic relationship which was generated by Algeria's development as France's pre-eminent settler colony. As a result, migration flows have to be seen as two-way, but performing different functions. One of the results of this relationship is that Algerian migration, unlike that of most countries of emigration, has had an almost exclusive destination. The result is that, with the exception of some relatively small Algerian communities outside France, most of the emigration which has taken place from Algeria in modern times has occurred between Algeria and France.

At the same time, the numbers and the political experience of Algerian workers in France have meant that they have been seen as of political significance in both Algeria and France. The early experiences of proletarization led to the formation of the *Étoile Nord Africaine* in the 1920s. During the Algerian War, Algerian workers in France while not all for the FLN would nevertheless provide material and moral support for the struggle culminating in the October 1961 demonstration. In the industrial disputes of the 1970s, among the car workers of the Paris plants of Renault and Citroën, Algerian workers were at the forefront of militancy. Thus there is a long-established Algerian working-class history in France which makes it to some extent ironic that, in the 1990s, it is Algerian Islamic militancy which is seen to threaten the French state. The ambivalent nature of this representation has, however, been translated into a series of other representations where political unrest in Algeria is perceived as a French issue. This perception is confirmed in practice by the bomb attacks which have occurred since 25 July 1995. These attacks have been consistently attributed to Algerian groups and have led to measures in which the issue of terrorism is simultaneously linked to questions of crime and both are used to create a picture of a community in which terrorism and crime are interchangeable leitmotivs which can be used to justify repressive measures such as *vigipirate*.

To explain the Algerian as criminal consequently requires a consideration of much the same processes as those which have criminalized sections of Britain's black communities, that is, the ghettoization of different Algerian communities, poor housing, political unrest in the country of origin. One of the ways in which this can be conceptualized is to depict the relationship between France and Algeria symbolically through the idea of Algeria in France. In fact, the issue of symbolism in the characterization of the relationship between France and Algeria is important because it provides a basis for understanding the complexity of the relations which need to be portrayed. Adopting this symbolic framework makes it then possible to examine the relationship of France to Algeria at a number of different levels, which involves configurating the following: the position of Algerians in France, internal developments within Algeria, and the relationship between the French and Algerian states. This also provides a means to explore the symbolic use of words, for example the words 'Algeria' and 'Algerian' themselves, as well as other words where the importance of the symbolic element is illustrated by the ways in which things Algerian become universalized in the discourses which are used. A useful way of illustrating both the nature of the discourses used and the process of universalization is to consider two words, namely 'Arab' and 'Beur'. The word Arab was used in popular discourse as a collective name for a person of Maghrebine origin resident in France who would usually be, but is not necessarily, a Muslim. By contrast, the word Beur became the word used by young Algerians born in France to identify themselves as neither French nor Algerian. It was a declaration of difference. This difference was then translated into a distinct form of youth culture.

In emphasizing the symbolic notion of Algeria in France, what is necessarily also being drawn upon is the nature of the French colonial enterprise in Algeria. However, colonization affected Algeria and Algerians in other ways; for example, the impact of French colonial power in Algeria resulted not only in the colonization of Algerian territory but also in the creation of an entirely new phenomenon, the migration of Muslims to non-Muslim countries for the purposes of work. Just as in the nineteenth century Algeria had become an important secondary labour market for France, so France in the twentieth century became a secondary labour market for Algeria and Algerians. The development of this labour market is partly explained by the special position which colonial Algeria held in the French overseas empire which meant that Algeria was considered to be an integral part of French territory.

The ambivalences which are evident in French government policy towards the Algerian community in France are also illustrated by its attitudes towards the FIS, and associated groups such as the AIS and the GIA. These also reflect a longer-term relationship over security issues, a key aspect of French foreign policy which in Algeria involves the stationing there of some 158 members of the French *gendarmerie* (*Le Monde*, 11.11.95). Furthermore, some 20 per cent of military technical assistance personnel in the region are *gendarmes* (*Le Monde*, 11.11.95). The continuing importance of Algeria as well as of Morocco and Tunisia in French foreign policy can also be illustrated by President Chirac's making Morocco the object of his first foreign excursion, while the ambivalence of this relationship is shown in the contrast between former President Mitterrand's 'threshold of tolerance' and President Chirac's 'Islam as the second religion in France'. It is in this context that one should view the anti-immigration rhetoric of the French extreme right, articulated by the National Front but in recent years also serving to set the agenda of government policy, particularly when the RPR (*Rassemblement pour la République*) have been the party in power and Charles Pasqua has been in charge of internal policy-making – for example, in the early 1980s and again after the 1993 elections to the French National Assembly. These led latterly to a series of anti-immigration laws in July 1993, many of which were then reversed by France's constitutional council. However, enough remained to fuel the current confrontation between immigrants and the French state, although the principal sufferers are African immigrants.

In looking at the role which has been played by Algeria and the Algerian in France, a number of themes have been suggested, in particular that, since the colonial expedition of 1830, the history of the two countries has been inextricably linked, with events in one having an effect on the other. Thus political upheavals in France in the nineteenth century created the conditions for different waves of emigration to Algeria; the increasing pace of industrialization in France in the first quarter of the twentieth century reversed the flow of migration and brought the first workers from Algeria to France. However, Algeria was not only present in France in the person of migrants; it was also present in symbolic form as a French colony at such events as the 1931 Paris Exhibition and the celebration of the centenary of the conquest of Algiers in 1930. Algeria would also embody the ambiguity of France under German occupation, as part of the colon population supported the Vichy regime and there was also some support from other colon groups for the Italian Fascists; yet it was from Algeria that de Gaulle would launch the Free French counter-offensive and, at the same time as liberation was declared in Europe, French forces would attack Muslim demonstrators at Sétif, Guelma and Kherrata (Mekhaled, 1995). The division of the French state during the period 1939–45 and the subsequent ambiguities and ambivalences which marked post-war France are also reflected in the treatment of the Algerian War in France, a war which for many French soldiers became 'a war without a name', but which also at a political and ideological level repeated curious parallels through the actions of individuals implicated in both events. One such example is embodied in the repression of the 17 October 1961 Paris demonstration by supporters of the FLN which was carried out under the orders of the Head of the Paris police force, Maurice Papon.

This chapter has sought both to respond to and to illustrate Bhabha's dictum of a 'repressed history' through an exploration of the relationship between Algeria and France. This has involved a discussion of the part which Algerian emigration has played and the manner in which the tensions within this relationship are expressed through the attitude of the French state to Islam and the linking of the issues of terrorism and crime. However, as Bhabha suggests, beneath the surface of this relationship is the question of French identity. An identity which as Silverman (1992) has argued is one in which a republican and secular tradition launched by the 1789 French Revolution struggled throughout the nineteenth century with the different attempts to recreate the monarchy and reinstall the Catholic Church, a struggle relived in 1896 (and again in 1996) through the celebration of the fourteenth centenary of the baptism of a Frankish king called Clovis who is reputed to be the creator of the French nation and therefore the ancestor of the modern French state. This concern with symbols and their evocation informs both the left and the right of politics but is most starkly portrayed by the French right of the National Front where another heroine of French history, Joan of Arc, is recalled to symbolize the resistance of the French nation against the invader. However, symbolic representations are not solely a prerogative of the National Front, as the French state once again recalled Clovis in September 1996 with celebrations of the links between France and central Christian power. In these celebrations, there is no place for the dialectic of the colonial relationship. Instead, colonization is viewed as a reflection of a conception of French imperial power which nourished the French state throughout the nineteeenth and the first half of the twentieth century, and therefore forms an integral element in the creation of French identity. Colonial territories provided opportunities for the development of scientific research (Lorcin, 1995) in which the categories which were elaborated are the basis today of policies and ideas. They also created the conditions for movements of peoples between the two countries. Algeria was a settler colony, which linked it much more closely to the French political scene than was any other French colony. At the same time, the geographical proximity of Algeria to France created additional notions of interconnectedness which subsequent migration from Algeria to France only served to reinforce. Its legacy, as Provost (1996) has argued, is that the French state has still not found the means to renegotiate its relationship with its former colony.

Notes

1. There is also an article by Provost in *Le Monde Diplomatique*, September 1996: 4–5, 'Paris et Alger entre brouilles et complicités', which contains an interesting Table of Events beginning with the Évian Agreement of 18 March 1962 which ended the original war and ending with the visit by French Foreign Minister M. Hervé de Charrette in August 1996 which was followed by the assassination in Algeria of the Bishop of Oran, Mgr Pierre Claverie.

2. A *rappelé* was someone who had completed his military service after which he agreed to be a reservist who could be called upon to defend French territory. However, this was not generally perceived to extend beyond mainland France. As a result,

many of them were opposed to service in Algeria as they did not consider the war there to be a threat to the integrity of France. Tavernier's film was made with the assistance of Georges Mattei who was a rappelé and François Sirkidji, a doctor from Grenoble, another rappelé. For further information about the impact of the Algerian War, proceedings of a conference held at Salford, 11–13 October 1996 entitled 'The Algerian War and the French Army: Experience, Image, Memory (1954–62)' are to be published.

3. A number of recent studies have illustrated the ways in which science served to engender racial categories. In the case of France, Algeria (as Lorcin illustrates) was one of the sources upon which such categories were constructed. However, parallel to these ethnographic studies was work focused on the issue of the decline and fall of civilizations and the impact of these on race and nation. One example is Ernest Renan's 1882 Sorbonne presentation (1992) 'What is a nation?' – this is translated by Martin Thom in Bhabha (1990) *Nation and Narration*. More generally, the French contribution to the generation of racialized categories is discussed in Robert J. C. Young (1995) *Colonial Desire*.

4. *Vigipirate* is the name given to the counter-insurgency measures which were instituted after the attack on the Jewish school at Villeurbanne (Rhône) on 7 September 1995. It involves increased spot checks by police services on foreigners/ immigrants; the presence of the CRS at airports and frontier crossings; as well as security guard checks on entry to shops, etc. However, it was reported in *Libération* (10.10.95) that after one month of operation, of

6,935 recorded cases by the customs authorities, 5,669 concerned drugs, 244 were for arms offences and 1,305 were people whose papers were not in order, of whom 13 were charged. Measures had been suspended but were reintroduced after the December 1996 Métro bomb in Paris. It continues to be one of the government's principal public responses to the bombings and is also intended to encourage the wider population to be 'vigilant' (President Jacques Chirac speaking on TF1, 12.12.96).

5. The September 1996 celebrations were also accompanied by extensive coverage in the press. *Le Monde* (19.9.96), for example, produced an eight-page supplement entitled 'Clovis, l'Église et la République', in addition to articles such as that of 17.9.96 written by the current Archbishop of Reims, Mgr Gérard Defois, entitled 'L'Héritage chrétien fait partie de notre patrimoine national' in which he made a plea for a better recognition of the place of Christianity in the history of the development of French identity.

6. Although the actual fine imposed against Body Shop was derisory, being for the sum of 1,000FF/£135.

7. Owing to the tightly regulated employment and social security system which operates in France, a person without papers usually does not have the right to work and in the absence of this right would usually not have the right to local publicly-provided housing or social security benefits. In a real sense, such a person does not exist.

8. See for example Catherine Wihtol de Wenden (1988) *Les Immigrés et la politique*; the collection of articles edited by Jacqueline Costa-Lascoux and Émile Temime (1985) *Les Algériens en France*; Patrick Weil

(1991) *La France et ses étrangers*; Mohand Khellil (1991) *L'Intégration des Maghrébins en France*; as well as the review of French writing on immigration in Silverman (1992: 10–11).

9. Guillaumin is, perhaps more than any French writer, closest to the English tradition in her focus on racism and sexism as against immigration. A translation of some of her major articles was published in 1995.

10. Arrested September 1996 for the part he played as General Secretary of the Gironde *préfecture* during the period 1942–44 for the arrest and deportation of Jews to Drancy, a transit camp on the outskirts of Paris for which the ultimate destination was the Nazi concentration camps. He was Head of the Paris police force in 1961 and would become a Minister in the government of Giscard d'Estaing.

11. Therborn's Table is derived from G. Tapinos (1973) *L'Immigration étrangère en France*; and G. Marc (1987) *Les Étrangers en France*.

12. One of the few other migrant groups to have been represented as both criminals and terrorists were Jewish migrants in late nineteenth-century London. The image of criminality was long established and is present famously in Dicken's portrayal of Fagin in *Oliver Twist*. It was the growth of Jewish immigration from Russia and Eastern Europe at the end of the nineteenth century which transformed this image into one of terrorism.

13. The particular significance of Pontecorvo's film is being re-interpreted in a number of different ways. In one instance, it is used as an example of Low Intensity Conflict at the Royal College of Defence Studies.

14. This episode formed the basis of a book by Frederick Forsythe entitled *The Day of the Jackal* which was later made into a film of the same name, starring Edward Fox.

15. The prestigious *Annuaire de l'Afrique du Nord* consecrated its 1988 issue to 'L'Islam en France', which was then republished as a separate volume in 1990 (Étienne, 1990). This contains a 15-page 'Selective Bibliography' of works written up to 1990 about Islam in France.

8

Algeria, Islam and European Policy

In this final chapter, we return to the question of the way in which the Algerian experience, represented by the failure of the post-independence political and economic project and the parallel growth of Islamist movements, illustrates the profound ambiguities which have marked the post-independence experiences of the former colonial states. In spite of the mass departure of the *colon* population on the eve of independence, expectations about Algeria's future were universally optimistic. The first critiques of post-independence policy were primarily concerned with the validity of Algeria's socialist project. However, as we have sought to suggest, while the project itself was certainly flawed, the critique was also flawed because no one actually knew what that project should be. Furthermore, much of what was attempted could equally well be situated within the model of the post-World War II French state's political and economic project. Although Chapter 7 was concerned with the very particular relationship which exists between Algeria and France, the focus has been primarily on the internal conditions of Algeria, particularly during the Boumediene period, for the failure of the project for which in many ways he was the principal agent. In this chapter, the aim is to examine the global dynamics of the Algerian project. Some of the ways in which the Algerian project was affected by its articulation with the global economy were discussed in relation to the limitations of the use of a petroleum-centred economic motor as the principal mechanism for economic development. However, although it was the limitations of the construction of an economic project based on oil which are necessarily central to the analysis of the economic aspects of the Algerian project, that project was also affected by the dynamics of its relationship with the wider world. In that relationship, one key player was the European Union whose role particularly in the Boumediene period will now be examined in more detail. The other global factor which will be considered is the role of the wider world of Islam in the search for Algerian identity.

Throughout the period under consideration there were clearly a number of competing discourses within the Algerian polity. These can be illustrated by an extract from a speech by Boumediene on the occasion of the opening of an Agrarian Revolution village, and a quote from the presentation in the press of the aims and objectives of the Second Four-Year Plan. On the first of these occasions, the opening of an Agrarian Revolution village in the Mostaganem wilaya, Boumediene told his audience that 'Your duties consist indeed of having an unshakeable faith in this Agrarian Revolution and taking on board your responsibilities for the success of the Socialist Revolution in your country. Because your future is irremediably bound up with the success of this Revolution' (*El Moudjahid*, 24.5.74). In fact the phrase 'The future is irremediably bound up with the success of the Socialist Revolution' was used as the headline for the report. In the second example, the presentation of the aims and objectives of the Second Four-Year Plan, each significant element is introduced with the words 'The Revolutionary Council and the Government'; the focus is particularly on the issue of education and, while talking about the need for an education system which is able 'to properly meet the enormous needs of the economy', the actual focus in the section on education is 'the transformation of the Algerian man and the recovery of his identity' which is to be achieved by 'actively pursuing the programme of arabization previously embarked on, which constitutes an essential instrument for the restoration of our national personality and which must come out from the use of the national language in all areas of economic, social and cultural life' (*El Moudjahid*, 15.5.74). The problem which these two speeches highlight is the division which is being made between the conception of the Revolution in the realm of the economic, with the conception of its meaning in the realm of the political. On the one hand, the individual is asked to put his or her faith in a future based on a socialist project and, on the other, is asked to put his or her faith in the discovery of the authentic Algerian through the use of a particular form of speech. However, the form of speech by which this authentic Algerian will be rediscovered is not the same form of speech as that in the first discourse. The tensions and the ambiguity which this presents in part helps to explain how it was possible for the Algerian state at the same time as it pursued one project to be also providing the base for the emergence of a different project, the rise of Islamist movements. Furthermore, it also helps to explain the actual inability of the state either to compromise with these movements or neutralize them because, in effect, the state itself was a partner in their development.

However, if the internal project of the post-independence Algerian state manifested itself through this dual discourse, it was also necessary for the state to pursue more than one external project. This is apparent in the post-independence Algerian state's relationship with its former colonial power and with the European Union, when these are set alongside the relations pursued with the Arab Middle East and in particular with Egypt where many of the FLN had found refuge; with the Third World in general exemplified by the 9 April 1974 speech to the United Nations; and of course with the former communist countries including the Soviet Union. However, the Algerian state was also the object of the competing discourses of others, among which can be counted the European Union. Within the European Union, these competing discourses can be observed through the tensions between economic and commercial policy initiatives and the politics of immigration control. Algeria also illustrates how a favoured partner of the 1970s, and a country whose ties with one member state – France – are long historically and complex in practice, can find itself no longer a favoured partner once the state becomes in-/af-fected by the rise of Islamist movements. It is then not simply a question of the relationship with an individual member state that is subject to scrutiny but its relationships with all member states.

The idea that what is present is in effect two faces of the same coin is important to an understanding of the apparent paradoxes of the growth of Islamist movements in Algeria. While Chapters 2 and 3 focused on the historical and ideological bases on which post-independence economic policy – and particularly that of the Boumediene era – were based, Chapters 4, 5 and 6 examined in more detail the ideological basis and the outcomes of economic policy-making during the Boumediene era and argued that the image and reality of economic decision-making were more complex than the international projection of the Algerian state as 'socialist'; in other words, that this naming of the state in fact obscured the bases of the economic model which was used – that is, the 1945 French *étatiste* model; and furthermore, that the nature of many of the subsequent problems which arose from its adoption and in particular the bureaucratization of the state are the same problems which are being faced by the French state in the 1990s. The difference being that because Algeria was an underdeveloped economy, these problems took less time to surface; and they arose more quickly and more starkly. In large part this was due to the fact that the basic political, ideological and economic infrastructures, or what in the context of Eastern Europe has been called 'civil society', were themselves insufficiently developed to provide the internal camouflage for the system. However, neither states nor economies operate autonomously, and Algeria also illustrates the role which a bilateral dependency established during the colonization process can continue to play – the subject of Chapter 7.

In Chapter 3 the different meanings which Islam has possessed in Algeria from the pre-colonial period to the rise of the Islamist movements during the 1980s were explored. In this chapter, it is the global context which is the focus and how external events within the Muslim world have generated new contradictions for Muslim states as a result of the impact of these developments on the other external dependencies of such states. Various authors have identified events which signify the turmoil which has been experienced within the Muslim world during the twentieth century. Among the events which are most commonly identified are colonization, decolonization, the foundation of Israel, the post-1979 Iranian state, the Gulf War and Afghanistan (A.S. Ahmed, 1992; Mernissi, 1993; Zubaida, 1993). It is argued that each of these events destabilized the internal political order of the Muslim world, a process which was then accentuated by economic relations. Colonization placed non-Muslim rulers in charge of Muslim peoples; while decolonization served to confirm the political and economic order established by colonization. The controversial circumstances of the foundation of Israel and the subsequent politics of the Israeli state served both to destabilize the old political centre of the Muslim world and also to divert attention from internal political and economic issues to external politics. The creation of the Islamic Republic of Iran in 1979 and its almost immediate seizure of the US Embassy suggested that western hegemony could be challenged, but the price was a legacy of western state antagonism and opposition which served to create western foreign policies in which there was only one possible enemy, Iran. The Gulf War's impact was the opposite as it showed Muslim states fighting Muslim states under the control of the west; this event more than any other seems to have been felt as deeply traumatizing (A.S. Ahmed, 1992; Mernissi, 1993). Finally, though, to Afghanistan which at first was a pawn in the struggle for hegemony between communism and capitalism but which, because of a profound misunderstanding of the political complexities of the region, has created a far more difficult legacy in which one important effect has been to contribute to a destabilization of other parts of the Muslim world.

In considering the specific impact of these events on Algeria, the impact of colonization and the aftermath of decolonization can be seen to have created the base conditions for the unfolding of the different trajectories forming the basis of the discourses of the contemporary state. The Algerian struggle for independence was a nationalist struggle and the FLN was, as its title indicates, a National Liberation Front. However, in the formulation of the nationalist project which was its base, the FLN built upon the formulations of the Association of Reformist Ulama of the

1930s whose project had been both nationalist and aimed at the transformation of the Muslim practices of the day. It has been argued (Colonna, 1995) that the Association aimed at, and succeeded in, creating the conditions for a reorientation of everyday Muslim practice. In particular, they sought the affirmation of the supremacy of the '*ulama* to that of the 'saints' (Colonna, 1995: 333). Colonna further argues that they seized control of the cultural/religious domain (Colonna, 1995: 338) and in so doing transformed the nationalist movement from a primarily secular project to a project in which there was a latent religious content (Colonna, 1995: 299). The implications of this shift and the impact which it would have were not immediately visible as first the events of World War II intervened, and then the FLN as an organization was able to subsume within it a variety of different ideological views. It can be seen that a number of factors contributed to a process which entailed a shift in primary identification from nationality and individually-based identification to a universalistic identification, and the abstracted notion of Muslim. These processes did not begin with the events of the 1980s and 1990s although these helped to give these processes form. In a general sense, they are also about finding ways to express unity, but in this case it is a unity between religious and secular life which the impact of colonization had disrupted but for which it had failed to provide alternatives. At the same time, as colonization affected the basic structures of everyday life and governance within the Muslim political community in Algeria, it also created the conditions for the development of a largely new phenomenon, the migration of Muslims to non-Muslim countries in which they would not only constitute minorities but also minorities of non-equal social status. The ways in which the institution of patterns of migration for work result in an inferior social status is something which is largely alien to Muslim thought, where principles of equality hold a fundamental position in the construction of the civil and economic community as well as of the religious community.[1]

This discussion has attempted to show that one of the processes of globalization was in effect colonization, and it was colonization which became the catalyst for a series of other processes of globalization, of which perhaps the most immediately important were migration and nationalism. However, at the same time, colonization also changed the character of the Muslim polity in such a way that the twentieth century has witnessed a series of movements in search of new ways to legitimize the realities which were created. Consequently, the roots of the Algerian Islamist movements of the 1990s are only partly to be found within Algeria itself. Certainly, they are an expression of the attempt to reconstitute Algerian society in the post-independence period and to define it as Muslim, that is 'The recovered Algerian morality – the Islamic and Arab morality' (*El Moudjahid*, 16.5.74).[2] The author of this piece makes some attempt to define what he means by arguing that the economic development process brings with it 'dangerous temptations' for the individual, and that the aim of the these policies is not 'the satisfaction of private egoisms' but 'the enrichment of the country and the people, and the promotion of the citizen and social justice'. What this short piece serves to illustrate is the difficulty which was faced in actually articulating a post-independence moral code. In other words, what did being Muslim mean, what was this 'Islamic and Arab morality' and once it was named would it be able to deliver what it promised?

The effect of colonial practices had been initially to shift the locus of Muslim practice away from the towns/urban centres and towards the popular Islam of the rural areas. However, this was to change in the 1930s with the emergence of the Association of Reformist Ulama and shift the locus back to the towns. In the years after independence, each Algerian regime sought to reconstitute the Islamic specificity of their new state, to recover an 'Islamic and Arab morality'. One of the methods which was used was to invite Muslim scholars and teachers from other parts of the Muslim world and in particular Egypt, Iraq and Pakistan to come and teach in its educational institutions and to help provide other kinds of welfare.

Algeria illustrates that the disruption and dislocation of colonization mean that it is not simply a case of being a Muslim state: what that Muslim state is has to be constructed and given meaning. However, while the focus here has been the individual state, Islam itself is global; consequently the construction of meaning requires to some extent the transcendence of the local in favour of the universal. Thus, while what was left of Islam in Algeria was largely rural, the focus of today's Islamist movements is the expanding urban areas. Such movements do not therefore draw upon the internal alone but are resourced from the external Islamic world. Consequently, they also reflect a new globalization of Islam in which there are a number of key players including Saudi Arabia and Pakistan. It is the capacity of Saudi Arabia and the Gulf in general to provide financial support to particular types of Islamist movements which allows those same movements the possibility of autonomous development. However, while Saudi Arabia can supply economic aid and also the sense of authority and power which it derives from its status as the guardian of the two holy cities of Mecca and Medina, it also requires other players to mediate and facilitate. In this role, an important actor is Egypt which, through its own long history of Muslim scholarship embodied in such institutions as the al-Azhar university/mosque in Cairo, provides a sense of continuity and permanence within a broader context of loss. These represent general processes of globalization within the Muslim world and the world in general (Guibernau, 1996).

A further example of the impact of globalization on Islam has been the war in Afghanistan (1980+) in which those forces opposed to communism were subsumed under the banner of Islam. The process was supported by financial and military aid from both Muslim and western states to the Muslim groups engaged in the fight against the Soviet-backed regime. However, the war also drew in as combatants young Muslims from the wider Muslim world, and some of these were Algerian. The war thus provided an opportunity for young men from many parts of the Muslim world to gain military experience and acquire weapons. Today, these fighters have the nickname of Afghani and such Afghani elements are to be found in the fighting wings of the Islamist movements in Algeria – that is, the AIS (Islamic Salvation Army) and the GIA (Islamic Armed Group). In the same spirit, young Muslims in other countries, particularly other European countries, offered themselves as fighters to the Bosnian government in their conflict against Serbia. In the light of the wider impact of the Afghan war, it may be useful to reflect that the impact of this more recent experience will probably depend on the management of the peace in Bosnia and whether that peace is perceived as just. In fact the ambiguities of the peace process are becoming apparent as post-independence Bosnia seeks to assume a Muslim character (*Le Monde*, 1.9.96).

European Union policy and the Maghreb

The focus so far having been primarily on the the ways in which globalization has affected the ideological construction of the Islamist movements in Algeria today, in this section I want to turn to the economic aspects of the globalization process and to look in particular at the role which is being and was played by the European Union particularly during the period of Boumediene. European Union policy must necessarily unite national state interests as well as articulating a common Union interest. In European Union policy, the Mediterranean Partner countries are more than the Maghreb and more than Algeria even though, from its origins in the Global Mediterranean Policy of 1972, Mediterranean policy has tended to reflect the French state's concern with the Maghreb. As the changing nomenclature suggests, European Union policy-making with regard to the southern Mediterranean is not static; current policy reflects Union and national state concerns over immigration (Title VI of the Treaty of European Union 1992) coupled to a recognition that more rigorous border controls are not a sufficient answer. As a result there is a visible shift in policy towards the encouragement of economic development in these countries. This contrasts to the position in the 1970s when concern with immigration was minimal and there were more fears about the impact that economic development policies in the south might have on European economies. As a result, European Union policy-making was actually restrictive of the kinds of development which it now favours. In order to give some idea of how priorities have changed, therefore, it is useful to reconsider the history of European Union relations with post-independence North Africa.

The pattern of the relationship between Algeria and the EEC after Algerian independence in 1962 illustrates the ambiguous nature of the relationship which exists between the economies of the Third World and those of the already industrialized nations in which the Third World country may have the appearance of power but where the reality of power remains with the West. Algeria illustrates the underlying structural weakness of these countries, and demonstrates that even a strongly articulated policy for national development was not sufficient to establish relations with the EEC and the other industrialized nations on a more equal basis and in accordance with internal national priorities. The reality of Algeria's relationship with the European Community shows that even where a Third World country has coherent policies and, in principle, the natural resources to implement those policies, its ability to manoeuvre and to obtain what is in its own best interests is circumscribed.

Although it is Algeria's relations with the EEC which are of primary concern, Algeria had economic ties with the United States particularly with regard to long term contracts for the supply of natural gas. For many of those contracts concluded in the late 1960s and early 1970s, the Algerian government would seek to renegotiate the terms of supply after the impact of the 1971 nationalizations. At the same time, links were developed with the former 'socialist countries' (the USSR and Eastern Europe). Indeed, at the beginning of the 1980s, the Soviet Union had a $715m aid programme in Algeria (*Financial Times*, 4.3.80). The programme was, however, largely directed into steel and aluminium production, hence Russian involvement in the construction of the iron and steel plant of El Hadjar, near Annaba in eastern Algeria. As important was the fact that the USSR also supplied Algeria with military equipment including their T54/55 tanks (*Financial Times*, 5.9.79). Finally, there were some attempts to develop relations with the People's Republic of China. However, although the significance of Algeria's relations with such countries (particularly perhaps at an ideological level) should not be ignored, nevertheless patterns of economic relations were shaped more by the impact of western Europe and the United States than they were by the former 'socialist countries'.

In the 1970s, the EEC viewed itself as 'a region specializing in the processing of raw materials from other continents which she then resells to them as finished products'.[3] This view, they argued, was based on the reality of its historical experience. While in one sense this may be interpreted as a somewhat crude statement of the form that relations have historically taken between the countries of the Third World and the member states of the European Union, it does nevertheless also illustrate that Europe was in a very real sense still dependent upon imported raw materials. Supplying states may have come to exercise some control over these raw materials: for example, the oil-producing states who both individually and through their umbrella organizations OPEC and OAPEC[4] did come to exercise a control over the terms of trade in the supply of petroleum and natural gas to the European nation states. However, there were no parallel changes in the terms of trade as they affected textiles and agricultural products.

The idea of the European Economic Community as a distinct geographical area can be seen as the beginnings of an attempt to transform an economic customs union born out of the trauma of World War II into a political entity which would articulate common interests and be sufficiently strong to counter the hegemonic power of the United States. However, in the EEC's relations with the Third World, it must be remembered that the majority of the original member states were ex-imperial centres. These were most notably France and the United Kingdom; but also The Netherlands, Belgium, Italy and Germany had all at some time had imperial possessions. The effects that the possession of colonies had on the economic development of the Community's individual member states while dependent on the particular characteristics of the colonies themselves nevertheless had produced a general pattern of reliance on importing raw materials cheaply from production centres outside Europe. Consequently, the Tariff arrangements, and the various Association Agreements which were made with countries outside Europe need to be understood within this general framework. The articulation of 'Global Mediterranean Policy' (EC, 1972) was a first response to the political and economic effects resulting from the decolonization process of the 1960s.

The Global Mediterranean Policy can be seen as the beginnings of a significant policy initiative aimed at all the countries which border upon the Mediterranean. It was based on an idea of a 'multiplicity of links due to proximity and tradition' (EC, 1972) between these countries and the Community. These links were seen as being reinforced by a 'considerable degree of interdependence, going beyond trade and extending to labour, tourism and all manner of invisible trade' (EC, 1972). The presence of this interdependence of political and economic interests, it was argued, provided the substantive basis for Europe's actual and envisaged influence in the Mediterranean region. Ideally the policy hoped for the conversion of this influence into a policy for 'making the development of the Mediterranean Basin a natural extension of European integration' (EC, 1972). In the 1974 General Report (EC, 1975), it was stated that cooperation between the Community and the Maghreb countries should have three principal aims. These were to be the promotion, *inter alia*, of the Maghreb countries' industrial output as well as their exports to the Community; the introduction of cooperation in the industrial, scientific and technical fields and on matters of the environment; and the encouragement of private investment particularly by the Community's operations with a view to promoting the transfer of European capital and know-how to the Maghreb countries and the opening up of North Africa's markets. There were perhaps two principal concerns here. The first was to ensure that the industrial development of the Maghreb countries would provide exports markets for European Community production; and secondly, that the actual process of industrialization would inevitably be dependent upon a supply of skilled manpower and technical advisors, a commodity which European countries were able to sell through companies like France's Technip and Italy's Snam Progretti, both of which were major operators in Algeria.

Although the main focus of EEC policy in the 1970s towards the Maghreb was economic policy, in the mid-1970s a shift in emphasis was noticeable with the development of the Euro-Arab Dialogue (EEC, 1977). The first meeting of this group was held in May 1976 and was followed by a second meeting in Tunis in February 1977 when a Euro-Arab Centre for the transfer of technology was established. At the same time, other projects under consideration were the setting-up of a Euro-Arab centre for trade cooperation and the negotiation of a multilateral convention on the protection of investments. However, the funding ($15 million) for feasibility studies for these proposed projects was supplied by Arab country participants, not by their European partners. A number of meetings were subsequently held but President Carter's Camp David talks between Israel and Egypt during 1978 resulted in the suspension of the Dialogue after its December 1978 meeting in Damascus. The history of the Dialogue illustrates well the uncertain relationship between Europe and the Arab-Muslim world throughout the 1970s in which the status of Israel was, as indicated earlier, an overriding consideration in the political dynamics of Arab states.

EEC activity in the Mediterranean area increased markedly throughout the 1970s, resulting on the one hand in a series of specific agreements with Mediterranean states on trade, and on the other, the first debate on widening, which led eventually to the entry of Greece in 1981 and Spain and Portugal in 1986; but in the initial debate, four countries were under consideration for membership. The accession of the fourth country, Turkey, in spite of repeated applications by the Turkish state for membership is still outstanding. The formalization of relations with the other states of the region were completed through the signature of bilateral agreements. However, in the execution of this policy, the position of Algeria continued to reflect the ambivalent status it had enjoyed as a French department. This meant that throughout the 1960s and early 1970s there was no formal agreement on relations between it and the Community. As a result, Algeria was not dealt with on the same third-party basis as her neighbours, Tunisia and Morocco. This had the effect of providing Algeria with a relatively privileged access to European markets, and for that reason, the Algerian government chose not to take any formal steps which might jeopardize this position. However, in 1969, negotiations were begun but their progress was slow as each party had an interest in the continuation of the existing relationship. The result was that a final agreement was not signed until April 1976 only to be almost immediately renegotiated in 1978.

The 1976 Agreement had provided for some cooperation in the energy sector but in the form of participation by EEC firms in exploration, production and processing programmes set in motion by the Algerian government. Provision was also made for the issue of invitations to tender where these involved less than 4 million dinars (or 1 million units of account).[5] The 1978 Agreement did not differ greatly from the earlier agreement, providing an overall commitment to assist industrial development in Algeria and to provide aid in the modernization of its agriculture. However, this assistance was somewhat circumscribed by the placing of restrictions on the import of certain products, including petroleum products and agricultural products such as olive oil. Thus action to encourage the development of the Algerian economy was constrained within a framework in which Algerian products were not to receive a more favourable treatment than that accorded to the same products in Member states, with the result that in agriculture, given that there was an overlap between Algerian agricultural exports and those of the Member states (olive oil, wine and citrus fruits), concessions made were in practice very limited. If the development of Algerian agriculture was not necessarily in the best interests of Community producers, neither was the development of industrial capacity, particularly in the area of 'refined petroleum products' which the 1976 Agreement had specifically excluded from free access to Community markets.[6] The April 1976 Agreement also provided for grants of 114 million units of account (456 million dinars) as assistance to Algeria in the financing of her development activities.

These Agreements reflected the traditional concerns of the countries of the European Community, and in particular those of France with its former North African colonies. At the same time, the 1970s witnessed the growing interest of countries such as West Germany in the Algerian market. For example, in the single month of July 1974 (*Bulletin Économique,* 1974), West German companies signed three exclusive contracts with Algerian state companies. These included SNMC (construction materials) with Klockner-Humboldt and Deutz (KHD) for the construction on a turnkey basis of an entirely automated cement plant (capacity: 1 million tons); Sonatrach (petroleum and gas) and Bittenfeld-Kuhng de Siehorg to construct a factory for the transformation of plastics; and Sonitex (textiles) and Uniomatex and Famatex for the supply of machinery, etc. for a textile plant at Tlemcen specializing in silks.

Throughout the 1970s, European firms were involved in a number of ways in Algerian industry. For example, the Italian firm Innocenti-Marelli were the consulting engineers for the construction of the hot-rolling mill at El Hadjar (near Annaba); while Snam Progretti (a member of the ENI group) were the consulting engineers for the construction of a polyethylene plant at Skikda; and Montfalcone was built as one of the collecting points for Algerian natural gas supplies to Europe. Britain was involved through Davy-Ashmore in the construction of the cold-rolling mill at El Hadjar; and W. S. Atkins were given the contract for the overall engineering supervision at El Hadjar for the period 1975–80.

Meanwhile Algeria itself was active on the international money market, so that by 1978 it had become the largest borrower within OPEC, having raised $3.2 bn in the financial markets (of which $721m was in bonds) as well as 'exim' credits from most of the major industrial countries. The strain of this kind of heavy borrowing began to have an effect internally within Algeria, leading in 1977 to a committee being set up in Algiers with the intention of providing better coordination of the activities of the Algerian state companies in their approaches to foreign banks. Although there was something of a pause in such activities following the death of Boumediene in 1978, they were resumed in 1983 when a loan of $800m was raised and was greeted in the *Financial Times* (28.12.83) with the headline 'Algeria brings big syndications back to life'. The question which is raised is over the extent to which western banks in fact not only colluded with such excessive borrowings but also were at least to some degree dependent upon such borrowings.

The Maghreb also illustrates how different regions slip in and out of focus. Economic problems in the North African economies in the 1980s led to a loss of interest in the area. It is only as political priorities in Europe have changed (particularly as a result of the 1992 Treaty of European Union and as a response to home pressures on the control of immigration to address fears about the transfer of the conflict in Algeria to France and the more general rise of Islamist movements within the three countries of the Maghreb) that the North African countries have once again become a focus of interest for European Union policy-makers. To illustrate this raised profile in European Union policy-making, a new policy framework is being established under the rubric of the Euro-Mediterranean policy. Under its aegis, a conference was held in Barcelona in November 1995. In addition, new Association agreements have been signed with both Tunisia and Morocco. However, these developments take place against a European Union policy over central and eastern Europe that promises not just Association but real possibilities of membership.

Looking at European Union policy with the Mediterranean Partner countries from the perspective of economic interest ignores perhaps the more dominant discourse of security. Security can be interpreted in a number of different ways: the European Council which was held in Cannes in June 1995 spoke of the Mediterranean Partner countries as having a strategic importance for the Union. However, translating this into practical policy depends upon the country, both the Maghrebine country and the European Union. For example, the association agreements signed with Morocco and Tunisia give some indication of the intended direction of policy in the region. The agreement with Tunisia was initialled in June 1995 and that with Morocco in November 1995. The agreement with Morocco means that from 1997 Morocco will have to begin to open up its market to European products, which means in the first instance to those products which are currently not manufactured in Morocco. However, from 2000 Morocco will be required to reduce its tariff barriers by 10 per cent each year for ten years (*FT Survey*, 19.12.95).

Another aspect of the policy is to provide technical aid to individual manufacturers, the idea being to prepare industry in each country for competition with European companies. Thus the European Union is providing financial aid to Tunisia to enable the Tunisian Ministry of Industry to help companies raise productivity levels, promote vocational training, etc. (*Financial Times*, 26.10.95). Algeria on the other hand is seen primarily as a threat to security, much as it is in France. Thus the European Council in Cannes appealed 'to all those involved in political life to break the cycle of violence and find a political solution through peaceful dialogue and free and fair elections' (EU, 1995). Should the parties do this satisfactorily then the EU would provide support for an economic restructuring policy in Algeria. The basis of European Union policy is as it has become in France, centred around the issue of security. Security in terms of the prevention of actions of terrorism on European Union soil; security in terms of the prevention of labour flows.

A third aspect of relations between the European Union and the Mediterranean partner countries occurs at the level of ideology, and is being negotiated around the question of the construction of a Mediterranean identity. The question of the existence of a distinct identity which might be called Mediterranean is not new. It formed the focus of the classic study by Fernand Braudel, first published in 1949: *The Mediterranean and the Mediterranean World in the Age of Philip II* (1975). Today, the European Union funds projects under this rubric such as the conference held in Cargèse, Corsica in September 1996 under the auspices of the travelling Euro-Arab University. There one of the participants, Edgar Morin, said of the Mediterranean that it was 'a sea saturated (*gorgée*) with history, cultures, religions, wars, a sea-mother, a matrix sea' but that 'The Mediterranean existed only in our subjective mind. If we cease to feel ourselves Mediterranean, there will no longer be a Mediterranean' (*Le Monde*, 8/9.9.96). The view of the Mediter-ranean as a totality, ironically, is one which has been successfully achieved only by two major Muslim powers: Muslim Spain, and the Ottoman Turkish Empire. European powers such as France have sought to unify north and south of the Mediterranean but have sought to do so on the basis of inequality – the relationship of imperial power to colony. Today, ideas of union are impeded by the desire to prevent labour migration from the south.

Relations between the European Union and the three countries of the Maghreb have always been characterized by a certain ambivalence in which opportunities for trade, industrial contracts, and markets have been encouraged, but Maghrebine emigration including Algerian emigration to the countries of the European Union has been frequently discouraged. An examination of Maghrebine migration patterns suggests, as might be expected, that there is no single pattern of migration. The individual nature of each of these migration patterns should perhaps be stressed as they reflect not only current social, political and economic circumstances but also each country's unique historical experience. The economic interpretation of migration tends towards a universalization of phenomena which can make it difficult to account for patterns of difference between countries where the underlying economic conditions appear to be the same. It also tends to mean that responses to each migration are also universalized. The superficial nature of such similiarities and therefore the limitations of globalized responses are clearly visible in the Maghrebine region.

Table 8.1 has been constructed from data available in the RIMET Report (1995) *The EC Member States and Immigration in 1993*. It should be noted that in the preparation of the Report, partial data was available from Spain, the United Kingdom and Ireland. In terms of Maghrebine migration, the inclusion of Spain would increase the figure for Moroccan migration into the European Union by a further 54,000 plus migrants.

Table 8.1   Maghrebine nationalities in the European Union 1993

	Algeria		Morocco		Tunisia	
	No.	%	No.	%	No.	%
Belgium			145,000	18.5		
France	614,207	21.9	572,652	20.4	206,336	7.7
Germany			80,278	1.7		
Italy			97,604	20.6	44,505	9.4
Netherlands			91,418	22.8		
Total	614,207	33.2	986,952	53.3	250,859	13.5

Source: RIMET (1995), *The EC Member States and Immigration in 1993.*

Percentage figures under individual receiving countries illustrate the proportion of the total foreign national population in that receiving country that is represented by this particular national grouping. Percentage figures in the totals row indicate the proprtion held by these sending countries of total immigration into the principal EU receiving countries.

Table 8.1 clearly shows that Algerian emigration into the European Union is uniquely an emigration to one member state, France, and as a percentage of the total migration by Maghrebine nationals into the

European Union, accounts for approximately a third of that migration. While France also has proportionately significant populations of both Moroccan and Tunisian migrants, in the case of the former, there is a wide geographic spread with the result that it is Moroccan nationals in the EU who comprise the largest group of Maghrebine migrants in the five main EU recipient countries. If one then adds Moroccan nationals in Spain to this number, there are over one million Moroccan migrants in the EU. In total then, Maghrebine migration in these five countries is around 1.8 million which represents approximately one-fifth of the total migrant population of 9.9 million for the nine countries covered in the Report. The significance of Algeria as a source of migrants is therefore not a universal issue for the EU but an issue limited to the interests of a single national member state: France. The question of whether this immigration has security implications for the Union can probably be answered in the negative in the sense that Algerian immigration is such a specific manifestation of a unique colonial relationship, which means that events which take place in France are in fact a reflection of that relationship and have no general application. In other words it is, as Provost (1996) suggests, as much French policy towards Algeria as it is events in Algeria itself which influences what happens within France proper. Moreover, it is by no means clear that Islamist group activity in France is an Algerian phenomenon, as indicated in the December 1996 trial of a group of Islamists where the nationality of origin of all the accused was Moroccan (*Le Monde*, 14.12.96). Furthermore, although Algerian connections were alleged, these were not only with Algerian Islamist groups but also with the Algerian security forces; and perhaps as important is that links were also shown with the 'counter-insurgency' movements in Afghanistan.

In other words, as Chapter 7 argued, even within France, concentrating the focus on the Algerian may not in practice be particularly helpful in understanding the current dynamics of political and ideological movements within the Muslim diaspora. Besides, within the European Union as a whole, other Muslim minorities are as important. Within the Union it is Moroccan migrants who form numerically the largest group of Maghrebine migrants; while in global numbers, the largest single Muslim minority comprises peoples of Turkish origin. The significance of this grouping can be explored briefly using data from the RIMET report. Table 8.2 illustrates where the principal communities of Turkish origin are to be found within the EU.

However, although Table 8.2 suggests the presence of another signific- ant Muslim minority community within the European Union, this data

Table 8.2 Turkish nationals: principal communities in the European Union

	No.	%
Belgium	83,300	6.5
Denmark	33,653	40.1
Germany	1,854,945	38.6
Netherlands	115,128	28.7
Total	2,087,026	21.1

Notes: see Table 8.1

also has to be treated with some circumspection, for in the same way that Maghrebine migrants of Algerian origin are concentrated in a single country, here migrants of Turkish origin are concentrated in a single country, namely Germany. Furthermore, the size of this population of Turkish foreign nationals within the German state arises not from the actions of the migrants themselves but from the actions of the German state through its nationality policies which mean that a largely long-term resident Turkish population has only limited access to German citizenship. The effect of this exclusion from citizenship is twofold. On the one hand, they appear in the statistics as foreign nationals and, on the other, they are denied the right to be full citizens of the country in which they live and work.

Finally, the picture of Muslim minority communities within the European Union would not be complete without including those communities settled within the United Kingdom. The size of this population has been variously calculated (Peach, 1990) but probably accounts for some 1 million people. However, the national composition is equally varied although the principal countries of origin are Pakistan, Bangladesh and India; there are also Muslims from Malaysia and the Gulf states as well as from Morocco, Tunisia and Algeria. It is after all in London that the Algerian Abou Fares/Rachid Ramda, reputed to have been involved in the July 1995 bomb attacks in France, was arrested in November 1995 and continues to be held in custody. His arrest and detention confirm the assurances given by President Chirac, in his 12 December 1996 response to a question by the journalist Marine Jacquemin, that in matters of security there was full cooperation between national security forces.

Conclusion

In thinking about Islam and Muslim minorities in the European Union, it is necessary to consider them not only in terms of resident migrant communities whose members may or may not have citizenship but also in terms of the post-colonial relationships which their presence reflects. At the same time, the post-colonial world has produced new processes of globalization within Muslim communities themselves in which flows of labour are only one part. The resolution of conflicts generated by the imperial past poses fundamental questions to the old metropoles, questions which, if Provost (1996) is right in respect of the Franco-Algerian relationship, ask the West to rethink its relationships completely. Algeria illustrates how difficult it is for a country to resolve this past independently even with an apparent surplus of natural resources if the infrastructural base is not there. The discussion throughout this book has aimed to illustrate that understanding the present and future role of Muslim communities in Europe requires an appreciation of a complex interplay of events in Europe as a whole, within individual European states and between individual member states of the Union, but in conjunction with an appreciation of developments both in the internal politics of Muslim states and in the Muslim world globally.

The annulment of the 1992 second round of elections after the December 1991 first-round initial victory of the Muslim party, the FIS (Front Islamique du Salut) illustrates the unfinished nature of this struggle. However, in spite of this victory, it is important to remember that in these elections around 41 per cent of the electorate abstained, and in practice the vote in which FIS was the majority was divided between three parties: FIS, the FLN (the party of government), and the FFS (*Front des Forces Socialistes* of Aït Ahmed, largely representing interests in the region of Kabylia). The narrow base on which this victory would have been achieved is an indication of the ambivalences which populations in states such as Algeria feel about the political conduct of their governments; thus it can be argued that what that near victory also represented is the essentially problematic nature of the systems of government and popular legitimacy in the post-independence Muslim world.

The apparent direction of the 1991 elections, if taken in this context, becomes less surprising and more comprehensible if they are seen as part of the processes which are in progress to define what an Algerian Muslim is, and in what kind of society and state an Algerian Muslim of various complexions might wish to live. In other words, the struggle for identity and meaning brings with it new conflicts in which Islam comes to play a defining role. This process of redefinition is not unique to Algeria and in practice can be seen to be taking place throughout the Muslim world. For evidence of similar processes, the recent success in the Turkish elections (24 December 1995) of the Islamist Welfare Party, *Refah* (RP) (*Le Monde*, 26.12.95) may be cited, particularly as with the FIS success in 1991, the actual margins of victory are narrow; the RP gained 21.25 per cent of the vote with its two closest rivals (including the Government party) gaining respectively 19.7 per cent and 19.2 per cent of the vote. In other words, what provokes concern is not massive shifts in popular support for Islamist parties but democratic procedures which result in narrow victories for such parties. Given this, why do such victories provoke in the non-Muslim world the fear that they do? Perhaps part of the answer may be found by drawing a comparison with the series of recent victories by communist parties in the former communist countries following democratic elections. Some writers (of whom Ernest Gellner is one example) would argue that such victories reflect the recent and as yet incomplete development of *civil society* (Gellner, 1994) in such societies. Incomplete in the sense that the range of civil institutions is not extensive, with the result that there is an absence of a balance of competing institutions to offset potentially non-democratic victories. If the development of civil institutions in the former communist countries is weak, it is equally weak in the former colonial countries. The primary impact of colonization was to destabilize structures but, having destabilized them, it sought to reconstruct them in a way which would best accommodate the colonial project. Consequently the particular manner in which French colonization was pursued also had a specific impact on the direction and formation of Muslim society within the colonial complex. It is clear therefore that the present Algerian state not only reflects the values of and a history attributable to Islam but is also a product of the interaction between Islam and the experience and aftermath of French colonization. Decolonization and the discourse adopted by the post-independence Algerian state initially gave the impression that Algeria was engaged in a project to build a 'socialist' state. However, the basis for its construction was theoretically and structurally weak. The implosion of the contemporary Algerian state reflects the underlying weakness of this project.

Notes

1. For a discussion of the theoretical principles underlying the creation of an economic community of Muslims, see for example Naqvi (1994).
2. 'La morale algérienne retrouvée – la morale islamique et arabe'; the word *retrouvée* can be interpreted to mean either 'recovered' or 'rediscovered' and there is a sense in which both these meanings are intended here.
3. Bulletin of the European Communities 1/75 'The Community's supplies of raw materials'.
4. OPEC stands for the Organization of Petroleum Exporting Countries and was set up in 1960 as an attempt by oil producers to enhance their bargaining power (Odell, 1975: 18). OAPEC attempted to do the same thing but for Arab producing countries only.
5. Units of account were subsequently replaced by the *ecu* (or European Currency Unit). Both represent a method of a nominal central monetary accounting system.
6. The seriousness with which the threat from Middle East producers of oil and gas products was treated at this time is illustrated by this report on SABIC (*Financial Times*, 29.3.84) which argued that its potential growth would be constrained by the fact that European production of basic chemicals was already under serious threat from Middle Eastern producers, including Algeria. SABIC: Saudi Arabian Basic Industries Corporation.

Bibliography

Documentary sources

Administration des douanes 1827 à 1836 (1838) *Tableau décennal du commerce de la France avec ses colonies et les puissances étrangères.* Paris: Imprimerie royale.

Algerian Export Year Book, 1973/74.

Algérie, naissance d'une société nouvelle: charte nationale du peuple algérien 1976, Paris, Éditions sociales, introduction by Robert Lambotte.

Bulletin économique (1974), nos 2–4, Algiers: Algérie Presse Service.

Cannes European Council, 26–27 June 1995, *Presidency Conclusions.* Doc/95/6.

Chambre de Commerce et d'Industrie d'Alger (1974) *Algérie, situation économique 1972–73.*

Documents sur les relations entre l'Algérie et les sociétés pétrolières françaises (1971). Algiers.

European Commission (1995) *The EC Member States and Immigration in 1993. Synthesis Report 1993: Closed Borders, Stringent Attitudes.* (RIMET Report), Luxembourg: Office for Official Publications of the European Communities.

European Communities, Commission of (1972) *Memorandum on a Community Policy on Development Cooperation.*

European Communities, Commission of (1975) *Eighth Report.* Brussels-Luxembourg.

European Communities, Commission of (1976) *EEC-Algeria.* Brussels: Information, Cooperation and Development 120/76.

European Communities, Commission of (1977) *The Community and the Arab World.* Background Report, ISEC/869/77.

European Communities, Commission of (1978) *Official Journal,* L263, 21(2), 27 September.

European Communities, Council of (1992), *Treaty on European Union.* Maastricht, 7 February 1992.

FLN (1962), *Projet de Programme pour la réalisation de la révolution démocratique populaire.* The Tripoli Programme. Algiers: Al-Chaab.

FLN (1964) *Charte d'Alger.* First Congress 16–21 April.

RADP (République Algérienne Democratique et Populaire (1970) *Données 1969 sur la commerce de gros privé.* Algiers.

RADP (1970) *Listes des sociétés nationales à activité industrielle en 1970.* Algiers.

RADP (1970) *Plan quadriennal 1970–1973. Rapport général.* Algiers: Éditions Populaires de l'Armée.

RADP (1971) *Annuaire statistique de l'Algérie 1970.*

RADP (1978) *Annuaire statistique de l'Algérie 1977–8.*

RADP (1980) *Listes des sociétés nationales ayant une activité industrielle et leurs unités de production.* Algiers.

RADP, Direction des Statistiques et de la Comptabilité Nationales (1978) *Recensement général de la population et de l'habitat 1977 – données abrégées, résultats du sondage.*

RADP, MARA: Commission Nationale de la Réforme Agraire (no date) *Coopération et révolution agraire – recueil des textes relatifs à la coopération agricole.* Algiers: Imp. El Baath.

RADP, Ministère d'État chargé des Finances et du Plan (no date) *Note rapide sur la situation de l'emploi avant et après l'indépendence (1960–1966),* PIT No. 17. Algiers: Direction Générale du Plan et des Études Économiques, Sous-direction des Statistiques.

RADP, Ministry of Information and Culture (1970) *Education.* Algiers: The Faces of Algeria 7.

RADP, Ministry of Information and Culture (1971) *Hydrocarbons.* Algiers: The Faces of Algeria 15.

RADP, Ministry of Information and Culture (1971) *Basic Industries.* Algiers: The Faces of Algeria 17.

RADP, Ministère de l'Information et de la Culture (1973) *L'Organisation socialiste des entreprises.* Visages de l'Algérie 22.

RADP, Ministry of Primary and Secondary Education (no date) *Enseigner en Algérie.* Algiers.

RADP, Secrétariat d'État au Plan (1970) *La Situation de l'emploi et des salaires 1970.* Algiers: Imp. Direction des Statistiques.

RADP, Secrétariat d'État au Plan (1971) *L'Emploi 1971.* Algiers: Imp. Direction des Statistiques.

RADP, Secrétariat d'État au Plan (1972) *Industrie 1969,* vol. IV. Algiers: Imp. Direction des Statistiques.

RADP, Secrétariat d'État au Plan (1974) *IIe Plan quadriennal 1974–1977.*

RADP, Secrétariat d'État au Plan (1978) *Les Résultats de l'enquête emploi et salaires de 1977,* Algiers: Direction des Statistiques et de la Comptabilité Nationale.

Sonatrach (1968) *Sonatrach.* Paris: Public Relations Department.

Secondary Sources

Abdel-Malek, A. (1965) *Anthologie de la littérature arabe contemporaine.* Paris: Éditions du Seuil.

Abun-Nasr, J. M. (1965) *The Tijaniyya. A Sufi Order in the Modern World.* London: Oxford University Press.

Ageron, Ch-R. (1968) *Les Algériens musulmans et la France I.* Paris: PUF.

Ageron, Ch-R. (1970) *Histoire de l'Algérie contemporaine, 1830–1964,* Paris: PUF; English edition translated and edited by Michael Brett (1991) *Modern Algeria – A History from 1830 to the Present.* London: Hurst & Company.

Ahmed, A. S. (1992) *Postmodernism and Islam: Predicament and Promise,* London: Routledge.

Ahmed, A. S. (1993) *Living Islam.* London: BBC Books.

Ahmed, K. (1972) Plan et planification, in *Révolution Africaine,* **451,** 13/19 (octobre).

Ahmed, L. (1992) *Women and Gender in Islam.* New Haven and London: Yale University Press.

Aït Ahmed, H. (1983) *Mémoires d'un combattant: l'esprit d'indépendance 1942–1952.* Paris: Sylvie Messinger.

Akkache, A. (1971) *Capitaux étrangers et libération économique: l'expérience algérienne.* Paris: François Maspero.

Akkache, A. (1973) *L'Évasion.* Algiers: SNED.

Al-Azmeh, A. (1993) *Islams and Modernities.* London: Verso.

Amin, S. (1965) *L'Économie du Maghreb.* Paris: Les Éditions de Minuit, 2 volumes.

Amin, S. (1970) *The Maghreb in the Modern World.* Harmondsworth: Penguin.

Amin, S. (1973) *Le Développement inégal: essai sur les formations sociales du capitalisme périphérique.* Paris: Les Éditions de Minuit.

Amin, Samir (1989) *Eurocentrism.* London: Zed Books.

Ammour, K., Leucate, C., Moulin, J.-J. (1970) *La Voie algérienne: les contradictions d'un développement national*. Paris: François Maspero.

Amott, T. and Matthaei, J. (1991) *Race, Gender and Work – A Multicultural Economic History of Women in the U.S.* Montreal/New York: Black Rose Books.

Anderson, B. (1991) *Imagined Communities*. London: Verso.

Anderson, P. (1974) *Lineages of the Absolutist State*. London: Verso.

Ansky, M. (1950) *Les Juifs d'Algérie. Du décret Crémieux à la libération*. Paris.

Anthias, F. and Yuval-Davis N. (1990) *Woman – Nation – State*. London: Macmillan. Also *Feminist Review* 44.

Appiah, A. (1992) *In My Father's House: Africa in the Philosophy of Culture*. London: Methuen.

Ardagh, J. (1977) *The New France*. Harmondsworth: Penguin.

Association France-Algérie (1966) *Colloque sur la migration algérienne en France*. Paris.

Badillo, D. (1980) *Stratégies agro-alimentaires pour l'Algérie. Prospective 2000*. Aix-en-Provence: Coll. 'Maghreb Contemporain', EDISUD.

Baghli, S-A. (1978) *Aspects of Algerian Cultural Policy*. Paris: UNESCO.

Barbé, R. (1959) Les Classes sociales en Algérie, in *Économie et Politique* 12: pp. 7–23; and Les Classes sociales en Algérie II. Les Activités agricoles, in *Économie et Politique* 13, pp. 22–45.

Barone, E. (1908/1972) The Ministry of Production in the Collectivist State, in A. Nove and D. M. Nuti *Socialist Economics*. Harmondsworth: Penguin.

Bauchet, P. (1964) *Economic Planning, the French Experience*. London: Heineman.

Beauge, G. (1985) Migrations internes et migrations externes: exode rural et offre de travail algérienne en France entre 1840 et 1940, in J. Costa-Lascoux and E. Temime, *Les Algériens en France*, Paris: Publisud.

Beauvoir, S. de and Halimi, G. (1962) *Djamila Boupacha*. London: André Deutsch/Weidenfeld & Nicolson.

Bedrani, S. (1982) *L'Agriculture algérienne depuis 1966 – étatisation ou privatisation?* Paris: Economica.

Benamrane, D. (1980) *Agriculture et développement en Algérie*. Algiers: SNED.

Benissad, M. E. (1979) *Économie et développement de l'Algérie (1962–78): sans-développement de l'Algérie*. Paris: Economica.

Berbrugger, A. (1871) La Régence d'Alger sous le consulat et l'empire, in *Revue Africaine* 15, pp. 241–60.

Bernis, G. D. de (1963) L'Industrialisation en Algérie, in F. Perroux *Problèmes de l'Algérie indépendente, étude présentée par François Perroux*. Paris: PUF.

Bernis, G. D. de (1971a) L'Économie algérienne depuis l'indépendance, in Ch. Debbasch *et al. Les Économies maghrébines*. Paris: CNRS 1971.

Bernis, G. D. de (1971b) Les Industries industrialisantes et les options algériennes, in *Tiers Monde*, 47, pp. 545–63.

Bernis, G. D. de (1975) L'Algérie à la recherche de son indépendance: nationalisation et industrialisation, in J. D. Esseks, *L'Afrique de l'indépendance politique à l'indépendance économique*, Paris: François Maspero/PUG, 19–61.

Berque, J. (1955) *Structures sociales du Haut Atlas*. Paris: PUF.

Berque, J. (1967) *French North Africa: The Maghrib Between Two World Wars*. London: Faber and Faber; English translation by Jean Stewart.

Bhabha, H. K. (1990) *Nation and Narration*. London: Routledge.

Bhabha, H. K. (1990a) The Third Space, in J. Rutherford, *Identity*. London: Lawrence and Wishart, 207–21.

Bhabha, H. K. (1994) *The Location of Culture*. London: Routledge.

Bloc-Laine, F. (1956) *La Zone Franc*. Paris: PUF.

Bontems, C. (1976) *Manuel des institutions algériennes de la domination turque à l'indépendance*. Paris: Éditions Ceyas.

Borrmans, M. (1977) *Statut personnel et famille au Maghreb de 1940 à nos jours*. Paris/La Haye: Mouton.

Bourdieu, P. (1977) *Algérie 60*. Paris: Les Éditions de Minuit.

Boyer, P. (1963) *La Vie quotidienne à Alger à la veille de l'intervention française*. Paris: Hachette.

Braudel, F. (1975) *The Mediterranean and the Mediterranean World in the Age of Philip II*. London: Fontana/Collins, 2 vols.

Braudel, F. (1989) *The Identity of France, Volume I: History and Environment*. London: Fontana Press.

Braudel, F. (1990) *The Identity of France, Volume II: People and Production*. London: Collins.

Brubaker, R. (1992) *Citizenship and Nationhood in France and Germany*. Cambridge (Mass.): Harvard University Press.

Brunschwig, H. (1964) *French Colonialism 1871–1914, Myths and Realities*. London: Pall Mall Press.

Bugéja, M. (1929) *Visions d'Algérie*. Algiers: Baconnier Frères.

Bulliet, R. W. (1994) *Islam – The View from the Edge*. New York: Columbia University Press.

Callinicos, A. (1995) *Theories and Narratives: Reflections on the Philosophy of History*. Cambridge: Polity Press.

Camus, A. (1946/1961) *The Outsider*. Harmondsworth: Penguin.

Camus, A. (1958) *Exile and the Kingdom*. Harmondsworth: Penguin.

Centre d'Études et de Recherches Marxistes (1971) *Sur le féodalisme*. Paris: Éditions Sociales.

Chaliand, G. (1964) *L'Algérie est-elle socialiste?* Paris: François Maspero.

Chaliand, G. and Minces J. (1972) *L'Algérie indépendante*. Paris: François Maspero.

Charles-Roux, F. (1932) *France et Afrique du Nord avant 1830, les précursors de la conquête*. Paris: Librairie Félix Alcan.

Charnay, J.-P. (1965) *La Vie musulmane en Algérie, d'après la jurisprudence de la première moitié du XXe siècle*. Paris: PUF.

Clegg, I. (1971) *Workers' Self-Management in Algeria*. London: Allen Lane.

Colonna, F. (1975) *Instituteurs algériens: 1883–1939*. Paris: Presses de la Fondation Nationale des Sciences Politiques.

Colonna, F. (1995) *Les Versets de l'invincibilité. Permanence et changements religieux dans l'Algérie contemporaine*. Paris: Presses de la Fondation Nationale des Sciences Politiques.

Costa-Lascoux, J. and Temine, E. (1985) *Les Algériens en France*. Paris: Publisud.

Costa-Lascoux, J. and Weil, P. (1992) *Logiques d'états et immigrations*. Paris: Éditions Kimé.

Coulson, N. (1971) *A History of Islamic Law*. Edinburgh: Edinburgh University Press.

Courrière, Y. (1968–71) *La Guerre de l'Algérie*. Paris: Fayard, 4 volumes: *Les Fils de la Toussaint* (1968); *Le Temps des léopards* (1969); *L'Heure des colonels* (1970); *Les Feux du désespoir* (1971).

Crowder, M. (1968) *West Africa under Colonial Rule*. London: Hutchinson.

Crowder, M. (1984) The Impact of Two World Wars on Africa, in *History Today*, 34, pp. 11–18.

d'Arcy, F., Krieger, A., Marill, A. (1965) *Essais sur l'économie de l'Algérie nouvelle*. Paris: Presses Universitaires de France.

Daumas, General (1912) *La Femme arabe*. Algiers: Adolphe Jourdan – posthumous.

Davidson, B. (1992) *The Black Man's Burden: Africa and the Curse of the Nation-State*. London: James Currey.

Debbasch, Ch. *et al.* (1971) *Les Économies maghrébines, l'indépendance à l'épreuve du développement économique*. Paris: CNRS.

Depont, O. and Coppolani, X. (1897) *Les confréries religieuses musulmanes*. Algiers: np.

DiMaggio, P. J. and Powell, W. W. (1991) The Iron Cage Revisited: Institutional Isomorphism and Collective Rationality in Organizational Fields, in W. W. Powell and P. J. DiMaggio *The New Institutionalism in Organizational Analysis*. Chicago and London: University of Chicago Press.

Dumont, R. (1957) *Types of Rural Economy: Studies in World Agriculture*. London: Methuen.

Dumoulin, R. (1959) *La Structure asymétrique de l'économie algérienne d'après une analyse de la région de Bône*. Paris: Éditions M.-Th. Geurin.

Durkheim, E. (1960) *Les Formes élémentaires de la vie religieuse. Le Système totémique en Australie*. Paris: PUF.

Durkheim, E. (1964) *The Division of Labour in Society*. New York: The Free Press.

Eisenbeth, M. (1952) Les Juifs en Algérie et en Tunisie à l'époque turque (1516–1830), in *Revue Africaine*, 96, pp. 114–87 and 343–84.

Eisenbeth, S. N. (1970) Problems of Emerging Bureaucracies in Developing Areas and New States, in B.F. Hoselitz and W.E. Moore *Industrialization and Society*. UNESCO: Mouton.

Ellman, Michael (1972) *Soviet Planning Today*. Cambridge: Cambridge University Press.

Esposito, J. (1995) *The Oxford Encyclopedia of the Modern Islamic World*. New York and Oxford: Oxford University Press, 4 volumes (OEMIW).

Esseks, J. D. (1975) *L'Afrique de l'indépendance politique à l'indépendance économique*. Paris: François Maspero/PUG.

Fanjul, Serafin y Arbos, Federico (1987) *Ibn Battuta: a través del Islam*. Madrid: Alianza Editorial.

Fanon, F. (1972) *Sociologie d'une révolution (L'An V de la révolution algérienne)*. Paris: François Maspero.

Feraud, L-Ch. (1877) Causes de l'abandon du comptoir de Collo par la Compagnie française en 1795, in *Revue Africaine*, 21, pp. 124–40.

Fleury, G. (1996) *La Guerre en Algérie*. Paris: Éditions Payot & Rivages.

Foucauld, Vicomte Ch. de (1988) *Reconnaissance au Maroc, 1883–1884*. Paris.

Friedman, J. (1994) *Cultural Identity and Global Process*. London: Sage.

Gallissot, R. (1971) L'Algérie précoloniale, in Centre d'Études et de Recherches Marxistes *Sur le féodalisme*. Paris: Éditions Sociales, 147–87.

Gallissot, R. and Valensi L. (1962) Le Maghreb précolonial: mode de production archaïque ou mode de production féodal?, in *La Pensée*, (December), pp. 57–93.

Gaudry, M. (1929) *La Femme chaouia de l'Aurès*. Paris: Librairie Orientaliste, Paul Gauthner.

Gaudry, M. (1961) *La Société féminine au Djebel Amour et au Ksel*. Algiers: Société algérienne des impressions diverses.

Geertz, C. (1968) *Islam Observed*. Chicago and London: University of Chicago Press.

Gellner, E. (1969) *Saints of the Atlas*. London: Weidenfeld & Nicolson.

Gellner, E. (1981) *Muslim Society*. Cambridge: Cambridge University Press.

Gellner, E. (1983) *Nations and Nationalism*. Oxford: Basil Blackwell.

Gellner, E. (1992) *Postmodernism, Reason and Religion*. London: Routledge.

Gellner, E. (1994) *Encounters with Nationalism*. Oxford: Blackwell.

Gendarme, R. (1959) *L'Économie de l'Algérie*. Paris: Armand Colin.

Gerth, H. H. and Mills, C. Wright (1948) *From Max Weber: Essays in Sociology*. London: Routledge & Kegan Paul.

Ghozali, S. and Bernis, G. D. de (1969) Les Hydrocarbures et l'industrialisation de l'Algérie, in *Revue Algérienne*, 1, pp. 253–94.

Giddens, A. (1971) *Capitalism and Modern Social Theory*. Cambridge: Cambridge University Press.

Gide, A. (1990) *The Immoralist*. Harmondsworth: Penguin.

Gilroy, P. (1987) *There Ain't No Black in the Union Jack*. London: Unwin Hyman.

Gordon, D. C. (1966) *The Passing of French Algeria*. London: Oxford University Press.

Goscinny and Uderzo (1977) *Astérix and the Goths*. London: Hodder Dargaud – English translation.

Granotier, B. (1979) *Les Travailleurs immigrés en France*. Paris: François Maspero, 3rd edn.

Grice-Hutchinson, M. (1978) *Early Economic Thought in Spain, 1177–1740*. London: George Allen & Unwin.

Guibernau, M. (1996) *Nationalisms: The Nation-state and Nationalism in the Twentieth Century*. Cambridge: Polity Press.

Guichard, P. (1976) *Al-Andalus – estructura antropológica de una sociedad islámica en occidente*. Barcelona: Barral Editores – Breve Biblioteca de Reforma.

Guillaumin, C. (1995) *Racism, Sexism, Power and Ideology*. London: Routledge.

Hall, S. (1995) Negotiating Caribbean Identities, in *New Left Review*, 209, pp. 3–14.

Halliday, F. (1974) *Arabia without Sultans*. Harmondsworth: Penguin.

Halliday, F. (1995) *Islam and the Myth of Confrontation: Religion and Politics in the Middle East*. London: I. B. Tauris.

Harbi, M. (1975) *Aux Origines du FLN. Le Populisme révolutionnaire en Algérie*. Paris: Christian Bourgois.

Harbi, M. (1980) *Le FLN. Mirage et réalité: des origines à la prise du pouvoir (1945–1962)*. Paris: Éditions JA.

Hargreaves, A. G. (1987) *Immigration in Post-War France: A Documentary Anthology*. London: Methuen.

Hargreaves, A. G. (1995) *Immigration, 'Race' and Ethnicity in Contemporary France*. London: Routledge.

Heper, M. (1985) *The State Tradition in Turkey*. Hull: The Eothen Press.

Historama Special (1993) Afrique du Nord – 2 ans d'histoire, 33.

Hobsbawm, E. and Ranger, T. O. (1983) *The Invention of Tradition*. Cambridge: Cambridge University Press.

Hoselitz, B. F. and Moore, W. E. (1970, 1st edn 1963) *Industrialization and Society*. UNESCO: Mouton.

Hourani, A. (1962) *Arabic Thought in the Liberal Age 1798-1939*. London: Oxford University Press.

Hourani, A. (1991) *Islam in European Thought*. Cambridge: Cambridge University Press.

Ibn Khaldūn (1967) *The Muqaddimah*. 3 vols translated by Franz Rosenthal, 2nd edn. London and Henley: Routledge & Kegan Paul.

Inalcik, H. (1969) Capital formation in the Ottoman Empire, in *Journal of Economic History*, **XXIX**, 1, pp. 97–140.

Inalcik, H. (1973) *The Ottoman Empire. The Classical Age 1300–1600*. London: Weidenfeld & Nicolson; translated by N. Itzkowitz and C. Imber.

Itoh, M. (1980) *Value and Crisis: Essays on Marxian Economics in Japan*. London: Pluto.

James, C.L.R. (1991) *The Black Jacobins*. London: Virgin Publishing.

Julien, A. (1919) Marseille et la question d'Alger à la veille de la conquête, *Revue Africaine*, 60, pp. 16–61.

Julien, Ch.-A. (1952) *L'Afrique du Nord en marche*. Paris: Juillard.

Julien, Ch.-A. (1970) *Histoire de l'Algérie contemporaine*. Paris: PUF.

Keddie, N. R. (1972) *Scholars, Saints, and Sufis: Muslim Religious Institutions in the Middle East since 1500*. Berkeley and Los Angeles: University of California Press.

Kedouri, E. (1966) *Afghani and 'Abduh*. London: Frank Cass.

Khellil, M. (1991) *L'Intégration des Maghrébins en France*. Paris: PUF.

Koulytchizky, S. (1974) *L'Autogestion, l'homme et l'état – l'expérience algérienne*. Paris: Mouton.

Krieger, A. (1965) Les Prémices d'une réforme agraire en Algérie, in F. d'Arcy, A. Krieger and A. Marill *Essais sur l'économie de l'Algérie nouvelle*. Paris: PUF.

Lacheraf, M. (1965) *L'Algérie: nation et société*. Paris: François Maspero.

Lacoste, Y. (1984) *Ibn Khaldun: The Birth of History and the Past of the Third World*. London: Verso – English translation; French original François Maspero (1966).

Lacoste, Y., Nouschi, A. and Prenant, A. (1966) *L'Algérie: passé et présent*. Paris: Éditions Sociales.

Lamchichi, A. (1992) *L'Islamisme en Algérie*. Paris: L'Harmattan.

Laroui, A. (1970) *L'Histoire du Maghreb: un essai de synthèse*. Paris: François Maspero.

Lazreg, M. (1994) *The Eloquence of Silence: Algerian Women in Question*. New York/London: Routledge.

Lebjaoui, M. (1970) *Vérités sur la révolution algérienne*. Paris: Gallimard.

Lebovics, H. (1992) *True France*. Ithaca and London: Cornell University Press.

Lenin, V. I. (1966) *Collected Works*. 31, London: Lawrence & Wishart.

Lenin, V. I. (1967) *The Development of Capitalism in Russia*. Moscow: Progress Publishers.

Lenin, V. I. (1970) *Questions of National Policy and Proletarian Internationalism*. Moscow: Progress Publishers.

Lerner, D. (1964) *The Passing of Traditional Society*. New York: Free Press.

Lespès, R. (1930) Bône, port minier, in *Revue Africaine*, 71, pp. 129–53.

Lespès, R. (1934) Oran, ville et port, avant l'occupation française (1831), *Revue Africaine*, 75, pp. 277–335.

Le Tourneau, R. (1957) *Les Villes musulmanes de l'Afrique du Nord*. Algiers: Maison des Livres.

Le Tourneau, R. (1962) *Évolution politique de l'Afrique du nord musulmane, 1920–1961*. Paris: Armand Colin.

Le Tourneau, R. (1965) *La Vie quotidienne à Fez en 1900*. Paris: Hachette.

Lewis, B. (1937) The Islamic Guilds, in *The Economic History Review*, VIII, (1), pp. 20–37.

Lewis, B. (1982) *The Muslim Discovery of Europe*. London: Weidenfeld and Nicolson.

Lewis, B. (1984) *The Jews of Islam*. London: Routledge & Kegan Paul.

Lewis, B. (1995) *The Middle East*. London: Weidenfeld & Nicolson.

Lloyd, C. (1991) Concepts, models and anti-racist strategies in Britain and France, in *New Community*, 18, (1), pp. 63–73.

Lorcin, P. M. E. (1995) *Imperial Identities: Stereotyping, Prejudice and Race in Colonial Algeria*. London: I.B. Tauris.

Lord, P. B. (1855) *Algiers with Notices of the Neighbouring States of Barbary*. London: Whittaker & Co.

Lucas, P. and Vatin, J.-C. (1975) *L'Algérie des anthropologues*. Paris: Maspero.

Mabro, J. (1991) *Veiled Half-Truths*. London: I.B. Tauris.

Mahiout, R. (1974) *Le Pétrole algérien*. Algiers: Éditions En AP.

Mameri, K. (1975) *Citations du Président Boumediene*. Algiers: SNED.

Marill, A. (1965) L'Expérience algérienne d'autogestion industrielle, in F. d'Arcy, A. Krieger and A. Marill *Essais sur l'économie de l'Algérie nouvelle*. Paris: PUF.

Maschino, T. M. and M'rabet, F. (1972) *L'Algérie des illusions. La Révolution confisquée*. Paris: Éditions Robert Laffont.

Maspero, F. (1993) La Conquête d'Alger, in *Historama, 33*, pp. 113–20.

Masqueray, E. (1886) *Formation des cités chez les populations sédentaires de l'Algérie*. Paris: Ernest Leroux.

Mazri, H. (1975) *Les Hydrocarbures dans l'économie algérienne*. Algiers: SNED.

McClelland, D. C. (1961) *The Achieving Society*. Princeton: Van Nostrand.

McClelland, D. C. (1970) The Achievement Motive in Economic Growth, in B.F. Hoselitz and W.E. Moore *Industrialization and Society*. UNESCO: Mouton.

Méducin, D. Y. (1974) Le Modèle algérien de coopération pour le développement, Mémoire pour le Diplôme d'Études Supérieures de droit public, Université d'Aix-Marseille.

Mekhaled, B. (1995) *Chroniques d'un massacre, 8 mai 1945*. Paris: Syros/Au Nom de la Mémoire.

Melman, B. (1992) *Women's Orients – English women and the Middle East, 1718–1918 (Sexuality, Religion and Work)*. London: Macmillan.

Merad, A. (1967) *Le Réformisme musulmane*. Paris: Mouton.

Merad, A. (1987) *L'Islam contemporaine*. Paris: PUF Que sais-je?, 2nd edn.

Mernissi, F. (1975) *Beyond the Veil*. New York: Schenkman Publishing Company.

Mernissi, F. (1991) *Women and Islam*. Oxford: Blackwell, translated by Mary Jo Lakeland.

Mernissi, F. (1993) *Islam and Democracy*. London: Virago, translated by Mary Jo Lakeland.

Miles, R. (1989) *Racism*. London: Routledge.

Mises, L. von (1920/1972) Economic Calculation in the Socialist Commonwealth, in A. Nove, and D. M. Nuti *Socialist Economics*. Harmondsworth: Penguin.

Modood, T. (1991) The Indian Economic Success: a Challenge to some Race Relations Assumptions, in *Policy & Politics*, 19, (3), pp. 177–89.

Montagne, R. (1930) *Les Berbères et le Makhzen au sud du Maroc*. Paris: Éditions Félix Alcan.

Montagne, R. (1931) *La Vie sociale et la vie politique des Berbères*. Paris: Comité de l'Afrique Française.

Morell, J. P. (1854) *Algeria: The Topography and History, Political, Social and Natural of French Africa*. London: Nathaniel Cooke.

Mwayila, T. (1987) *Francophonie et géopolitique africaine*. Paris: Éditions OKEM.

Naqvi, S. N. H. (1994) *Islam, Economics and Society*. London: Kegan Paul.

Norbye, O. (1968) The economy of Algeria, chapter 10 in P. Robson and D. A. Lury *The Economies of Africa*. London: George Allen & Unwin.

Nouschi, A. (1961) *Enquête sur le niveau de vie des populations rurales constantinoises de la conquête jusqu'en 1919*. Paris: PUF.

Nouschi, A. (1971) Réflexions critiques sur le dossier: l'Algérie précoloniale, in Centre d'Études et de Recherches Marxistes *Sur le Féodalisme*. Paris: Éditions Sociales, pp. 181–7.

Nouschi, A. (1978) *La Naissance du nationalisme algérien*. Paris: Éditions du Minuit, 2nd edn.

Nouschi, A. (1995) *L'Algérie amère 1914–1994*. Paris: Éditions de la Maison des Sciences de l'Homme.

Nove, A. (1986) *The Soviet Economic System, third edition.* Boston: Unwin Hyman.

Nove, A. and Nuti, D. M. (1972) *Socialist Economics.* Harmondsworth: Penguin.

Odell, P. R. (1975) *Oil and World Power: Background to the Oil Crisis.* London: Penguin, 4th edn.

OECD (1972) *The Pulp and Paper Industry 1971–72.* Paris: OECD.

Ogden, P. E. and White, P. E. (1989) *Migrants in Modern France.* London: Unwin Hyman.

Ottoway, D. and M. (1970) *Algeria: The Politics of a Socialist Revolution.* Berkeley and Los Angeles: University of California Press.

Ouzegane, A. (1963) Perspectives de la Réforme agraire en Algérie, in F. Perroux *Problèmes de l'Algérie indépendante, étude présentée par François Perroux.* Paris: PUF.

Pagden, A. (1995) *Lords of All the World: Ideologies of Empire in Spain, Britain and France c1500–c1800.* New Haven & London: Yale University Press.

Peach, C. (1990) The Muslim Population of Great Britain, in *Ethnic & Racial Studies*, 13 (3), pp. 414–19.

Perennes, J.-J. (1979) *Structures agraires et décolonisation: les oasis de l'Oued-Rhir (Algérie).* Algiers: Office des Publications Universitaires.

Perroux, F. (1963) *Problèmes de l'Algérie indépendante, étude présentée par François Perroux.* Paris: PUF.

Perroux, F. (1965) *Les Techniques quantitatives de la planification.* Paris: PUF.

Perroux, F. (1991) *L'Économie du XXe siècle.* Grenoble: Presses Universitaires de Grenoble; 3rd edn/part V of his complete works first published in 1961.

Powell, W. W. and Dimaggio, P. J. (1991) *The New Institutionalism in Organizational Analysis.* Chicago and London: University of Chicago Press.

Provost, L. (1996) *La Seconde Guerre d'Algérie, le quiproquo franco-algérien.* Paris: Flammarion.

Raffinot, M. and Jacquemot, P. (1977) *Le Capitalisme d'état algérien.* Paris: François Maspéro.

Ramet, S. P. (1992) *Nationalism and Federalism in Yugoslavia, 1962–1991.* Bloomington and Indianapolis: Indiana University Press.

Rassam, A. (1995) Mernissi, Fatima, in J. Esposito *The Oxford Encyclopedia of the Modern Islamic World*, volume III. New York and Oxford: Oxford University Press.

Renan, E. (1992) *Qu'est-ce qu'une nation?* Presses Pocket; also in English translation with commentary by Martin Thom in H.K. Bhabha (1990) *Nation and narration.* London: Routledge.

Reporters Sans Frontières (1994) *Le Drame algérien – un peuple en ôtage,* Paris: Éditions La Découverte.

Rinn, L. (1884) *Marabouts et Khouans, étude sur l'Islam en Algérie.* Algiers: Adolphe Jourdan.

Rinn, L. (1891) *Histoire de l'insurrection de 1871 en Algérie,* Algiers: Adolphe Jourdan.

Robertson, R. (1992) *Globalization: Social Theory and Global Culture.* London: Sage.

Rodinson, M. (1966) *Islam et capitalisme.* Paris: Éditions du Seuil (English edn 1974, London: Allen Lane).

Rodinson, M. (1988) *Europe and the Mystique of Islam.* London: I.B. Tauris.

Roediger, D. (1991) *The Wages of Whiteness. Race and the Making of the American Working Class.* London: Verso.

Rushdie, S. (1988) *The Satanic Verses.* Harmondsworth: Viking Penguin

Rutherford, J. (1990) *Identity.* London: Lawrence & Wishart.

Said, E. (1978) *Orientalism.* London: Routledge.

Said, E. (1993) *Culture and Imperialism*. London: Chatto & Windus.

Schacht, J. (1964) *An Introduction to Islamic Law*. Oxford: Oxford University Press.

Schacht, J. and Bosworth, C. E. (1974) *The Legacy of Islam*. Oxford: The Clarendon Press, 2nd edn.

Schliephake, K. (1977) *Oil and Regional Development, Examples from Algeria and Tunisia*. New York: Praeger.

Sheahan, J. (1969) *An Introduction to the French Economy*. Charles E. Merrill Publishing Co.

Silverman, M. (1992) *Deconstructing the Nation: Immigration, Racism and Citizenship in Modern France*. London: Routledge.

Smith, A. (1991) *National Identity*. Harmondsworth: Penguin.

Spencer, W. (1976) *Algiers in the Age of the Corsairs*. Norman: University of Oklahoma Press.

Steele, D. R. (1992) *From Marx to Mises*. La Salle (Illinois): Open Court.

Stora, B. (1993) *Histoire de la guerre d'Algérie (1954–1962)*. Paris: Éditions La Découverte.

Tanzer, M. (1970) *The Political Economy of International Oil and the Underdeveloped Countries*. London: Temple Smith.

Teillac, J. (1965) *Autogestion en Algérie*. Paris: J. Peyronnet et Cie.

Therborn, G. (1995) *European Modernity and Beyond*. London: Sage.

Tiano, A. (1967) *Le Maghreb entre les mythes*. Paris: PUF.

Trebous, M. (1970) *Migration and Development, the Case of Algeria*. Paris: OECD Development Centre.

Tritton, A. S. (1954) *Islam*. London: Hutchinson University Library.

Turner, B. S. (1978) *Marx and the End of Orientalism*. London: George Allen & Unwin.

Turner, B. S. (1994) *Orientalism, Postmodernism & Globalism*. London: Routledge.

Uno, K. (1980) *Principles of Political Economy*. London: Harvester Press.

Valensi, L. (1969) *Le Maghreb avant la prise d'Alger*. Paris: Flammarion.

Valensi, L. (1971) Archaïsme de la société maghrébine, in Centre d'Études et de Recherches Marxistes *Sur le Féodalisme*. Paris: Éditions Sociales, pp. 223–32.

Vanek, J. (1972) *The Economics of Workers' Management – a Yugoslav Case Study*. London: George Allen & Unwin.

Vatikiotis, P. J. (1987) *Islam and the State*. London: Routledge.

Vatin, J.-C. (1970) L'Algérie en 1830, essai d'interprétation des recherches historiques sous l'angle de la science politique, *Revue Algérienne des Sciences Juristiques, Economiques, et Politiques*, 8 (4), pp. 977–1058.

Vatin, J.-C. (1974) *L'Algérie politique, histoire et sociéte*. Paris: Armand Colin.

Vayssettes, M. (1858–59) Histoire des derniers beys de Constantine, in *Revue Africaine*, 3, pp. 107–28 and 193–8.

Viollette, M. (1931) *L'Algérie vivra-t-elle?* Paris: F. Alcan.

Waterbury, J. (1970) *The Commander of the Faithful*. London: Weidenfeld & Nicolson.

Weber, M. (1976) *The Protestant Ethic and the Spirit of Capitalism*. London: George Allen & Unwin, 3rd edn.

Weil, P. (1991) *La France et ses étrangers*. Paris: Calmann-Lévy.

Weiss, F. (1970) *Doctrine et action syndicales en Algérie*. Paris: Éditions Cujas.

Wihtol de Wenden, C. (1988) *Les Immigrés et la politique*. Paris: Presses de la Fondation Nationale des Sciences Politiques.

Willis, J. R. (1995) Tijaniyah, in J. Esposito, *The Oxford Encyclopedia of the Modern Islamic World*. New York and Oxford: Oxford University Press, volume IV.

Yacono, X. (1953) *Les Bureaux arabes*. Paris: Larose.

Young, R. J. C. (1995) *Colonial Desire – Hybridity in Theory, Culture and Race*. London: Routledge.

Zubaida, S. (1993) *Islam, the People and the State*. London: I.B. Tauris.

Newspapers

Algérie-Actualité

L'Algérien en Europe (organe de l'émigration algérienne)

CARF (Campaign Against Racism and Fascism) bimonthly (London)

El Djazaïria (revue de l'union des femmes algériennes)

El Djeich (revue de l'armée nationale populaire)

Financial Times (London)

El Moudjahid (Algiers)

Le Figaro (Paris)

Le Monde (Paris)

Libération (Paris)

La République (Oran)

Révolution africaine (organe central du FLN)

Révolution et Travail (organe central de l'Union Générale des Travailleurs Algériens)

Terre et Progrès (MARA)

Other

Amrane, Djamila (1992) *Algerian Women at War*. Channel 4.

Pontecorvo, Gillo (1966) *The Battle of Algiers*.

Tavernier, Bernard (1992) *La Guerre sans nom*.

Téchiné, André (1994) *Les Roseaux sauvages*.

Index